Paul Sturrock's
Championship Diary
The inside story

with Richard Cowdery

Acknowledgements

AS is always the case, many more people than just those whose names appear on the cover and between the covers of this publication have played some part in the creation and execution of it during an unforgettable season. My thanks to all of them, but especially: Margaret; Christopher; Scott Squires; Mike Sampson; Griz; everyone at Kingfisher; Plymouth Argyle club photographer Dave Rowntree, and his freelance colleagues Tony Carney and Richard Austin; friends and colleagues on the *Western Morning News* Sports Desk (especially Exeter City fan Stuart for his proof-reading) and in the Argyle Press Box; Paul Roberts and the rest of the Green Army; Martin Hesp; the board of directors, management, players and staff at Home Park, of course; and, last, but by no means least, the anonymous people whose names have been accidentally and undeservedly omitted from the above.

Published by PAFC Books. First published in 2002
Designed by mediasolve and Richard Cowdery
For PAFC Books, Home Park, Outland Road, Plymouth, Devon PL2 3DQ
Printed in Great Britain by Kingfisher Print & Design Ltd, Wills Road, Totnes, Devon TQ9 5XN
Produced in conjunction with Media Print Consultants, 23 Eliot Street, Plymouth PL5 1AX
ISBN: 0-9543200-0-X
Front and back cover photographs: Tony Carney
All other photographs: Dave Rowntree, except page 172 – Richard Austin

(c) Plymouth Argyle FC and Richard Cowdery
All rights reserved. No part of this publication may be reproduced, stored in a retrieval system or transmitted in any form or by any means – electronic, mechanical, recording or otherwise – without the prior permission of the copyright owner.

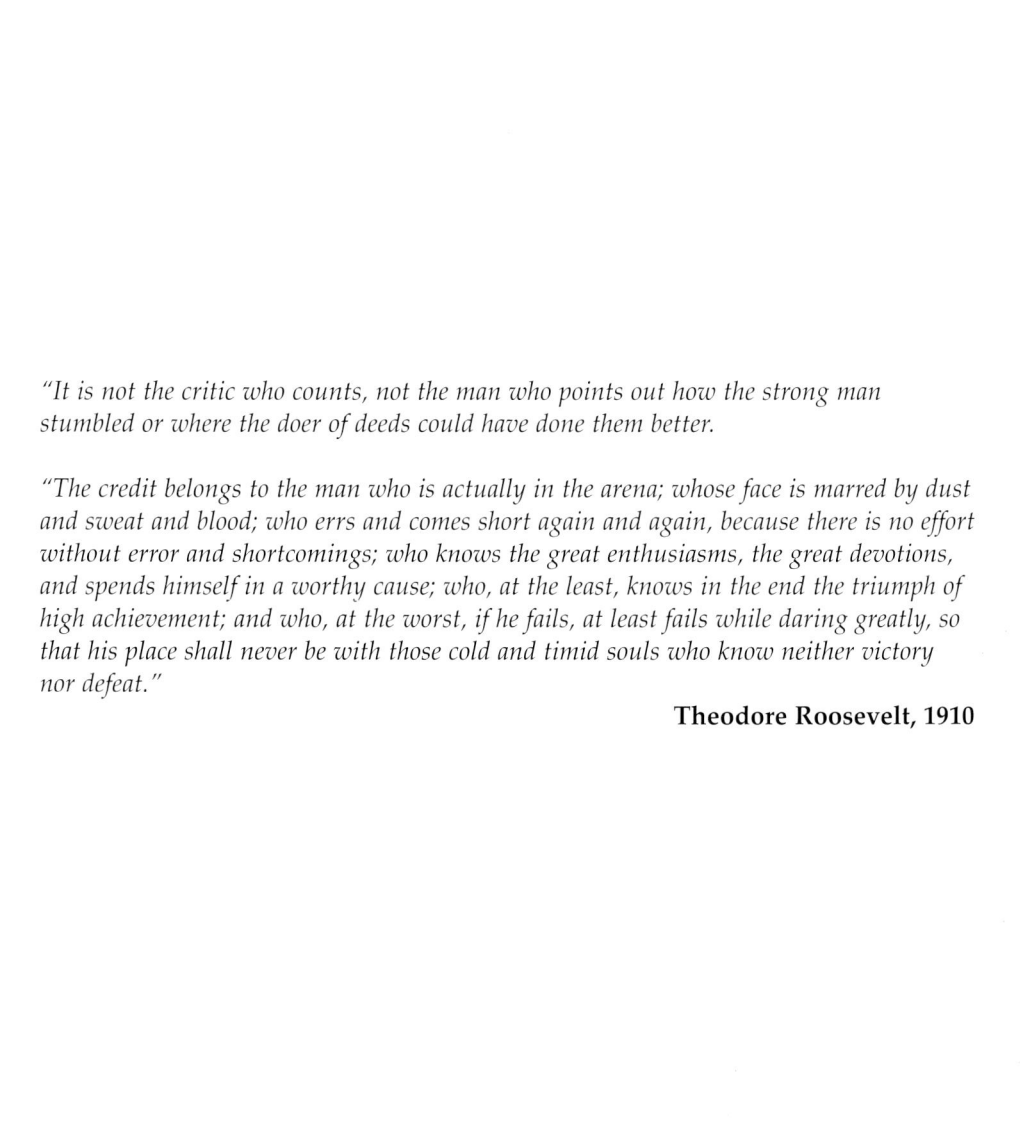

"It is not the critic who counts, not the man who points out how the strong man stumbled or where the doer of deeds could have done them better.

"The credit belongs to the man who is actually in the arena; whose face is marred by dust and sweat and blood; who errs and comes short again and again, because there is no effort without error and shortcomings; who knows the great enthusiasms, the great devotions, and spends himself in a worthy cause; who, at the least, knows in the end the triumph of high achievement; and who, at the worst, if he fails, at least fails while daring greatly, so that his place shall never be with those cold and timid souls who know neither victory nor defeat."

Theodore Roosevelt, 1910

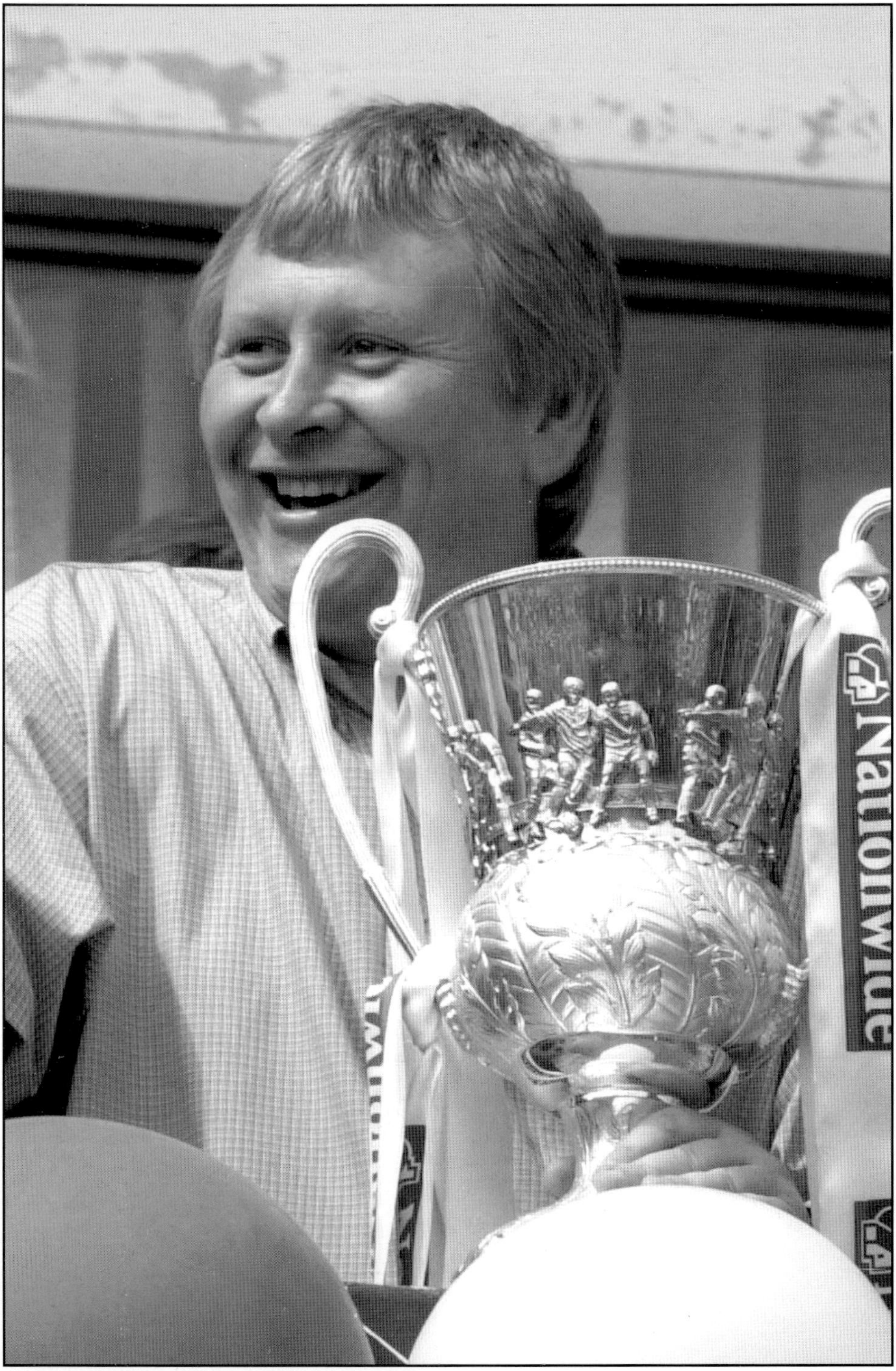
Nationwide

FINAL 2001-02 NATIONWIDE LEAGUE THIRD DIVISION TABLE

			HOME					AWAY						
		Pld	W	D	L	F	A	W	D	L	F	A	GD	Pts
1	Plymouth Argyle	46	19	2	2	41	11	12	7	4	30	17	43	102
2	Luton Town	46	15	5	3	50	18	15	2	6	46	30	48	97
3	Mansfield Town	46	17	3	3	49	24	7	4	12	23	36	12	79
4	Cheltenham Town	46	11	11	1	40	20	10	4	9	26	29	17	78
5	Rochdale	46	13	8	2	41	22	8	7	8	24	30	13	78
6	Rushden & Diamonds	46	14	5	4	40	20	6	8	9	29	33	16	73
7	Hartlepool United	46	12	6	5	53	23	8	5	10	21	25	26	71
8	Scunthorpe United	46	14	5	4	43	22	5	9	9	31	34	18	71
9	Shrewsbury Town	46	13	4	6	36	19	7	6	10	28	34	11	70
10	Kidderminster Harriers	46	13	6	4	35	17	6	3	14	21	30	9	66
11	Hull City	46	12	6	5	38	18	4	7	12	19	33	6	61
12	Southend United	46	12	5	6	36	22	3	8	12	15	32	-3	58
13	Macclesfield Town	46	7	7	9	23	25	8	6	9	18	27	-11	58
14	York City	46	11	5	7	26	20	5	4	14	28	47	-13	57
15	Darlington	46	11	6	6	37	25	4	5	14	23	46	-11	56
16	Exeter City	46	7	9	7	25	32	7	4	12	23	41	-25	55
17	Carlisle United	46	11	5	7	31	21	1	11	11	18	35	-7	52
18	Leyton Orient	46	10	7	6	37	25	3	6	14	18	46	-16	52
19	Torquay United	46	8	6	9	27	31	4	9	10	19	32	-17	51
20	Swansea City	46	7	8	8	26	26	6	4	13	27	51	-24	51
21	Oxford United	46	8	7	8	34	28	3	7	13	19	34	-9	47
22	Lincoln City	46	8	4	11	25	27	2	12	9	19	35	-18	46
23	Bristol Rovers	46	8	7	8	28	28	3	5	15	12	32	-20	45
24	Halifax Town	46	5	9	9	24	28	3	3	17	15	56	-45	36

INTRODUCTION

THIS is the book which Plymouth Argyle fans have been waiting 43 years to read.

The last of the Pilgrims three divisional championship success had been in 1958-59, when former Manchester United player Jack Rowley steered the club to the Third Division title. When the 2001-02 season kicked off, there were precious few Argyle supporters who gave the amiable Scot Paul Sturrock a chance of replicating Rowley's achievement.

Four games into the campaign, with no victories, no goals (apart from a solitary own goal) and a cup exit against their name, that number had dwindled further. Yet, from 22nd place in the Third Division, Sturrock and his assistant Kevin Summerfield rallied the troops to such effect that Argyle ended the season with a points total that has been bettered by only one club in the entire history of English football; and they did it – setting club records almost weekly – with a style and panache that elicited many flattering comments.

They did it, too, amid a backdrop of unprecedented upheaval off the field. Their Home Park ground was steadily rebuilt during the campaign and, on the eve of the season, there was a change in the board-room, with Dan McCauley standing down as chairman and handing over control to a consortium of supporters led by Paul Stapleton. Yet, unbeknown to Argyle fans, that hand-over progressed far from smoothly and, at one point, matters became so fractious that Sturrock and the entire board considered walking away midseason.

This is the exclusive inside story of that incredible and eminently enjoyable season – Bank Holiday Monday at Rushden; Are You Watching, Joe Kinnear?; the tunnel bust-up at Cheltenham; beating Bristol Rovers on the telly; flying to Whitby; four Devon derbies; glory nights at Rochdale and Darlington; the lot – as told by Paul Sturrock, Kevin Summerfield, Paul Stapleton and his fellow directors Peter Jones and Phill Gill. I've provided the facts and figures to give context to their insights.

Richard Cowdery, 2002

CHAPTER ONE

THEY came in their thousands – men, women, teenagers, toddlers and some barely able to crawl – decked out in green and white, with a touch of tangerine thrown in. They came to sing, they came to cheer, and, most of all, they came to pay homage to Plymouth Argyle manager Paul Sturrock and his players – the 2001-02 champions of the Nationwide Third Division.

More than 10,000 of the self-styled Green Army's volunteers witnessed Argyle's sunshine-blessed open-top bus pilgrimage around Plymouth City centre on Sunday, April 21, 2002, which preceded a suitably lavish Civic Centre reception where each of Sturrock's heroes was welcomed in turn by the noisy and ecstatic throng.

Two buses had left Argyle's Home Park headquarters at around 11am – the first containing the players, directors, respective partners, and, following the previous night's champions' do at the Plymouth Novotel, more than one or two hangovers; the second – a nice touch, this – Home Park staff and the Argyle youth team.

A small crowd had gathered at the ground to bid them on their way, and all down Alma Road and Western Approach people cheered, waved and whistled. A small company of vehicles formed an impromptu convoy, drivers honking their horns and shouting their approval, and youngsters ran alongside the slow-moving procession.

It was only when the buses turned into Royal Parade, Plymouth's main drag, that you understood how deeply this triumph of Argyle's had touched the very souls of thousands of ordinary men and women, many of whom have never met Sturrock or the players, and who never will. Plymouth's main street was simply crammed with humanity. Both sides of the road were packed. The buses, already at a crawl, had to slow down for fear of an accident.

Among this throng was Steve Morris, a 43-year-old machinist, who had travelled from Hull for the weekend – "This is the best day of my life...apart from my wedding,"he said – and Jenny Nowell, a 64-year-old housewife from the Stoke area of Plymouth, who was in Paraguay when she learnt that Argyle had been promoted. She immediately flew home to see the team that she had supported since 1949.

At the top of Royal Parade, the Plymouth Highland Pipe Band joined the parade, marching Argyle's Scottish manager towards the Civic Centre, and an ear-splitting welcome for each and every one of the players, introduced by BBC Radio

Devon's hopelessly biased commentator Gordon Sparks, until finally, Paul Sturrock and his assistant Kevin Summerfield – Luggy and Summers – arrived with the championship trophy.

Then, after a few words from the proud young Plymothian captain, Paul Wotton, the crowd sang, the players sang and the sun shone. Days like these do not come along too often.

"Today, was a Plymouth day, rather than an Argyle day," said Sturrock. "People are proud of their city – the whole of it, rather than just the football club. We've waited a long time for it. We should enjoy it."

CHAPTER TWO

PLYMOUTH Argyle's 1-0 victory over Darlington in the 1996 Third Division play-off final ought to have been the springboard for a sustained period of success.

After all, they had a chairman, Dan McCauley, who was not only wealthy (he has consistently featured in the *Times* Top 500 Rich List) but had also shown a willingness to invest many hundreds of thousands of pounds in the club; and they had a manager, Neil Warnock, who was adept at coaxing the best out of lower league players and whose reputation in that respect had been enhanced by the fact that he had won promotion in his first – and, as it turned out, only – full season in charge of Argyle.

They had a squad which many believed could do well in the echelon to which they had won promotion, as was proved when they briefly led the Second Division at the start of the 1996-97 season; they were in discussions with Plymouth City Council to build a 23,000 all-seater state-of-the-art stadium; and they had a following which was the envy of many First Division chairmen – 33,000 pilgrims from all parts of Planet Earth who converged on Wembley to see Ronnie Maugé head Argyle out of the Third Division underlined the club's potential.

Potential. The one word guaranteed to have an Argyle fan grinding his or her teeth. For generations, they have been told about their club's potential and yet have rarely caught a glimpse of it: Warnock's success was only the sixth time in the Pilgrims' 100-year-plus history that they had won promotion. Needless to say, none of those successes included promotion to the top flight, so it does not take a genius to realise that most of Argyle's seasons have been spent swilling around in the middle two divisions of the English professional game.

Surely this time, though: the combination of McCauley, Warnock, the squad, the new stadium and the fans would ensure the potential was realised. Predictably, no. Less predictably, within two seasons, all that remained from that irresistible list of positives was McCauley, and even he, in many people's eyes, had become something of a negative.

First to go was Warnock. The whole 1996-97 season had been liberally sprinkled with public and private spats between the manager and the chairman, so the only real surprise about his sacking was that it took place as late in the season as February, by which time the squad's potential, overshadowed by events off the field, had resolved itself into mid-table obscurity.

Fans, disillusioned and divided by the bickering between McCauley and Warnock, and disappointed with the team's failure to rise above halfway, quickly

drifted back to pre-Wembley levels, while the stadium project, which had never really been a favourite of McCauley's, was put on the back-burner.

In a moment now enshrined in Pilgrims' folklore, Warnock was sacked while driving home when he answered his mobile phone and found Argyle chief executive Roger Matthews on the other end. There might have been footballing reasons behind the dismissal, but there was clearly something personal, too. "He thought he was God and could walk on water," said McCauley.

"Neil Warnock can always get a job," retorted Warnock, "but I'm not sure Plymouth can always get the right manager." Within a month, he had proved the first part of his self-penned epitaph right by landing the vacant Oldham manager's job, and the next three seasons apparently vindicated the second part.

Warnock's long-time assistant and close friend Mick Jones was the only one to win promotion in the 1996-97 season, taking over the Argyle top job on a caretaker basis. As the partnership ended, so did the friendship. He was never able to inspire the Pilgrims to great heights but he did enough to ensure another season of Second Division football and was given the dubious reward of the manager's chair on a permanent basis.

There is a macabre symmetry in that, while Warnock won promotion and provided Argyle fans with one of the best moments in his only season in charge at Home Park, Jones was relegated in one of the most awful years in the club's history in his sole season at the helm.

To some extent, Jones – a thoroughly likeable and pleasant man – was in the wrong place at the wrong time, albeit at his own choosing. He could barely be held responsible for failing to reverse a trend that, one or two blips aside, had been downward for the duration of McCauley's chairmanship which began in 1991.

The 1997-98 season, in which Argyle were tantalisingly never out of the mire or never swamped by it, ended in tears – famously those of young home-grown centre-back Paul Wotton – at Burnley on the the season's final day. Argyle were back in the lowest rank of the Football League for only the second season in their history.

Despite unequivocal post-season assurances from McCauley that the club was not considering a fifth change of manager in less than four seasons, Jones was sacked. Like Warnock, he discovered his fate after answering his mobile; unlike Warnock, he was on a family holiday aboard at the time.

The poisoned chalice passed to Kevin Hodges, the Pilgrims' former head-down-no-nonsense midfielder whose club-record 670 appearances is never likely to be

beaten. The previous season Hodges, in conjunction with another Argyle Old Boy, Steve McCall, had taken Torquay United to the Third Division play-off final, where they had lost to Colchester.

The fact that he had achieved the feat on a relatively small budget appealed to McCauley, who had now entered the most parsimonious period of his chairmanship. The appointment also had the approval of the largely disenchanted supporters, who held Hodges and McCall in high esteem. Both knew the ropes at Argyle (McCall had even been player-manager of the club for 17 games post Peter Shilton) and approached their new task with enthusiasm and confidence – admirable traits which unfortunately counted for nothing.

In the cold light of mere statistics, Hodges' management was the worst in Argyle's history. In his first season – 1998-99 – the club finished 13th in the Third Division, their lowest ever final league position, and in his second, he improved their standing by only one place. Yet, there was considerable sympathy for the manager, who did not have the financial backing that Warnock, and, earlier, Shilton, had enjoyed, and who gave the job his all.

Hodges began the 2000-01 season having survived longer than the average McCauley appointment, but was unable to extend his managerial tenure much further. Optimism off the pitch after McCauley reached an agreement with Plymouth City Council to rebuild Home Park was not translated into success on it. Seven games into the campaign, Argyle had one win and were one place ahead of bottom side Halifax. Successive defeats – a 5-2 reverse at Cheltenham that the manager himself called "a disgrace", and a 3-2 home loss to Barnet – sealed his fate.

For once, the parting of the ways was dignified, with not a mobile phone in sight. The club issued a statement calling the decision to sack Hodges and McCall "particularly sad" and Hodges said only: "I know that I can hold my head up high and say I always did my best. I wanted to do well for the club but sometimes things don't always work out the way you would like."

Hodges' former Argyle team-mate Kevin Summerfield, the club's youth-team coach, was put in temporary control as the club began its search for what would be McCauley's seventh manager in less than ten seasons. It was a decision he could not afford to get wrong.

CHAPTER THREE

THE day after Kevin Hodges' sacking, the *Western Morning News* reported that Paul Sturrock was interested in filling the Argyle vacancy. On the face of it, there was nothing to link a man whose entire playing and managerial career had been based in a few square miles about as far as you could get from Plymouth and still be involved in British football.

Sturrock, though, was interested, and the *Morning News* knew he was because they had a solid tip-off from another former Pilgrim who was the largely anonymous and unheralded key player in arranging the marriage between Argyle and the man who, within 18 months, would lead the club to only the fourth championship in its history.

David Byrne was an old fashioned winger signed by then Argyle manager Ken Brown from Millwall in the late 1980s, and who played under Brown and his successor David Kemp before winding up his career in Scotland.

Byrne had since returned to Plymouth but kept in touch with contacts he had made north of the border, one of who was Sturrock, remembered vaguely by Sassenachs as a half-tidy Scottish international of the 1980s. In fact, he is a living legend in Dundee and beyond.

After signing for United manager Jim McLean in 1974, and making his debut two months later in the European Cup-Winners' Cup, Sturrock exploded onto the Scottish scene in April 1975 when, as a mere 18-year-old, he scored twice in a 2-2 draw against Rangers. It was the beginning of a glittering playing career in which he was a vital member of the most successful ever Dundee United side – two League Cups, the League title, European glory nights – an international regular and Scottish Footballer of the Year.

He was a hero to the half of Tayside proud to wear the tangerine of Dundee United – and grudgingly admired by those who didn't – and one of those rare sportsman who are honoured to be known instantly by their nickname alone. Although the epithet Luggy, on account of the generous size of his ears, or lugholes, is hardly flattering, it says plenty about his affability and approachability that he allows everyone to address him so familiarly.

After retiring from playing for the only senior club of his career in 1989, Sturrock had taken up coaching at Tannadice and gone on to manage St Johnstone, winning promotion and Premier League respectability after relegation in his first season, before returning to Tayside to take up the reins at Dundee United. Along the way, he had gained the reputation north of the border as first-class coach and someone adept at rebuilding a club from the foundations.

"I seem to be the type of manager who likes challenges," he said later. "Who likes to get into the guts of a club: cleaning out, making players better, moulding a squad, developing players. I enjoy restructuring clubs."

Sturrock had quit United earlier that season, suddenly and unexpectedly. The unique problems associated with managing a club so close to his heart, one at which he had spent virtually his entire adult life, had, he explained, become too much. He felt too close to things and took too much too personally.

Sturrock might have quit Dundee United, but he had no intentions of quitting football and was up for a new challenge. Byrne knew this and knew that Plymouth Argyle could offer Sturrock the challenge he was seeking. He had few hesitations in recommending Argyle to Sturrock and fewer still in recommending Sturrock to the Argyle board.

Byrne is nothing if not persuasive, and it was no surprise that, as a result of his matchmaking and lobbying, Sturrock was one of five candidates interviewed for the managerial vacancy, in addition to caretaker Summerfield, who had put up a good case for permanent elevation with two refreshing wins from his five matches in charge.

Byrne's involvement in the appointment process did not end there, however. After the interviews, Sturrock and the Argyle board were poles apart on certain conditions of his employment. After the first day of interviews, when four of the six candidates had been seen, McCauley called for a somewhat premature straw-poll of the directors – only one, John McNulty, voted for Sturrock, with Paul Stapleton among those who felt the Scot's potential wage requirements would price him out of their range. Ironically, it was the last input McNulty was to have on the decision process as he resigned the next day for personal reasons.

Sturrock returned to Scotland under the impression that his chances of getting the job were slim, and McCauley let it be known to his favoured candidate, Ian Atkins, then in charge of Argyle's Third Division rivals Carlisle United, that he was now in prime position.

It might have ended there, if it had not been for Byrne. He contacted Sturrock, then Stapleton, to find out if a compromise could be found. Sturrock bent a little, and the board reconvened at Home Park on the afternoon of Saturday, October 28, following the late postponement of the Pilgrims' match against Kidderminster, due to waterlogging. They spoke to Summerfield, then discussd the appointment during three long, often tortuous, hours in the board-room as they tried to come to a unanimous decision.

McCauley relistened to the arguments for Sturrock and against his preferred

choice Atkins and eventually decided against his self-confessed impetuosity. So it was that Sturrock was presented to the Plymouth public as the new board's unanimous choice on October 31, 2000.

"The quick-fix went out of the window," said McCauley, "and we felt we had to look at the long-term solution. That's why we all switched to Paul.

"We are in a perilous position. The crowds are low and we do not intend to face relegation. It disturbs me that we are not good enough. That has got to change and I think Paul is the man to do that for us.

"I hope it will be a really long stay. I want him to be here ten years and to outlive me."

For his part, Sturrock breezed into Home Park like a gust of braw air off the Tay. Within half-an-hour of his introductory Press conference in the Home Park boardroom, he had blown away, one by one, any misgivings Anglocentric Argyle fans might have had about his appointment, initially, it was announced, until the summer of 2003.

He showed himself quite ready to answer queries before they were posed. "I'm surprised no-one's asked me the million-pound question," he said, and, when no-one still did, revealed: "I'm very much up on the English game. I have often talked with Scottish managers who know the English game, and with English managers as well, dare I say it? When we were in Scotland, we travelled everywhere in England to watch games."

It was strange, anyway, that Sturrock's nationality should have given some Argyle fans pause for thought. After all, of the six men to have previously led the club to promotion, three (Bob Jack, Jimmy Rae and Dave Smith) were Scots.

He also frankly addressed his resignation from Dundee United after two games of the season, and before Argyle's own miserable campaign had even begun. "I felt I was banging my head against a brick wall," he said. "I made one or two mistakes as well, which annoyed me. I thought it was appropriate and the right thing for the club for me to leave." After two months off, calluses on his hands from too much gardening persuaded him that the merits of the daily managerial grind were perhaps underrated and he reviewed his options.

"I am still ambitious," he said, "and one of my ambitions has been to work in England."

England, yes, but Plymouth? "People I spoke to down here said that it was a club with potential but that it was going the wrong way. I have never gone for a

job I didn't want. One of the reasons why I was excited about taking this job was talking to the chairman and directors. They are so desperate for success."

Still in the confessional, Sturrock came clean on his famous dug-out collapse during a game at Tannadice when he was manager of St Johnstone, since when his heart (literally, not colloquially) had been questioned.

"That was more than five years ago," he said, "and it was entirely stress-related. I was trying to do everything myself and it was too much. It won't happen again. I hyperventilated – I forgot to breathe." (Despite the explanation, which has been patiently repeated to people who believe Sturrock has a dodgy ticker, the myth is still strong – when Argyle played Joe Kinnear's Luton in February 2002, one national newspaper reporter made great play that both managers "had suffered heart-attacks.")

Sturrock revealed that his quest to right the good ship Pilgrim would involve a healthy injection of youth, a tried and trusted tactic at St Johnstone and Dundee United, where the likes of Duncan Ferguson, Christian Dailly, Billy McKinley and Kevin Gallacher – to name but £20 million of Sturrock-produced talent – cut their teeth.

He said: "In management, you have to look at the whole picture. The short-term is that it is important to get this club out of where it is (21st in the Third Division); in the long term, you have to build foundations at a football club. Hopefully I can bring a bit of experience in that sphere to Plymouth."

Almost imperceptibly, Sturrock slipped easily from 'Plymouth' to 'we' when talking about his new club, and his self-confidence and enthusiasm-without-naivete relaxed everyone in the room.

"It's been difficult times at the club," he said, revealing that he had done more than some cursory homework on recent seasons. "Hopefully we can now go in the right direction." Probably no-one was hoping for that more than the white-haired man on his left.

He moved into *Braveheart* territory when he pledged to bring "a bit of confidence, a bit of spirit, a bit of Scottish passion" to Home Park, but revealed he had come with a "clean sheet of paper" with no pre-conceived idea of the players (except, coincidentally, given his nationality, Argyle's two Macs, Paul McGregor and Sean McCarthy) or his coaching staff.

With that, it was off to pose for the stereotypical new-man-in-charge pictures for the following day's papers – 'Can you hold the scarf above your head, Paul?'; 'one by the home dug-out, Paul'; 'shaking hands with the chairman, Paul' – and to 'do' TV and radio, before talking privately with the newspaper boys.

"I don't do interviews over the phone, boys," he said. "If you want me, you'll have to come to the ground." Fair enough. "One other thing," he said, pointing to a rather loud number around one reporter's neck and smiling. "Dinnae wear that tie." Life under Sturrock was going to be nothing, if not interesting.

PAUL STURROCK: "I was quite surprised with the phone call. It was something like a week after I had shown an interest. It might shock a lot of people to know that my first thoughts were to use the experience of an interview, more than anything else. I had never been interviewed by anyone for any job in my life before, so I did feel that, with the situation I was in, the experience of an interview would hold me in good stead for other interviews that were to come.

"That was more in my mind than the job, but I travelled down to Bristol Airport, rented a car and drove to Rotolok [McCauley's company], in Tiverton, where the board and Dan had arranged interviews right through the Sunday. I arrived – one of the other managers was coming out as I was coming in – and I was interviewed for the job.

"I didn't know what to expect. I'd never had an interview for some reason, but it was a bit of an eye-opener in lots of ways. I found the interview was strange. The board kept going off at tangents and explaining themselves. I felt they were trying to sell the club to me, rather than me having to sell myself to them, which surprised me, and worried me also. I thought there must be something awry if they felt they had to counter-balance the questions they were asking me, and virtually answer them themselves.

"To be fair, I took a liking to all of them – I found them a friendly bunch – and, going back up the road on Sunday night, I felt quite content that the interview had gone well. They seemed to be the type of people who wanted to do the same things as me: youth development was a big key to some of them, and obviously relegation was big worry for them.

"Forward-planning and long-term planning seemed to be a concern of most of the board. I think Dan had a short-term plan as far as relegation was concerned – anyone who owned a football club would be similar – but the others seemed to be very receptive to my long-term thoughts on how a football club should be run.

"I had wanted to make sure that whatever job I took, I was comfortable with the people I worked with, and I think I changed my mind on the flight home. It seemed to be the type of job that I could get my teeth into because there was a lot more asked of me than normal.

"I was glad they had a chief executive because I did not want to be involved in the general running of the club and the transfers – I was quite choosy about that. I felt I had to have a relationship with the players like the one that I had at St Johnstone, which probably wasn't as forthcoming as I would have liked at Dundee United. That's a vitally important part of the job.

"I refused to speak personal terms at the first interview – I needed to know them and they needed to know me. If I told them what I had been on at Dundee United; that wasn't going to be forthcoming, the situation they were in, so I felt it was important to just get over the first hurdle. I went away, and waited to hear from them. After two weeks, I had heard nothing – no contact at all apart from a courtesy call just to thank me for coming down – so I started to think that it had slipped away and other options were coming into play. Abroad had reared its head at three or four clubs, the agents were keen, and there were some coaching jobs in Scotland around. I was still involved with coaching at the Scottish FA and they had said there would be more work if I was still out of a job.

"I thought Summers, who had done reasonably well, had convinced the board, which normally happens. I think it's well documented that someone down here who knew me had eventually made comment to one of the directors that, if they were interested in me, I was beginning to make decisions to go elsewhere. I got a phone call from Paul Stapleton on Friday saying they would much appreciate if I could hang on for a few days as they still hadn't made up their minds about the manager's job and there was a meeting due to be held soon.

"On the Sunday, I had another call from Paul Stapleton asking if we could come to some personal terms. To be fair, I took a huge wage-cut to come down here, but I had walked out on a job and that was a factor. I then had to sit down with my wife, who took a bit of convincing. I wanted away from Scotland. I felt, at that time in my career, it was time to go. It's very insular there, you don't really get your head above the trees and it gets stagnant – going into the same job, seeing the same teams, the same players, same media coverage. It was getting tighter and tighter because we were fighting relegation all the time: winning cups and chasing championships was never going to be part of your make-up; it was to make sure you weren't the last team or the second-last team in the league.

"I didn't enjoy that. I felt I was making decisions just to safeguard the club and myself, rather than making long-term decisions. At Dundee United, I felt that decisions were being forced upon me to try and get them back to the giddy heights and people did not appreciate that, after the transition they had been through, it might take another four years for that to happen. I didn't think the board or the supporters could wait that long, or seemed to want to wait that long, when I tried to explain it to them.

"I think my wife appreciated I had to move out of the country. It was time to start anew. The decision was made when I agreed the job that I would come down alone to find out whether I enjoyed it. I didn't mention to the board that this was a huge step for me and that, if things didn't work out properly for me, I would be telling them very quickly. At the end of the day, the family was the most important thing.

"Dan picked me up at the airport and gave me the history of his thoughts of how his chairmanship had went, managers he'd had, mistakes he'd made. He poured his heart out, really, which made me closer to him because he did appreciate he'd made a lot of personal mistakes – the way he had run the club and decisions on management – and he wanted me to change things as much as possible, my way. All the negative stories I hear about Dan very rarely raised their head in the time I was his manager. He was very, very supportive to what I was trying to achieve at his football club. I hear all these things, but, at the end of the day, I take people at face value and Dan's been a gentleman and a friend, which is the only way I can explain our relationship.

"To the extent that I must admit that when I heard about the boardroom changeover at the start of our title-winning season, I was a bit disappointed at first, although it was good men that had taken over. I wasn't taken into the loop very early, not until nearly the day that it all went through. When I heard about it, I thought Dan and I were going in the right direction – I have always found that successful clubs have chairman-manager relationships that are very, very strong. At the end of the day, I could appreciate where Dan was coming from; he'd done ten years and I think he realised it was time to give other people a go.
"Dan had tried to map out as much as possible, but, when I got here, it was a culture shock. Everything was a bit run down.

"I had an hour with Summers, an hour and a half with the chief executive [Roger Matthews], and then I sat down with the board. We were still at the ground at 8pm, chatting, until I went back to the Copthorne Hotel and just readied myself for the Press conference the next day, when I also had training to take.

"I said to Summers very early on that he had the job at that time, but there was no point in me beating around the bush – I'd had an assistant [John Blackley] in the past, who I was used to working with. But I said that we'd go down the road and see what happened. It's never easy. I've had to come into a situation like that two or three times. To be fair, the first training session we had together, I found we had similar ideas about the way that the game should be played. I could tell he was very disappointed, as anybody in his position would be because he felt he was the man for the job, but he dived straight in and was a great benefit. I was able to tap into his opinions, although I'm a great believer in that you judge every situation for yourself. It enabled me to have a clearer picture of the squad of players.

"At that time, Summers was still running the youth development. I would have taken John Blackley – I think we had a fantastic relationship – but circumstances at home for him were very difficult to change. He had a good job – a highly paid job – at Dundee United, so for him to uproot and take a dramatic wage decrease was never on, to be fair. Although he got the offer, it was never a goer in my mind, so it meant that my relationship with Summers grew. It was no-brainer after that. It was very easy. We seemed to be quite friendly and seemed to go from there. That was that."

CHAPTER FOUR

PAUL Sturrock's first game as manager was a Devon derby against Torquay United at Plainmoor, although it was not his first game in charge. He confessed to having had "a wee input" during his initial three days on the training-ground, but let Kevin Summerfield have the final say. "Kevin's picked the team and he's obviously in charge of tactics, the team-talk and everything else," he said.

Sturrock watched from the Torquay directors' box, alongside Dan McCauley, behind one of the goals and saw for himself the myriad of problems that he had been brought to Home Park to solve. The Pilgrims took an early lead through Sean McCarthy, who later went off injured, but were pegged back by Eifion Williams' leveller.

For the record, and as a measure of the changes Sturrock was quickly to bring to Home Park, the Argyle team that day, lining up 4-4-2, was: John Hodges; Paul Wotton, Steve Adams, Craig Taylor, Jon Beswetherick; Lee Phillips (Kevin Wills 63), Martin Barlow, Chris Leadbitter, Buster Phillips; Paul McGregor (Jason Peake 82), McCarthy (Steve Guinan 26). Substitutes (not used): Luke McCormick (gk), Adam Barrett.

The tangible and symbolic evidence that Sturrock had taken full control came after the game, when he conducted his first post-match Press conference. He was obviously eager to get to work, and realised he had plenty to do. "We defended too deep and our strikers never really held up the ball," he said. "I think it's a reason behind Plymouth's poor away results in the past and it's something we are going to work on."

By the time he was ready to take charge of his first game as Argyle manager, his scheduled home bow against Lincoln City was seen, not so much as a Third Division relegation scrap, more the start of the Sturrock revolution. His blend of Celtic pragmatism infused with a dash of Highland romanticism had immediately captivated all that encountered him, and those qualities were soon to become his stamp of office.

"We'll still have the dark days," he warned expectant fans. "There will be times when the whole world's against us at 4.45pm. This is a slow process, but the slower you go, the fruit is much better at the end, I can assure you."

No doubt the dark days will still come, but the day that greeted Sturrock on the morning of his anticipated Home Park debut was merely wet. So wet, that the game was postponed well before noon due to a waterlogged pitch.

Little can Sturrock have guessed then, but it would be another two weeks until he was to send his team into league action – 33 days after his appointment – as matches at home to Kidderminster and at Rochdale were also called off because of the wet weather.

His first two games were, therefore, an extended first-round FA Cup tie against Nationwide Conference side Chester City, who became only the second non-league side to knock Argyle out of the competition – and first on Argyle's own territory – when they won a replay at Home Park 2-1 after a 1-1 draw at the Deva Stadium.

Overseeing the worst result in the club's history was hardly the most auspicious of starts, but Sturrock was happy to be in the dug-out once again. "It's very pleasing to be back," he said. "I missed it – I wouldn't tell the wife that, though!"

In between the two matches, Sturrock had warmed to his task of rebuilding and reshaping his side and he brought in defender David Worrell on a three-month loan deal from his former club Dundee United. Worrell, a 22-year-old former Republic of Ireland Under-21 captain, joined Sturrock for a second time, having signed for United from Blackburn Rovers for £50,000 a year and a half previously.

With 20 Scottish Premier League matches under his belt – and it probably would have been more had it not been for injury – Worrell was earmarked by Sturrock for a right-back role, which would allow Wotton to move into the centre in place of the unfancied Barrett.

Sturrock said: "He's a true full-back and I haven't seen anyone else here who can play out-and-out full-back. Paul Wotton has done a sterling job at right-back but there's other positions he can fill. I've got two left-sided centre-halves and I don't think the balance of the team would be correct playing both of them together."

Barrett, one of those two left-sided centre-backs who had played more than 60 games for the Pilgrims during the previous two seasons, was summarily put up for transfer, alongside midfielders Kevin Nancekivell and Jamie Morrison-Hill. The decisions showed Sturrock was his own man: Barrett was a firm favourite with Pilgrims' fans, while Nancekivell was also something of a local hero, having been signed from Dr Martens League side Tiverton Town only three months previously.

"I don't want people of his age [29] playing reserve-team football," said Sturrock, of Nancekivell, who returned to Tiverton where he once again shone on the non-league stage. "I've told him his opportunities would be very limited with the first team.

"Barrett's a wee bit different. He's a 60-game man, but Craig Taylor's got his strip at this moment and I'm going to play a back four. He's done reasonably well, but I've already got a left-sided centre-half [Taylor] and there are other areas that need strengthening. I don't want that quality of player lying about in the reserves and being disappointed with the chances he's getting, so I thought being honest with him was the better idea.

"If there's people to be overstretched, it's my younger ones playing in reserve-team football: that's how this club will benefit. In the long-term-planning of a club, you sometimes have to assess your staff very quickly. People might say I've been too quick, but I feel that's a job a manager has to take on.

"He's got to bring in his own players; to know the areas he wants to strengthen; he's got to be a realist on finances – sometimes you have to move people out to bring people in."

After the cup exit against Chester, for which new signing Worrell was ineligible, Sturrock was in half a mind whether or not to move the whole squad out immediately. He unequivocally labelled the defeat as "unacceptable" and berated his players for their slow start. "It seems it's a habit of certain players," he said. "If they keep showing the habit, they will just go out of the team. I'm not waiting on anybody. If they will not change themselves, they will not play.

"I want 11 players who give me every ounce of effort; who appreciate that, when the other team has the ball, it is just as important as when we have it; who, when we walk in at half-time, are absolutely knackered; and who are out on their feet at the end of the game.

"If we have 11 boys like that, we will start climbing the league, but I don't believe some of these players are in that kind of mode at the minute and we've got to change that. Either they change or we have to change them. I'll tell them once, I'll tell them twice, but I won't tell them again.

"Alex Ferguson said to me 'Football managers make one mistake – they try to change the mental approach of players. That's impossible. If they are not brave, don't work hard, or are lazy, you will never, ever, instill that into a player.' "We have got to make sure we have 11 boys who want to play and who want to work."

Fate decreed that Sturrock's league debut would eventually come - on December 2, 2000 – at St James' Park, Exeter, home of Argyle's bitterest enemies, and, although he appreciated the intense rivalry, it paled in the light of the Tayside head-to-heads in which he had been involved on both sides of the touchline. On the eve of the game, Sturrock made his first permanent addition to his squad

in the shape of Brian McGlinchey, a 23-year-old Northern Ireland B international, on a free transfer from First Division Gillingham. McGlinchey had played in a trial game against Yeovil two weeks' previously (though not particularly well, the player himself later admitted), fulfilling Sturrock's promise not to sign players he had not personally seen in action, and arrived on the same day as Barrett completed a £10,000 move to Mansfield.

Former Manchester United schoolboy and Manchester City YTS trainee, McGlinchey, a left-sided defender/midfielder, was signed by Gills manager Peter Taylor from Port Vale and became a regular member of the Kent side. He fell out of favour with Taylor's successor Andy Hessenthaler after Taylor moved on to Leicester. "I'm coming down here to get in the first team and hopefully to better myself and better Plymouth," said the Derryman, who started the derby on the substitutes' bench.

There was, however, a surprise selection included in the Pilgrims' starting line-up: David Friio, a 27-year-old French midfielder who had been signed on a one-month trial contract earlier in the week – along with his countryman and former team-mate at French Third Division side ASOA Valence, Romain Larrieu, a 24-year-old, 6ft 4in goalkeeper.

Larrieu watched from the stands as Friio, deputising for the injured Martin Barlow, made an impressive debut on the pitch, Sturrock made his own league debut in the dug-out and Argyle, by now the third-worst team in the Football League, made Exeter suffer. Two goals from stand-in captain McCarthy ensured Sturrock's reign proper began with a victory – Argyle's first away from their Home Park base since the previous season – in the camp of his club's deadliest rivals. To put it in perspective, it was only Argyle's fourth win at St James' Park in 70 years.

Another Westcountry derby victory followed four days later, when Sturrock notched his first home win, a 3-0 victory over Second Division Bristol City in the opening game of the LDV Vans Trophy. As is the habit with managers in the early stages of this competition, Sturrock used the opportunity to run the rule over half-a-dozen players he had not previously seen in what he liked to call "battle conditions", among them strikers Ian Stonebridge and Martin Gritton; midfielder Wills; previously injured centre-back Mick Heathcote, the club captain; and Larrieu, who, like Friio, had not played regular competitive football for six months.

Larrieu's first contribution to affairs was to come for a cross and miss it by half the length of Armada Way, but he ended up making some spectacular saves, which boded well for the future. Stonebridge, Gritton and Taylor scored. Argyle were foiled from immediately building on their two wins in a week when

their re-arranged match at Rochdale was again called off, but they duly made it three wins – and three clean-sheets – in a row when Sturrock finally enjoyed his home league bow against York City on December 16, seven weeks after becoming manager. Taylor's second successive goal, after 160 seconds, proved to be the difference between two poor sides.

A third Frenchman joined Larrieu and Friio at Home Park over Christmas, although Sacha Opinel, a left-sided defender, was to enjoy considerably less success than his countrymen did. Like Sturrock, he made an inauspicious start to life at Home Park, putting Worrell out of action for a week after a clash of heads in training left the Dubliner with 12 stitches above his eye and a beautiful shiner.

A 2-0 defeat at Halifax on the Saturday before Christmas was followed by a 2-1 home victory over Cardiff the day after Boxing Day, with McCarthy again scoring twice against a side that was ultimately to win promotion. Wills made his full league debut.

Argyle's next two games – at home to Hull on December 30 and at Leyton Orient on New Year's Day – fell victim to the weather, with frost this time being the cause. The postponement of the away game at Brisbane Road was particularly disappointing for supporters who had spent several months organising a terrace-party-cum-friendly-protest at the way the club had been allowed to decline. Since most of the organisation was arranged over the Internet, the day had been christened 'NYD@LOFC' and had been expected to attract more than 3,000 fans.

Disappointing it might have been, but the knock-on effect of the postponement would have a significant, but totally unforeseeable, way in determining how the club would be run in the future.

Argyle's first action of 2001 came at Field Mill, where they held a Mansfield side that included Barrett 0-0, hardly a major cause for celebration but, with a rare away point and first clean-sheet outside Devon for 12 months in the bag, another small step in the right direction. Barrett won the man of the match award after the sort of performance players generally reserve for clubs that have binned them.

Opinel made his one and only appearance for the Argyle first-team in their next match, the LDV Vans Trophy second-round game against Bristol's other team. According to those who were there, it was a horrifying experience as the French trialist was turned so much by Rovers' winger Michael Meaker that he ended the match with twisted blood. Sturrock politely admitted that he looked 'ring-rusty'. Rovers won 3-0, with former Pilgrim Michael Evans scoring the Gas's third.

Sturrock called in his Tayside connections again to borrow Scottish Under-21

international defender Lee Wilkie from Dundee, allowing his footballing concerns to take priority over his distaste for all things Dundonian not coloured electric-tangerine. Wilkie, 20, came to Home Park hot from a trial with Everton and had previously spent a week at Elland Road to let Leeds run the rule over him.

Wilkie was confined to the substitutes' bench as Argyle continued their steady progress away from danger with a 1-1 draw at home to Darlington, Taylor again scoring, after which Sturrock announced that Friio and Larrieu would be staying at Home Park until the end of the season. They followed that with a ground-out 1-0 win against Lincoln in the game re-arranged from Sturrock's first week, Stonebridge netting in the second of three minutes stoppage-time.

Portuguese trialists Paulinho da Costa and Bruno Viejas were watched against Saltash United, and immediately rejected, despite both scoring in a 6-1 win, as Sturrock continued his search for the right blend of talent to build on the firm foundations he had laid, before Wilkie made his full debut at Cardiff on January 22, when the Welshmen took full revenge for their Home Park beating the previous month.

McCarthy and McGlinchey were both sent off, along with Cardiff's James Harper, but Sturrock was pleased with the way his nine men had acquitted themselves. "In many ways, it was our best performance of the season," he said. "The final score was a bit false because, when we were 2-1 down, we still played to win the match and that gifted Cardiff's two late goals."

It was McCarthy's second red card of the season, and Argyle's seventh, giving them the worst record in the Football League – another aspect of the Pilgrims' failings that Sturrock would soon have to address.

Worrell made his temporary move from Tayside permanent at the end of January, following in the studmarks of the man who signed him. "The words I would have to use are 'absolutely delighted'," said Sturrock, as the ink was drying on Worrell's contract. "Absolutely delighted," concurred Worrell. "I've enjoyed being here. It's a decent standard. We've managed to have a few results, and the fans have been brilliant. The lads we have got here, we're in a false position; there are some good footballers here." Sturrock, who would reveal only that the fee for Worrell had been 'nominal', said: "He's been near enough our best player in every game he's played so far. If we can bring another five or six players like that to the club, we should be going in the right direction."

In his pursuit of other Worrells, and maintaining his far-ranging eye, he gave a second trial to Portsmouth striker Steve Lovell and ran the rule over Chelsea midfielder Jay Richardson, who later joined Exeter City, and wing-back Karim El

Khabir – yet another Frenchman – in a 6-0 reserve-team win over Barnstaple. None scored and none really impressed.

A third 1-0 win from Sturrock's five undefeated home league games followed, when Wayne O'Sullivan scored against Halifax and lifted Argyle nearer to the Third Division play-off places than the one relegation spot for the first time in the season. It was a measure of both the new man's impact, and the expectations he had engendered, that fans had changed their requests to him.

He said: "When I arrived, I got letter after letter say 'Please, Paul, just make sure we don't go down into the Conference.' Now, I'm getting letters saying 'Please, Paul, make sure we get into the play-offs'."

His mail-bag would have increased after a 4-0 beating of Kidderminster at Home Park on January 30 lifted the Pilgrims into the division's top ten for the first time during the season. Taylor, again, Stonebridge, twice, and Wotton, with a late penalty, ensured Jan Molby's side's first ever visit to Plymouth was not a happy one.

Argyle and their supporters came back down to earth with a bump the following Saturday at Moss Rose, where a Macclesfield side coached by Sturrock's close friend Allan Preston won 3-1 to extend the Pilgrims' sorry record of not having won outside Devon to 15 months.

"Our away form has to improve if we are going to do what everyone wants us to do," said Sturrock, who, after the game, shared a car to Perth with Preston – known all over Scotland and beyond by the sobriquet of 'Biscuits'- for Preston's testimonial dinner at their former club St Johnstone. "The quicker we break this, the better. It's grating on us. The longer it goes on, the more apprehension we have during games."

It must have been all the more galling for Sturrock, as Argyle led through Stonebridge's goal until a familiar collapse in the final 20 minutes. "Selection is the only way I am going to turn this round," he said. "We are carrying too many players away from home and I just can't pick them any more. If that means we change teams every week, then we'll do that."

If Argyle's poor away form was a familiar refrain throughout the 2000-01 season, so was the weather and the state of the Home Park pitch, and the subsequent home match against Southend was called off when torrential rain turned the surface into a quagmire. It was the eighth postponement suffered by the Pilgrims that season, and fifth at Home Park.

Before Argyle's next attempt to break their abysmal run of away results at Carlisle, they made three new signings: Ivor Jones, a financial advisor, returned

to the board of directors which he had left in 1996 after a three-and-a-half year stint, to join McCauley, vice-chairman Peter Bloom, Ken Jones and Paul Stapleton; while Sturrock took Coventry City's Rob Betts on loan from fellow Scot Gordon Strachan, and signed Opinel's LDV Vans tormentor Meaker until the end of the season after he was released by Bristol Rovers.

Betts, 19, had captained Coventry to the FA Youth Cup final the previous season and was described by Sturrock as a "playmaking, footballing type of midfielder, but with aggression as well", while Wales B international Meaker, 29, a right-sided winger, had played four times for the Pilgrims 10 years previously while on loan from Queens Park Rangers.

Neither player featured at Brunton Park as Argyle again took the lead, courtesy of Friio's first goal for the club, only to concede a late equaliser as they sat back and tried to defend their advantage.

Both made their debuts, as substitutes, the following Tuesday when Argyle returned home and, predictably, returned to winning ways against Shrewsbury. Another Friio goal and another Stonebridge double, after Matt Redmile had been sent off, took the Pilgrims' home tally to 31 points from 14 matches: away from Home Park, they had taken just nine points from 15 games.

Sturrock had a bid for Macclesfield midfielder Chris Priest turned down, his valuation of £25,000 for the 27-year-old who had scored twice for the Silkmen against Argyle earlier in the year falling £50,000 below the Moss Rose side's estimation, before signalling his rebuilding work was beginning in earnest.

'Semper Fidelis' may be Argyle's motto but Pilgrims' fans have long since subscribed to the unofficial saw that every silver lining has a cloud. So it was that, in a week when they raised a glass of claret to celebrate a new midfield hero in the shape of French playmaker Friio, they learnt they were about to lose another whose contributions they often toasted in cider: Martin Barlow, an Argyle journeyman and boy, had reached the end of his 12-year pilgrimage.

Sturrock announced his decision not to renew the 29-year-old's contract when it expired at the end of the season on the eve of the Pilgrims' home match against Cheltenham, and Barlow was told he could leave Home Park – his only footballing home – immediately if he could arrange a move before the following month's seasonal transfer deadline.

"I wanted to let him know my decision early enough to give him the opportunity to find a new club so he's not one of the two or three hundred players scrambling for a job in the summer," said Sturrock. "He's been a superb servant to the

club and a new challenge at this stage of his career could help prolong his career. Obviously, though, he's gutted."

Barlow eventually signed for Exeter, prolonging his stay in his native Devon. He had twice before come close to leaving Argyle when he had responded to demands from Peter Shilton and, then, Neil Warnock to play on the right wing by, frankly, sulking. His days look numbered but both managers soon came to appreciate his playmaking abilities as much as his fans on the terraces, and he stuck around long enough to rack up his appearance total to 378 (in which he scored a disproportionate 29 goals) and enjoy the club's finest hour and a half. Being one of only two Janners in the 1996 play-off triumph against Darlington meant that spring day was particularly special.

Injury, though, curtailed his contribution during Hodges' last season and Sturrock's first, and one battle the combative midfielder was always destined to lose was that against the calendar. "I'm very much thinking long-term," said Sturrock. "I've got to tell four of my scholarship boys – 18-year-olds with dreams – that they are not part of my plans, which is ten times worse than telling Martin Barlow he's being released."

Also on his way out of Home Park was another midfielder, Jason Peake, who barely featured for the Pilgrims after scoring the club's first goal under Sturrock's management in the FA Cup tie at Chester and who made a loan move to non-league Nuneaton permanent. On the credit side, Paignton youngster Wills was given a year's extension to a contract that had been due to expire in the summer.

With the future taken care of, Sturrock turned his thoughts to the home game against Cheltenham, victory from which would extend fans' hopes of sneaking a play-off spot. "It's a strange scenario when you want to grow something but the top of the flower is the most important thing," said Sturrock, revealing green fingers to go with his Green heart. "I'm trying to nurture the top and bed down the roots at the same time. It's very difficult."

The following witless 0-0 draw against the Robins in front of 5,209 people who will surely never endure a more meaningless 90 minutes in their lives was described by Sturrock as "probably our most disappointing performance since I got here" and he would have found few dissenters if he had substituted the words 'since I got here' with 'ever.' The only plus was another shut-out – which kept the goals conceded at Home Park to three in ten games since Sturrock's arrival – shared between goalkeepers Jon Sheffield and Romain Larrieu, who made his league debut as a half-time substitute when the former succumbed to a back injury.

Almost incredibly, Argyle's attempt to play their away fixture at Rochdale four

days later fell victim to the weather for the third time in the season. Having been turned away from Spotland in November and December because of the rain, they this time did not even leave the Westcountry after frost left Dale's pitch rutted and unplayable.

Sturrock's rebuilding plans took a dent the following Saturday when Worrell broke his ankle at Barnet, ruling him out beyond the end of the season. The game was notable on two other fronts: a travelling support of around 1,000 of the Green Army's footsoldiers, the cancelled 'NYD@LOFC' having mutated into 'BIG@Barnet'; and the surprise debut of Jean-Phillipe Javary, a French midfielder who had recently been released by Brentford after falling out with team-mates during a reserve game.

Javary, an international at every level bar full, had been training with the Pilgrims during the previous week and had so impressed that he had signed non-contract forms which allowed him to line up alongside compatriots Friio and Larrieu.

Argyle took the lead against the side that would ultimately be relegated from the Nationwide League at the end of the season, through Wotton's 13th minute free-kick, but were pegged back to a 1-1 draw by former Home Park midfielder Darren Currie.

Betts finally made his full debut in midweek, when the Pilgrims lost 1-0 to a goal in the fourth minute of injury-time by Richard Walker at Blackpool, who ended the season by winning promotion via the play-offs. Blackpool manager Steve McMahon criticised Argyle's defensive mindset, saying that they got exactly what they deserved, but Sturrock took heart from another solid display. "I proved to the players what tactical awareness, shape and organisation can do for a team away from home," he said.

A busy week for Sturrock ended with him signing 23-year-old midfielder Sean Evers, from Reading, and defender Stuart Elliott, also 23, from Darlington, as well as letting midfielder Terry Fleming join Cambridge United and telling injury-hit young goalkeeper John Hodges that he would not be retained when his contract expired in the summer.

Evers, who signed a two-year-plus deal, came on a free transfer, having only two years previously cost Reading £500,000 when he moved to Berkshire from Luton, and was described by Sturrock as "a key piece of the jigsaw puzzle."

He said: "He's one of my long-termers. Getting him in now means he can bed himself down and it's enabling me to start structuring the midfield the way I want it. I have been looking for an attack-minded midfielder who will maybe get

six to eight goals a season. Sean has scored goals in the Second Division and we are hoping he's going to come in and do the same in the Third."

Elliott joined until the end of the season, but Sturrock denied he was a simply a short-term replacement for Worrell. Given that, even at his relatively young age, Elliott had played for ten different clubs, it seemed a forlorn hope.

Elliott and Evers made their debuts, the latter as a substitute, at the end of the week against Third Division leaders Chesterfield – managed by Home Park alumni Nicky Law. It was only the third defeat of the season for Chesterfield, who led the division at that stage by 13 points. Friio scored the first and made the second for Buster Phillips, with McCarthy rounding matters off.

Off the field, it was announced that Argyle had increased their quota of Joneses on the board of directors, following the appointment of Peter Jones, a former Plymouth College student and a managing director with Grey Advertising in London, who joined namesakes Ken and Ivor in the boardroom.

Argyle came back down to earth with a bump the following Tuesday when they squandered a long-time lead at home to Hull given them by Paul McGregor's third-minute goal – his first since Sturrock's arrival the previous November – to draw 1-1, the unfortunate Elliott putting through his own net in the 84th minute against rivals who also harboured play-off ambitions. The match marked Betts' last contribution to the Green cause as he returned to Coventry after a cameo role as substitute.

Evers, Meaker and McGlinchey were recalled for the subsequent trip to Scunthorpe, where Stonebridge's 90th-minute headed goal was scant consolation in a comprehensive 4-1 defeat that extended Argyle's run without a league win outside their native Devon to 29 league games and left Sturrock to admit that the play-offs were nothing but a distant dream. The Pilgrims were nine points away from seventh place with 11 games left.

"We're not good enough to go up," he said. "Plain, simple and easy. I would say that, hand on heart, it has slipped away from us. We will keep plugging away and I have got to find a winning formula away from home – for the start of next season, if nothing else.

"It would be the biggest travesty if we went up. It would be a false dawn. I'm not saying I wouldn't take it – I'd just have to do my job as quickly as possible – but I want a solid base. What I want to do is put a team on the park that progresses next year. Whether that progression takes us into the play-offs or we are promoted, fine, but we're up in the top half of that table all season and, if we are promoted, we have a consistent side that is comfortable in the Second Division."

Having previously ruled out any transfer deadline-day signings, Sturrock made two, bringing 28-year-old Plymothian striker Michael Evans back to the club he had left four years previously for Premiership Southampton, and handing fellow forward Gritton, who was on loan at Yeovil, a two-year extension to his contract. Another forward, Lee Phillips, made his loan deal to Weymouth a permanent move.

Evans, the other Janner alongside Barlow in the 1996 Third Division play-off final, had since been on a fairly brisk journey around the Premiership and Nationwide League, been capped (once) by the Republic of Ireland, and commanded fees totalling £1.75 million – which made the £30,000 that Bristol Rovers received form Argyle pretty small beer, but, then again, you know what they say about the Scottish.

"I watched him in the play-off final and kept tabs on him when Plymouth were playing in the north the following season," said Sturrock, revealing that his purchase of Evans had been no impulse buy. "I was interested in buying him for St Johnstone, but the price was going to be a problem. This season, I intentionally went upstairs when we played Bristol Rovers in the LDV Vans game to have a look at him and I thought he definitely had attributes like holding the ball up very, very well and bringing people into the game.

"That's something our mix of strikers is not very good at. The key to our game, especially away from home, is how our strikers develop the game for us. We can't seem to get ourselves in the right areas of the pitch because of our lack of linkage from our strikers."

Evans made his debut the following Saturday, when Hartlepool became the first team to lower the Greens' colours at Home Park since Sturrock's arrival. McGregor, one of six players whose contract was up in the summer, was a notable absence from the squad as Pools won 2-0, and Sturrock revealed that the former Nottingham Forest man would not be part of the following season's campaign. "He feels he will be moving on at the end of the season," said Sturrock of the striker who scored 24 goals in 90 appearances for the Pilgrims and was a firm crowd favourite. "That's his decision. I've been having conversations with him and we were quite prepared to make him one of our highest earners.

"He hummed and hawed and, really, the geography of this city is where he's having a problem. His family, which he sees very little of, is very important to him – with midweek games and training Sundays, he's never got himself home. There's no way we're kicking him out of the door – we wanted him to stay and lengthen his contract – but there's no point in forcing the laddie to stay here and him not enjoying himself."

Another Pilgrim trying to carve out a new career for himself, Barlow, joined Yeovil on loan until the end of the season, with Gritton returning to Home Park from the Glovers.

March 31, 2000 was a watershed in Sturrock's management of Argyle – a first away victory outside Devon since his appointment in November. Evans scored both goals in a 2-1 victory at York, who had taken the lead, and Sturrock was pleased to see his theory come to fruition. He said: "Mickey ran the line, held the ball up very well, and was definitely a factor in the game for us. We have had a problem with our strike-force being able to hold the ball up, and he has come in and started to do that."

Sturrock's relief at his first Nationwide points away from base in his 10th away match was nothing compared to Pilgrims' supporters, who had waited 511 days and seen 33 games slip by since their previous triumph on their travels – at Chester City in November, 1999.

Argyle trumped that by completing the double over Exeter at Home Park at the end of the first week of April, Friio scoring the only goal of the game in a match which had less passion than items on a fishmonger's slab that have had their spines removed. "Bad pitch, bad wind, bad game," summarised Sturrock, "but a good result for us. It was the poorest home performance since I have been here and it was a shame there was such a big crowd [8,671] here to see it."

One ray of light amid the gloom was the performance of 20-year-old home-grown product Steve Adams, who impressed as a substitute after previously catching the eye at York. 'Impressed' is probably an understatement as Sturrock immediately called off his search for a defensive midfielder.

"Stevie showed me that, what I thought he could do, he will do," said Sturrock, but you knew what he meant. "He has showed me he is tactically aware, wants to do things I know he can do, and his physique, which I think was a problem to him at centre-half, is not apparent in midfield. He's quick, sees a pass and wants to play. We have found someone in our own camp, which I'm very pleased about."

The re-arranged match at fifth-placed Leyton Orient ended in a 1-1 draw, with Meaker scoring a spectacular equaliser for Argyle after he was set up by Steve Guinan, who was recalled to the starting line-up as Sturrock maintained an earlier promise to look at all his players in what he was fond of calling 'battle conditions'.

Argyle were unable to kick sand in the face of fellow seasiders Brighton the following Saturday, when the visitors ensured their promotion to the Second Division with a 2-0 victory. The Pilgrims were clearly in the party mood on and

off the terraces. The team contributed two defensive howlers to gift Brighton their goals, while the fans staged yet another celebration/protest against the way the club had been run – after 'BIG@Barnet', this was 'BIGGER@Home Park'.

Those perverse celebrations continued on the city's Barbican later that day, where supporters gathered at the Cooperage (a successful Argyle piss-up in a brewery – now there was a first) for an evening whose far-reaching significance would only become apparent months later.

Sturrock was in anything but a party mood after a 3-0 Easter Bank Holiday Monday defeat at Kidderminster. The scoreline flattered Argyle and Sturrock said: "I'm totally embarrassed to be associated with some of the players out there today. It's the worst they have played for me. It won't be tolerated. Some people's heads will roll for that kind of standard. People today have probably played their last game for Argyle."

That number included surprise debutant Danny Bance, an 18-year-old defender, who Sturrock admitted feeling sorry for. "You can't blame the kid," he said. "I took him off because I didn't want him to taste any more of what was happening. It was nothing to do with his performance."

After two excoriating defeats, the news that Friio had agreed a two-year deal with the club was some sort of balm, but Sturrock wasted no time in carrying out his promise: Javary was released from his short-term deal immediately and goalkeeper Sheffield was told that he was no longer required by the club and, like Peake, Fleming, Nancekivell and Phillips, would be paid up.

Sturrock said: "When it comes to shot-stopping, I have the best 'keeper in the league, but, in the Third Division, there are lots of corners, goal-kicks and long throws and we have got to find two goalkeepers who are very confident with that style of play." On the credit side, 27-year-old captain Craig Taylor agreed a new deal taking him to the summer of 2003, and 19-year-old forward Stonebridge extended his current deal until the summer of 2004.

Argyle bounced back to winning ways with a 3-1 home victory over Torquay which pushed their neighbours nearer to the relegation trap-door, Stonebridge scoring twice and Torbay-raised midfielder Wills once as the Gulls fell apart following Khalid Chalqi's sending-off in the 40th minute, at which time they led 1-0. Happily, Torquay famously survived on the final day of the season.

The Pilgrims hit another three at Home Park four days later in an entertaining 3-3 draw against Southend. They led 2-0 through the newly-committed Friio and Evans, were pegged back to 2-2, led again through Wotton's 86th-minute penalty, but surrendered two points to Rob Newman's injury-time equaliser. Part of their

frailty in defence can be explained by the loss of Taylor in the 19th minute with a double break of his ankle.

Sturrock missed both games, and the subsequent visit to Lincoln, when he returned to Scotland to take care of the funeral arrangements for his father, George, who passed away suddenly, aged 77. In his absence, his right-hand man Summerfield took charge of affairs and was at the helm when it was announced that McGregor had been paid up the remaining few weeks of his contract.

Argyle dominated at Sincil Bank but went down 2-1 after Stonebridge had given them parity for most of the match, with McCarthy again playing as an emergency centre-back in Taylor's absence, and Sturrock was back in charge as the Pilgrims finished their season with back-to-back matches against play-off chasing Rochdale.

They lost the first, thrice-postponed, match at Spotland 2-1, Evans scoring, after which Sturrock said: "I can assure everyone we are definitely going in the right direction. We have played a team who could be in the play-offs and never looked out of sorts with them. We have only gained 14 points from our away games this season: if we can add another 10 to 12 next year and have the same home form, we are going to be sitting in the right area of the league."

Before the return at Home Park, Sturrock had declared his hand for the following season. O'Sullivan, Guinan, Chris Leadbitter, Meaker and Elliott all parted company with the club – the Pilgrims' manager might have made his reputation as a striker, but it was as a sweeper in the final week of his first English season that he will be remembered. That's sweeper as in 'sweeping out dead wood'.

Guinan, who was halfway through a two-year contract, was told he would not be considered for the first team, while Meaker and Elliott were released from short-term contracts. Leadbitter, plagued by knee problems, retired and O'Sullivan went to play for Parramatta Power in Australia – which critics of the game Down Under might say amounted to the same thing. Gritton, who had two years of his relatively new contract left, was warned not to expect to see it out as a first-teamer unless he improved.

Sturrock said: "Wayne has decided to move to Australia. We are a bit disappointed because we wanted him to be one of our players for next year, but that's football. I've decided not to give contracts to Stuart and Michael. They have worked very hard and are good lads, but we need a different type of player.

"Steve Guinan has been told he's surplus to requirements. Saying that, he's one player who maybe didn't get the opportunities he thought he should have but, after trying to get a pairing together, I feel Stonebridge and Evans got better and

better together every time I watched them. Martin Gritton has been given a warning. He has not achieved the standards I expect from him over the last two or three months and has not progressed as I would have expected. He has been warned he'd better reach those standards come pre-season training or I will be having words with him.

"Ledsy's had to retire. His knee's just not standing up to things. The one area we have missed has been a ball-winning midfielder and I'd hoped Ledsy was going to turn my head, so it's a big disappointment.

"I had to clear the decks, clear my mind, which means targeting players, starting now and working through the close season and into next season. I want to get 21 first-team squad players. The quicker I do that, the better, but I will not be rushed into it for the sake of getting bodies in for the start of the season, because I've got kids here who deserve a chance. I want to give them the opportunity to progress into my first team."

True to his word, Sturrock blooded three youngsters against Rochdale as the season ended, not with a bang, but a whimper, especially for Rochdale, who missed out on a play-off spot by the two points denied them by the Pilgrims in a 0-0 draw which saw goalkeeper Luke McCormick start and Ryan Trudgian and Paul Connolly come on as substitutes. Connolly became the 39th player to make a first-team appearance in the troubled season.

So ended Plymouth Argyle's worst ever season. Yet, there was room for optimism. Sturrock's clear-thinking and strong focus had seen him treat the weeks since he had taken the Pilgrims to the safety of mid-table as an extended pre-season, trying out players, working on formations, assessing the strength of a division of which he had only a passing knowledge until the previous November.

When he was appointed, Argyle were one position off the relegation place: they finished the season in 12th spot, the new manager's record having a pleasingly symmetrical look to it: played 34, won 12, drawn 10, lost 12. He said: "No team that we've played this season has made me think we cannot be in the right area in the league next season."

While Sturrock's methods looked sound, there was the x-factor over which he had no control: his chairman. Although there was nothing to suggest there was anything remiss in his relationship with Dan McCauley, in banning a local journalist from Home Park for penning an article with which he disagreed, the chairman showed he remained the loose cannon which had already fired six managers in nine seasons.

PAUL STURROCK: "For my first match at Torquay, I never went near the

changing-room. It was quite a funny day. Dan and [Torquay owner] Mike Bateson seemed to be getting along reasonably well and the banter was very good, my kind of banter. It was my kind of craic. The strange thing was where the directors' box was. I have never watched a game from behind a goal, not even as a kiddy – I would be in the enclosure under the stand. When you go behind the goal, you are either trying to usher everything into the net or you're trying to clear every ball. That was also the last game I was ever going to sit in the stand the whole match. I'd done it at Dundee United and St Johnstone, but never enjoyed it. When I had my problem with hyperventilation, I got recommended that I stay away from the dug-out for two or three games, so I had a walkie-talkie, which was ten times worse. When I first started here, I decided I would sit upstairs because I could see the game better. In my first season, I started up there and came down towards the end of games; second season, I began by doing the same thing, but pretty soon felt it was important that I stayed at pitch level, plus we were having problems with walkie-talkies and everything else.

"It would be unprofessional of me to start rattling off about everything I thought about individual players in that first game. I would say I saw problems in certain areas of the team. I saw a lack of pace in the team, a lack of sharpness, and probably the most scary thing I saw was a lack of heart, which I didn't expect in a derby. We got a goal really easily but kind of sat on it. When there were battles to be won that day, I don't think we won them.

"Going away, I felt that the training-ground was the place for me – then the hundred days of rain came. From then on, I was battling. We had a wee run, which I sort of played down at the end of the season, but, if the hundred days of rain hadn't come and we'd had more time on the training-ground, we might have sneaked a play-off place.

"The first thing you have got to remember is that the team was third-bottom of the league – that means it wasn't good enough. We can put sugar-pills on it, hear all the explanations, and everything else, but, although you always get a wee kind of lift when a new manager comes in, I realised that a lot of them would revert to type. I felt that a clear-out was the most important thing: one, to show the players that the manger was in charge; two, to clear my mind of the five or six players who were here when I got here that were not up to standard. I'd made up my mind about them very quickly.

"I think the problem I had was that I was uncomfortable with some of the players I was going to have to use. If whatever became available was better than what I had, I chipped away at it. That was the main thing: fishing them in, fishing them out, whenever the fish became available.
"I was very lucky. I've got five or six agents in Scotland, which is probably a

wee bit of a bonus that no other manager in the Third Division enjoyed. I had a respect up there and I felt my name might stand me in good stead of grabbing one or two players. David Worrell came very quickly, which was very pleasing.

"I'd watched him at Blackburn for Dundee United five or six times and felt he was a bit quiet, didn't really stamp his authority on games. That worried me, but he actually went straight into the team and we finished third-top of the league the season before I resigned. He got injured at Christmas, but, up until then, he'd been in the team. But I was worried about his confidence and felt that the step from reserve football to the Scottish Premiership was probably just too much for him. I thought this might be a more comfortable stepping-stone for him and I've been proved right.

"Brian McGlinchey came to us through one of the agents I was very friendly with. My old assistant had seen him play twice for Gillingham and he recommended him to me as well, so I got him down for a trial and played him at left-back. He didn't look a left-back to me. I did feel that Buster Phillips would always play on the right for me, so I needed a left-side to give me balance. I felt he might be a squad player, in as much as he could play three or four positions. He's done very well. He's worked very hard at his game. He was another one who was a bit quiet, a bit insecure, a bit unsure of his place in life, so that was a wee bit of a worry for me. I didn't feel he had come out of his shell, which he has now.

"When you go to a football club, there are favourites. Adam Barrett was a young centre-half who'd come in and progressed very well but I see no point having two left-footed centre-halves at a club – I'd rather have more right-footed centre-halves than left-footed, especially when, a lot of the time, two of them were playing together. That was a surprise to me. I had to choose between Craig Taylor and Adam and, at the end of the day, I decided Craig Taylor was the player I would commit to. He became part of the jigsaw and, all of a sudden, I had a back four that had a wee run and lost very few goals until David Worrell got injured.

"I got David Friio from another agent that had done me a decent turn on a couple of deals, so I gave him the opportunity. Probably the big talking-point was my decision to give David his debut against Exeter away when I'd never seen him play a game. I think that epitomised my experimentation that season. Although every Argyle supporter in the world would hate to get beaten by Exeter, that really didn't concern me. The important thing was to get people in and to find out their strengths. I had no time to dilly-dally. The only way I could test trialists was to play them. He looked terribly unmatch-fit. I thought he might last an hour, but at least I could see him

under battle conditions. He had an up and down game, but he showed there was something there.

"Romain was always going to be the cover goalie to start off with. He had lost his way and hadn't played for eight or ten months. There was no way he was going to play that early. It would have been too much of a risk. Obviously, it got forced upon me later because Jon Sheffield got injured. First game, he had a very ropy opening 20 minutes – he panicked, I would imagine – but I saw enough in training to appreciate that there was more to him. I knew ring-rustiness would be a factor. I thought he grew that year and, at the end of the season, people were very impressed with him.

"Sean Evers has obviously been my disappointment. He's a nice lad, but at the end of the day, not everyone fits into the jobs that are available. I made a comment that I wanted to build my team around him and I stick by that. I needed a player to link me from the midfield to the front, but it never really materialised.

"Though Sean McCarthy had done a very good job for me, there were two telling factors: one, referees had their card marked as far as he was concerned. There was no way any longer for Sean to be aggressive, to take the things into the game that he wanted to take into them. Secondly, injury-wise, he was up and down, in and out; he always seemed to have a wee knock. Although he gave everything he'd got for me, his age wasn't going in the right direction, either.

"I felt I needed back-up in that area – I needed height – and I was very pleased that the chairman went out on a limb for Sean and Mickey Evans. They had come from bigger clubs and it meant changing our wage-structure – very, very slightly – but, if we'd stuck to the wage-structure that was at the club when I got here, we would never have signed those two. I tried to map out that what I was trying to do was cut the squad down, and bring in more quality by paying 21 players the same amount we'd previously paid 29.

"First and foremost, Chopsy [Martin Barlow] was injured very soon after I got here and was out for five or six weeks with niggling injuries. When he came back, Buster, Brian, David Friio and Wayne O'Sullivan had basically snapped up the jerseys and he had to play in a kind of back-up role. Kevin Wills and Steve Adams were now coming into contention. Ledsy [Chris Leadbitter] could never get fit, either, so I felt they were always just covering the squad. If I decide a player is no good other than as a squad player, if they are 19 or 20, they have got to go and, if they are 29 or 30, they have got to go. There is a middle range where you can keep them, but I did feel

Chopsy had to move on. That was a big decision – he was a fans' favourite; he had played more than 300 games for the club; nobody could understand my thinking, but that's my job. Decisions like that have to be made.

"I thought I might be able to get to McGregor's psyche. I probably played him more than I should have because I think his performances for me were not up to standard. I had been told how scintillating his performances had been but I always believe what you see is what's been painted. I thought I could mould him to what I wanted but he was going out of contract and, in his own mind, he was leaving. I felt the laddie let himself down when I brought him back in the team. I didn't think he was committed to the football club, so he didn't play from then on.

"I received letters from fans saying they just couldn't believe that I was letting these players go, but hard decisions had to be made. It's no detriment to the players concerned, but we were third-bottom from the league. Sometimes losing gets imprinted on your brain and I had to break the mould. The only way I could do that was to change the personnel. I find it easier to tell a 29-year old man he's going to be surplus to my requirements because of a younger buck than I do breaking the heart of an eager 18-year-old. He's experienced enough to take it and I think players appreciate honesty.

"I've never flanneled anybody – I tell them what I think. Although I won't be on Guinan's Christmas card list, I think the one thing he will admit is that I marked his card very early. Circumstances that developed between us from then on as he negotiated his pay-off and wasn't involved for a year is the way football is these days. Time's a problem. I don't think Guinan and I could pass the time of day with each other now. At the beginning, I think we could have sat down and had a chat. At the end, quite rightly for him, not getting a game and not training with the first team, the situation had deteriorated.

"Generally, if you tell people, the mutual respect is much better. I think even Chopsy, although totally disappointed, appreciated the fact that I told him early. We tried to do a deal to wherever he wanted to go early, so that he didn't have that scramble at the end of the season, and I was delighted that he and Sean were picked up by Exeter.

"When I make a decision to release a player, it's absolute. These decisions are not made lightly and, at the end of the day, there's one thing to remember about football managers: you make your decisions and you stand or fall by them. If I'm going to get sacked, I'm going to do things my way. If it's not the way that gets results, I'll put my hands up and move on and try

and learn from the mistakes I made for next time. My wife says I'm a hard person – in football, not at home – no heart. Even with the relationship I've got with this lot. We can have a bit of banter but there's them, a fence, and there's me. Now and then, I'll jump the fence and be a lad, but they can't come the other way. I think the players appreciate that.

"There's no room for sentiment. I learnt that at St Johnstone. We battled ourselves out of relegation trouble when I took over. We were dead and buried when I got there and we eventually ended up losing our place by a goal. Hearts hit Partick Thistle's bar with two minutes to go and, if that went in, we were up and they were down. I was sat in the bus on the way down the road, and I had four people tell me they were too good for the First Division, they had to get away.

"The second scary thing was that I made a very poor decision that the squad we had was good enough to get us back up again – but at Christmas they had me sitting in a dressing-room at Stenhousemuir, losing 4-1 to a part-time football club. I was contemplating chucking it in and I'll always remember the chairman coming in and saying: 'I've made a mistake because I've put you down the road of thinking that, for financial reasons, this lot were able to take you back up. I apologise, I made a mistake.' I said: 'No, chairman, I made a mistake.' He said: 'Well, the two of us are here now. I can't give you much money, but whether whatever money I give you takes us to 15th in the country or third in the country, it'll be where we are. This is what your budget it is, if it's not enough, we'll just stay where we are. I'm with you and I'm staying with you, now go and change the team.' So we went and changed the team. That was something I learnt about sentiment and listening to other people."

CHAPTER FIVE

IF Argyle's players thought they could relax over the summer, they were quickly dispraised of the notion. Sturrock sent them on their break with a warning that any of them returning for pre-season training overweight would be fined.

"I'm not prepared to be committed to the cause and not have the players committed," he said. "I expect the players to be in the best possible condition for my pre-season, which is going to be the hardest they have had in their lives. Next year, I want to make sure we are the fittest team in the league."

The atmosphere of change at Home Park continued a week after the end of the 2000-01 season when chief executive Roger Matthews resigned five years after being appointed to the role by McCauley. Matthews, citing a desire to dedicate more time to his catering business as the reason for leaving, said: "I have become very fond of the club and I'm delighted that it is on the brink of a new era. However, five years is a long time in football and I would now like to concentrate on other interests which have had to take a back seat for half a decade."

McCauley paid tribute to the man who had often acted as a conduit between board and management, saying: "I'm disappointed that Roger is leaving. He has a great personality, he's a nice guy and he's well liked by everyone at the club."

His departure coincided with the decision of goalkeeper Romain Larrieu to commit himself to the club for two years. Sturrock said: "He's a young goalkeeper who showed a bit of inexperience at times last season, but he also showed that he's going to be a confident 'keeper in years to come. My squad is going to be a young squad, but I quite like the idea of that."

Sturrock revealed he had decided to make Larrieu his number one number one, despite the Frenchman having made only 17 appearances the previous season and initially deciding he was not yet ready to be a first choice. Luke McCormick would be Larrieu's understudy at the tender age of 18.

Sturrock said: "Larrieu and McCormick did enough at the end of last season to merit their opportunity at the beginning of this year. I felt it would be a backward step in their progress if I brought in another goalkeeper now. It will be up to them to make sure I don't have to go out and get another goalkeeper."

Next on board the good ship Pilgrim was 26-year-old centre-back Graham Coughlan, a long-time target for Sturrock, who made his move when the Dubliner was released by Scottish Premier League newcomers Livingston, who Coughlan had captained to successive divisional titles north of the border.

Not considered good enough to cut it at the highest level north of the border, Coughlan had been released on a free transfer. Sturrock said: "He's the type of centre-back we could do with: he's a rugged type, wears his heart on his sleeve, and has a burning desire to win. He also makes himself heard on the pitch, and we haven't got enough of those."

Sturrock, though, was denied from making it a double swoop when another target, St Johnstone striker Paddy Connolly, signed a three-year extension to his McDiarmid Park deal. "Obviously, we're very disappointed not to get him," said Sturrock, "because he would have added something to our squad, but St Johnstone made him an offer he couldn't refuse. The pleasing thing for me is we are targeting this standard of player and they are interested in talking to us. That bodes well for the future."

The comings and goings continued when Sturrock decided not to offer a new contract to veteran Welsh striker Sean McCarthy, despite earlier indications that the pair were trying to work out a deal. The 33-year-old thus finished his second spell at the club, which he quit for the first time in the summer of 1990 when he left to join Bradford after two seasons at Home Park in which he scored 26 goals.

He had returned three years previously and, in between injuries and the inevitable suspensions his abrasive style attracted, scored another 22 goals and proved to be a more than useful emergency centre-back.

Sturrock said: "Sean did well for me, but I felt that, with me looking to start with Evans and Stonebridge, looking to bring another striker in, and Gritton already here, it would be unfair on him at this stage of his career not to be involved every week."

McCarthy took the news of his estrangement philosophically. "It's disappointing," he said, "but these things happen in football. I've really enjoyed it. The fans have always been very supportive, and I think the club will do well next season and it will be shame not to be a part of it."

McCarthy's optimism was not shared by the bookies who, following the release of the fixtures for the new season which gave Argyle a home start against Shrewsbury, installed them at 14-1 to win the title. Bristol Rovers, demoted the previous season from the Second Division, were 5-1 favourites, with Luton and newcomers Rushden & Diamonds 7-1. Exeter City, who McCarthy joined in a two-year deal the following week to link up with fellow ex-Pilgrim Martin Barlow, were outsiders.

Argyle players returned for pre-season training on Thursday, July 5 and 23-year-old centre-back Paul Wotton eased some of the pain by signing a three-year

extension to his contract. "My immediate aim is to get myself into the first team and play well enough to stay there," he said. Given such modest ambitions, the following season was to surpass his wildest expectations.

Among the trialists who turned up for training were former Crystal Place striker Roscoe D'Sane; former Oxford United and Stranraer defender Neil McGowan; Plymothian Craig Swiggs, a midfield graduate of Crewe's successful youth academy; and French midfielder Romain Angelletti, whose previous club had been Corsica-based Ajaccio.

Goalkeeper Jon Sheffield spent just one more week at Home Park before signing for Nationwide Conference neighbours Yeovil, managed by former Cambridge United team-mate Gary Johnson, on a free transfer. Sheffield, signed for Argyle from Peterborough for £150,000 by Mick Jones in 1997, made 175 appearances for the Pilgrims before Sturrock decided he was surplus to requirements. He said: "An experienced 'keeper like Sheff needs to be playing first-team football and obviously he will receive that at Yeovil. He has been a very good servant to Plymouth Argyle and I wish him all the best."

Sheffield, who still had a year to run on his Pilgrims' contract, said: "Things weren't going according to plan at Plymouth and, with Yeovil having such a good record, it seems the right thing to do."

Just before the Pilgrims' first pre-season friendly at Carlsberg South Western League neighbours Saltash United on Monday, July 16, Argyle announced that David Tall OBE, would be Matthews' replacement as the club's chief executive.

Bristolian Tall, 55, a retired naval captain with 36 years experience in the senior service and a former chairman of the Royal Navy and Combined Services Football Associations, was a lifelong Argyle supporter. He said: "I don't think there are many people who can go from one job they love to another they already have affection for."

He promised to make the club more accessible to fans – "I can't guarantee their proposals will be put into action, but what I can guarantee is that they will be addressed" – and he often proved as good as his word.

All four Argyle trialists made their debuts at Saltash's tidy little Kimberley Stadium as, in front of a crowd of nearly 1,000, the Pilgrims beat their junior neighbours 2-0 with goals from Martin Gritton and Kevin Wills. None, however, staked a truly strong claim for a contract and Swiggs and Angelletii were immediately released, with Sturrock deeming that they offered nothing he did not already have at the club.

Playing alongside another debutant, Coughlan, in the centre of defence was club captain Mick Heathcote, who was making his first start in any Argyle team since suffering a serious groin injury the previous December. Heathcote, 35, had been given the pre-season to prove his return to fitness, and he said: "It's up to me to impress. The objective is to earn a new contract to stay at the club a little while longer and I will be working hard to do that. I still think I have something to offer."

Heathcote was back in action two days later, when the Pilgrims visited Blaise Park for a friendly against South Western League champions St Blazey. The match also served as a testimonial for former Pilgrim and Saint Mark Rowe, who will be most remembered at Home Park for a match in which he did not play – Rowe was the unused substitute when Argyle lost to Watford in the semi-finals of the 1984 FA Cup as a Third Division side.

Since then he had gone on to win every trophy available in Cornish football before retiring due to Achilles and calf injuries, and St Blazey manager Trevor Mewton heralded his achievements. "Mark Rowe is, and will always be, one of the great names of Cornish football," said Mewton, "He was one of the most gifted players around and always looked comfortable on the ball."

The match ended in a 1-1 draw, with Dominic Richardson, another former Pilgrim, scoring for the home side and Sean Evers equalising for the Pilgrims just after half-time. It could have been worse – Saints' midfielder Justin Harrington hit the crossbar twice in the dying minutes – and Sturrock was not happy. "The performance was not up to the standard I would expect from some of the players," he said.

With McGowan released, D'Sane was the only one of Argyle's original trialists to be included on a week-long pre-season tour of Scotland, which began on Saturday, July 21 with a match against Third Division Montrose. He was joined by another wannabe Green in Portuguese midfielder Miguel Reisinho, though neither new man started the game as Sturrock selected a side clearly geared towards the upcoming Nationwide Third Division campaign.

The tour's itinerary might have included a trip to a whisky distillery, a night out in Sturrock's hame frae hame, Dundee, and plenty of golf, but the Argyle manager was determined his players would not mistake the break from Plymouth as a lads' holiday.

"Pre-season starts here," he declared. "For anyone wanting to play on the first Saturday of the season, these four games will be taken into consideration. We have a lot of new players who have come together relatively quickly and it is good to get away as a team.

"As far as I am concerned, that is as important as the games we will be playing. Good team-spirit is vital if you are going to be a successful team."

Argyle began the tour on a winning note with a 68th-minute goal from Wills, who scored with his first touch after coming on as a substitute for Evers, leaving Sturrock to pick the bones out of generally unsatisfactory display. He said: "The first half was very ordinary but, in the second half, we began to show a wee bit of what we are capable. I'm pleased to get a result. Too many times, Plymouth go away and lose, so it's nice to have a win for a change."

More than 170 Argyle fans had travelled to Links Park for the dawn of the new era, many independently but some as part of the official tour party, for which they had paid £700. Among their number was Phill Gill, for whom the trip was the start of a much bigger journey in his life, and some, like 21-year-old student Ian Sherwood, from Salcombe, had been allowed to join in training sessions.

The Pilgrims' unbeaten start to their pre-season came to an end two days later on the coast at Methil, where they lost 1-0 at East Fife's Bayview Stadium. Midfielder James Allan scored the game's only goal direct from a 20-yard free-kick. Among the fans was Lewis Ridge, from Farnborough, who had not missed an Argyle game for 15 years – even going to the Gambia for a friendly in the mid-1990s. He once walked from his home to Swindon to Home Park for a Boxing Day fixture.

Alan Kernaghan, the 34-year-old Republic of Ireland centre-back who Sturrock knew from their time together at St Johnstone, joined trialists D'Sane and Reisinho in trying to impress the Argyle manager. Kernaghan, who had top-class experience with Manchester City and Middlesbrough, had made 19 appearances for the Saints the previous season before being released and had suffered from pelvic injuries.

"I have got to weigh things up," said Sturrock. "You have got to give the opportunity to his sort of quality." After weighing things up, he decided against pursuing his interest.

After a day off during which some Pilgrims' supporters went to watch a friendly between Arbroath and Dundee United reserves in the vain hope of seeing Sturrock's son Blair – he was injured – Argyle hit their stride two days later when they comfortably beat Second Division Forfar 3-0 at Station Park. David Friio, Ian Stonebridge and Reisinho scored, with Stonebridge's 20-yarder from open play being the pick of the quality triple. "It augurs well," said Sturrock, "I am normally a hard man to please, but even I have to admit partial satisfaction after that display. I think we showed the hard work we have put in over the past week. Our fitness looked good and we have now got to put a sharpness to the players."

The Scottish jaunt was concluded with a 2-1 win against part-timers Albion Rovers, immediately after which the players hopped on the team bus for a 12-hour journey home. They were probably already feeling a little sore from a match in which late tackles, shirt-pulling and raised elbows were all evident, but two set-piece goals inside four minutes from centre-backs Heathcote and Coughlan earned the victory. Sturrock said: "It wasn't a classic, but it was nice to finish the tour on a positive note."

PAUL STURROCK: "The P word – progression – was paramount. I wanted the players to appreciate that progress was what we were looking for. I talked to them on the last day of the season and said that progression had taken us so far and had to take us further the next season. I didn't have a holiday because I was transferring my wife down to Plymouth and because there was a lot to be done. I felt the effects of not having a break through the season.

"Mickey [Heathcote] was hampered by injury and was out of contract and Craig Taylor had been injured periodically throughout the season, meaning that Steve Adams, who had no comprehension of being a centre-half, had to play a couple of games there. Lee Wilkie had been brought in on loan to cover these two but, in the end, it annoyed me that we had to change the system to accommodate Lee Wilkie. I'll never do that again.

"Cocko became available. I couldn't believe that Livingston had let him go. I didn't like a couple of their other centre-halves but he was out of contract and they weren't. I met him in Perth, sat down, talked to the laddie, and liked him a lot. He wanted a three-year deal. I talked to Sloop [John Blackley], who had seen him twice the season before. Sloop, being a defender, said he was player who would battle his corner. I talked to three or four others – Darren Jackson, who had been at Livingston, and other mangers – and asked them what they thought. They marked my card that he was a player, so I went into negotiations. A couple of days later, he came down by train, walked in the door, signed a contract, walked back out and went back up the road.

"I just missed out on Paddy [Connolly] because St Johnstone upped their offer, but I still think he would have been a great influence on the football club. They were the only two key signings I wanted to make. I had only three strikers: Evans, Ian Stonebridge and Martin Gritton, and Gritts was a bit iffy with me. I'd given him a two-year deal and I was hoping I could mould him, but very quickly on the tour of Scotland, I discovered he wasn't going to fit into my style of how I wanted the game played.

"I got unbelievable letters about not buying players. Everyone was saying

we needed players. I didn't want to panic buy. I'd committed myself to certain things and didn't want to compromise.

"I don't think they'd ever had a real pre-season and they got it. I think it was huge culture shock to them. We started off running round Saltram House. It was something they'd never tasted before. At the same time, we were doing all the ball-work and, all of a sudden, we had games against Saltash and St Blazey and then we were off to Scotland. They must have thought they were getting a reprieve, but they were training morning and afternoon. Even on the days we had games, they were training in the morning.

"Pre-season puts a backbone of fitness into the players for the season. You have to keep topping it up every so often, but the general fitness is there. At the same time, you are working on tactics, which is why the Scotland tour was important, although I think I gave them too much information, for which we paid the penalty against Shrewsbury and Rochdale. A lot of stuff – systems of play, tactics, how I wanted things done – had been put into some people in a very short space of time, all sorts of things they had never been used to doing.

"Team-spirit was definitely enhanced in Scotland. A lot of bonding went on between players, because they were in each other's pockets the whole time. That's part of the psyche, because you've got a better chance of winning. No-one plays for the shirt any more – they play for the wage-packet and they play for their mates. That's what I tried to instill in them in Scotland.

"Also, they are cut off in Plymouth, which is a real benefit. They are training in the mornings and can't escape in the afternoons. So they will maybe play a bit of snooker, or golf, or go out for meals, are basically more friendly with each other.

"The chairman and directors, who are fans – and people forget that – wanted that closeness for everybody and that desire changed the mentality of the place. Everyone brightened up and the workers all changed here as well. The whole structure of the club, from chairman downwards, changed; it brought a breath of fresh air right through the whole club."

KEVIN SUMMERFIELD: "We had a lot of difficulties, pre-season, because our training pitch at Harper's Park was out of action. We were lucky that people provided for us. We went to Saltram, Keyham MOD, and Brickfields – all these sorts of places. Pre-season was tough. We had to get up and go to all these different places, carting everything we needed, including goals, about. Players drove their cars because the kids had the minibus; they took

all the balls, bibs, the cones. We were training twice a day, and it wasn't easy. If we could have had Harper's, it would have been a doddle. And the training kit didn't arrive until the day before we went away. We didn't have tracksuits at the beginning of the season. That's why it was great to get away to Scotland, where everything was there for us, away from all the hassle. That was a massive week, because we got loads of work done. The players become yours; you were in total control. Morning to night, we knew where they were. With four games and training twice a day, every day, they had no time to be lazy and they were ready to train because they had nothing else to do.

"Before we went away, there was one murder day – a run round Saltram. I don't think Romain enjoyed it. Basically, he was that far behind, there were woman with babies in prams walking past him and we thought he'd chucked himself in the river. He came in; it must have been 20-25 minutes later than everybody else.

"The squad was exactly the way Paul wanted it. We knew we had 14 or 15 and were ready to wait for Craig and Dave to get fit again, and search for the other ones. We were looking thin, but we knew that. You just don't know how it's going to go.

"In Scotland, we were trying people and we never really got to any shape until the third game, when we had the team on the pitch that was basically going to be the team that started the season.

"The football was fantastic during that Forfar game. It was exactly what we'd been working on throughout the week; the set-pieces worked, everything. So we thought at least we knew where we were going and the players knew what were looking for. It all worked exactly. I wrote in my notes: 'A glimpse of our true form, real quality'."

CHAPTER SIX

THREE days after returning from Scotland, Argyle played their first home friendly when Premiership Sunderland visited the Westcountry in a Benefit Match for club captain and fans' favourite Mick Heathcote. The match against the club at which he had begun his career represented Heathcote's first start at Home Park for eight months, during which time he had battled back from a career-threatening groin injury to force himself into Sturrock's planning for the new campaign.

Heathcote had been brought to Plymouth by Neil Warnock when he set about building his promotion-winning side in the summer of 1995. Warnock had far earlier earmarked the Cambridge United centre-back as the defensive rock on which he would lay his foundations and, ten months later, Heathcote led Argyle out at Wembley, and, after a 1-0 victory over Darlington, into the Second Division.

Heathcote – man of the match on that heady May day, player of the promotion campaign and a shoo-in for the PFA Third Division team of that season – had yet to agree a new contract with Sturrock, who had not seen him play under 'battle conditions' and the 35-year-old was hoping to convince the new manager that there was life in the old dog. There was a certain irony that the side providing him with a second chance with the Pilgrims should be Sunderland, and not just because the beneficiary of the Mackems' largesse was a Geordie Magpie at heart: it was the Black Cats who had given Heathcote a second life after he was rejected by Middlesbrough following a solitary, unproductive year as a young professional in the mid-1980s.

Heathcote was convinced his injury problems, healed by a Belgian surgeon in Bradford, were behind him. "There were times when I said I couldn't go on anymore," he said, reliving his time on the sidelines. "Now it's well out of the way. If I didn't believe I could do a good job for Plymouth Argyle week in, week out, I wouldn't waste everybody's time."

The fans' affection for the man known by many of them as 'Hoof' was evident as he received a standing ovation from a 5,000-plus crowd, and Heathcote let no-one down as Sunderland eased to a 3-0 win with two goals from England striker Kevin Phillips and another from his replacement Danny Dichio.

It was to be Heathcote's last appearance for the club. Sturrock offered him a one-year contract but the Argyle manager's Shrewsbury counterpart Kevin Ratcliffe was prepared to double that and Heathcote returned to the club for which he had made nearly 250 appearances earlier in his career.

He said: "Having proved my fitness to myself, the club and supporters, I was reasonably confident that I would be offered something with Argyle that would have taken me through to the end of the 2002-03 season. The contract I signed with Argyle last season included a clause that, if I was fit for the 2001-02 season, I would be offered a one-year extension.

"The manager said he would honour this but would not offer me the two-year contract I was seeking. Coincidentally, the next day, Kevin Ratcliffe, who had tried to sign me the previous season and who had been monitoring my progress this pre-season, contacted me with the offer of a two-year deal.

"Leaving Plymouth, with their wonderful supporters, is the hardest decision I have ever had to make in my life, particularly after the great support shown towards me at my Benefit Match. I hope they will understand that, above all, football is my living – I have a family to support and I have to continue my career as long as possible."

Sturrock stuck by his decision but expressed disappointment that his plans for the new campaign had been disrupted. He said: "I didn't think it would have been competent of me as manager of this football club to give him a two-year contract, with his recent medical history.

"I'm disappointed because I had pre-planned my defence for the start of the season and Mick was involved in that." To add spice to the situation, Argyle's first game of the season just one week later was against Shrewsbury Town.

PAUL STURROCK: "Mickey felt he merited two years. He had a clause in his contract guaranteeing him another year, but he felt he deserved another one on top of that. As a manager, you look at man-hours. Mickey was a fantastic servant for the football club, but I had to weigh up what it would mean for the club if he was sitting on the bench for another year. It would have been very unprofessional of me to sign him for another two years. He had another offer of a two-year deal and he would have been insane, in my mind, to turn it down, so Mickey moved on. There was more outcry and Coughlan had a couple of ropy games first up which I don't think helped the situation, but he soon won over their hearts.
"It's people's livelihoods and people's opinions. It was his opinion that he'd done enough but I don't think I would have convinced the board to give him a two-year deal even if I'd asked. If another 30 managers had been here, they would have made the same decision."

Sturrock had decided to offer a short-term contract to Portuguese former FC Porto midfielder Miguel Reisinho, who played a full 90 minutes in the next pre-season friendly, a disappointing 0-0 draw against Second Division Bournemouth

at Home Park. "I think Reisinho had the shock of his life as far as the pace of the game was concerned," said Sturrock afterwards. "David Friio was exactly the same when he arrived – the first three or four games passed him by until he learned and adapted. Reisinho is going to have to do the same very quickly."

KEVIN SUMMERFIELD: "There was a funny incident at half-time of the Bournemouth game. Brian [McGlinchey] played left midfield and they kept changing their system because they couldn't cope with us. I went in at half-time – Paul was upstairs for some reason – and Brian was getting caught between two stools. I sat him down and said 'Brian, we've got a bit of a problem. Have you got any idea what formation they play?' He looked at me and suddenly everyone's gone very quiet, listening. He looked at me and he started to stutter. He said: 'They're playing one in the hole, one deeper, and er, er...no I don't. Haven't got a clue.' The dressing-room erupted. He'd been trying to blather his way through it and gave up. It was so funny. You can't say anything to that."

Also in the Pilgrims' line-up at Bournemouth was another trialist, French winger Mickael Serreau, who Sturrock paired with countryman Vincent Petit in a friendly at Liskeard the following Tuesday. Petit, no relation to French World Cup-winning midfielder Emanuel, scored four of the Greens' goals in a 6-1 victory less than 36 hours after leaving Corsica. Sean Evers and teenage defender Paul Connolly scored Argyle's other two goals.

A notable absentee from Argyle's pre-season preparations had been Steve Guinan, and the 25-year-old signed by Kevin Hodges the previous season had correctly read the manager's intentions. With the club boasting only three strikers, all of who had struggled for goals in pre-season, Guinan was training with the youth team and had not been allocated a squad number.

"I'm pretty much finished here," he said, but he rejected an offer by the club to pay up the remaining 11 months on his contract as derogatory. "The offer they gave me was nowhere near the figure I'm after. The manager has said I'm not his type of player and that's fair enough, but there's no need for me to be treated like this."

As Guinan was contemplating his stalled career, Argyle's own future suddenly looked brighter when chairman Dan McCauley and Plymouth City Council leader Patrick Nicholson signed the legal documents which finally removed all obstacles to the redevelopment of Home Park.

A new 18,000 all-seater stadium for Home Park had been agreed in principle many months before, and construction company Barr had been on site for several weeks, awaiting the go-ahead to begin demolishing the old stadium. McCauley

had even taken the considerable gamble of paying out £1/2 million to start the redevelopment work, even though the contracts had not been signed. "If we don't get the contract with the council signed, we are going to be in a hell of a mess," he said.

The deal, including a new 125-year lease on Home Park for the club, was signed on Monday, August 6 and Barr wasted no time in moving in. As McCauley was hailing the deal – "At last it's all come to fruition," he said. "I understand from the previous board that discussions had been going on for 25 years, so you have got to give the [council] leader a lot of credit: he has fulfilled his pledge. I know it has taken a bit longer than we both wished but both teams have done a tremendous job and got Plymouth Argyle what it needed. All we need now is success on the pitch" – the diggers began ripping up the old Barn Park end.

Incredibly, around 600 Argyle supporters turned up to watch the first piece of the old stadium come down and one, Barry Bowden, voiced the question that was in the minds of most. "Once you've got the stadium, are you going to get the team to go with it?" he asked. With the new season just days away, he would not have to wait long to find out.

First, though, there was to be one unexpected and largely unforeseen event that would have a significant impact on the Pilgrims fortunes for the forthcoming campaign.

CHAPTER SEVEN

THE news that no-one had been expecting was broken by Argyle's shirt sponsors, the Plymouth *Evening Herald*, on the very eve of the 2001-02 season. The front page of their edition of Friday, August 10 carried their Argyle reporter Chris Errington's scoop that chairman Dan McCauley had agreed to relinquish his omnipotent controlling interest in the club after presiding over the most tumultuous decade in the club's history.

Errington's story detailed McCauley's agreement in principle to sell his shares to a five-man consortium headed by his fellow directors Paul Stapleton, who was to become the new chairman, and Peter Jones, who would be his deputy. The three others participating in the buy-out were revealed as former Labour Party leader Michael Foot, and London-based businessmen Phill Gill and Nic Warren, lifelong Argyle fans, like Stapleton and Jones, who had recently followed the club's tour of Scotland.

McCauley would remain on the board as one of six equal partners, until his new co-directors successfully repaid a £600,000 overdraft and the £1.8 million that McCauley's Rotolok company had invested in the club during ten years of his chairmanship that had seen six Argyle managers come and go and the Pilgrims relegated to the Third Division for the first time in their history. A period of nearly two years to settle the debt was envisaged.

It was the new consortium's collective passion for the club that finally persuaded McCauley, who had consistently refused to sell the club to a variety of interested parties, to sell. "There was a lot of people out there huffing and puffing, but nothing came of it and, in the end, you've got to buy the club from here," said McCauley, pointing to his heart. "A local consortium knows best – they know what goes on."

For Stapleton, a senior partner in city chartered accountants Parkhurst-Hill and a driving force behind the Argyle Youth Development Trust, his elevation to the chairmanship was another step in an extraordinary journey. From an eight-year-old tacker standing on the Barn Park terracing watching the likes of Johnny Williams and Wilf Carter, he became one of McCauley's biggest critics before joining the board in 1998. He said: "I feel very proud. It hasn't really sunk in. I'm just pleased to be joining an elite band of 16 people who have been chairman of the club since it started.

"We've got a new stadium; it's a new millennium, more or less; a new manager. I have got great faith in Paul Sturrock. He's a brilliant chap – he lives and breathes football – and we have got to back him whatever way we can: financially, emotionally, whatever. Let's get us back where we belong."

Jones joined Stapleton in predicting a brighter future. "We're lucky," he said. "We're not coming into a bombsite. We're coming into a stadium that's happening, with a new manager. There's a huge amount we have to do, but I don't think we're starting at ground zero."

It will have come as a satisfying surprise to McCauley's many opponents – and a shock to McCauley – that the consortium to which he had agreed to cede his boardroom power had its roots in a protest against his often unpopular chairmanship.

The previous March's 'BIGGER@HomePark' had been organised by Argyle supporters to cheer themselves up during a fourth successive thoroughly miserable season. Originally, fans had wanted to voice their disgust at McCauley's unproductive ten-year chairmanship in traditional manner, but were persuaded that some sort of ironic positivism would make more of a statement to a chairman who had regularly criticised – and ignored – protesting supporters.

It was at the subsequent evening function at Plymouth's Cooperage following another uninspiring Saturday afternoon that the germ of the idea that blossomed on August 10, 2001, took hold.

Warren, an executive director at London-based trading and risk-management specialists Morgan Stanley and a Devonport High School Old Boy, had been so impressed with the day that he made a suggestion. To the background of the music of Jelly Roll Jackson and the Boogie Kings – including the anti-McCauley 'Ballard of a Fat Man' – he put forward the idea of bankrolling one of the organisers, Paul Roberts, for a place on the board. Roberts was tempted, but declined. However, he put Warren in touch with his friend Jones, then a relatively new Argyle director.

The next link in the intricate chain of events that led to the changing of the guard at Home Park came from McCauley himself. During a board meeting, he had told directors that he had received another in a long line of bids to buy the club, this time from a consortium based in the Bahamas. After the meeting, he encountered Stapleton and Jones in the car-park, and they told him they were disappointed he was considering selling the club. McCauley's response was to challenge Stapleton and Jones to put together a bid themselves. Stapleton thought he was joking.

With Warren already on board, the putative new consortium's next member proved an unlikely one.

Jones had been friends with the Plymouth-born former Devonport MP Foot since the pair met at an Argyle game in Newport a quarter of a century earlier. Though

an unwavering supporter since his days as a young politician in the city during the 1920s and 30s, Jones presumed 88-year-old Foot's days of active involvement were long gone and was not expecting anything other than removed interest when, during one of their regular conversations, he told Foot about the latest developments at Home Park. To his surprise, Foot wanted in.

The final member of the new Argyle board of directors joined the consortium late. Gill, an area director for Kinleigh, Folkard and Hayward, London's largest independent estate agents, was still just another Argyle supporter when he had joined the club on their pre-season tour of Scotland two weeks' previously. By the time he left, and after conversations with Jones and Warren (who followed the tour, not with the official party, but staying in B&Bs with other supporters) he was on his way to completing the line-up.

In 'Ballard of a Fat Man', Jelly Roll Jackson exhorted McCauley to "put your money where your mouth is." His new partners – fans all – had done just that.

PAUL STAPLETON: "It was the end of May and we had a board meeting. Afterwards, I walked out to the car-park with Peter Jones – we didn't really know each other that well, but we'd become friendly in the board meetings because we saw each other as an ally – and Dan walked up to us, which was unusual because Dan had Sean [Swales, McCauley's accountant for his company, Rotolok] with him, and would normally get in his car and disappear.

"He actually walked across the car-park to where my car was and said: 'I'll just have word.' Then he said: 'Right you boys, you've got all the contacts – you put together a consortium.' I sort of looked at him and said: 'Yeah, right Dan.' But he said: 'No, I'm serious – you say you know everybody, you say you are fans, put together a package and I'll be interested in going.'

"We looked at each other and Peter said: 'I know somebody in London – Nic Warren.' And we said: 'Okay Dan, we'll give it some thought, see what we can do, and come back to you.' Then Dan disappeared and we carried on our conversation. We thought it could be quite interesting. He obviously wanted to go.

"Then I went to the Football League Chairmen's conference with him a week later at Carden Park, a lovely hotel in Cheshire. We then carried on talking on the way up and I said: 'Are you serious about going? Because it's not the right time for you to go in some respects – we're going to get a new lease, we're going to rebuild three-quarters of the ground, we've got Paul Sturrock in situ and I've got a good feeling we're going places. Don't you think it's sensible for you to get to a tangible point of new stadium

and/or success and then bow out?' He'd had a lot of stick, but he could have a bit of success and then go.

"He said he'd made his mind up. He was old enough to go, he'd had a lot of people making offers, and it had been intimated that he should go. It was time. I was worried that I was wasting my time. While I was at Carden Park, another league chairman told Dan he had buyer for him and asked what the property was like, whether there was any scope for development. Then someone from somewhere else said he knew someone who was interested in buying a football club. It opened my eyes to see all these people who wanted to be in a football club. I didn't really realise that; maybe I was a bit naive. I thought: 'We'd better get cracking here because there are other people interested.' I kept on talking to him. It transpired that before the season would be the best time to do the deal, if we could do it.

"At the end of the meeting, usually the chairmen of the clubs go to the top table, sit in alphabetical order and vote on certain proposals. We went to the AGM and he said: 'Go on, you go up and vote.' I said: 'You want me to vote? You might not like what I vote for.' He said: 'I don't care – you do what you want. Vote for what you want to – you're Plymouth Argyle, you go and do it.'

"So I went and sat with the chairmen and we all voted. [Darlington chairman] George Reynolds was opposite me and he kept voting the same as me. I said: 'What are you doing George?' He said: 'I always follow Plymouth.' I said: 'Where's all your notes?' He said: 'I can't read or write – I'm just going with you.' And every time I voted, he did – it made me laugh. I said: 'Dan, that was nice, thanks for letting me do that.' He said: 'That's fine – you've got to get used to it.' I think he'd made his mind up. It was a relaxed weekend and I think he'd made up his mind he wanted to go.

"I came back and rang Peter Jones and said: 'He's serious – we've got to get cracking.' I approached [the vice-chairman] Peter Bloom, because it was political to do so, to see if he was interested. I don't think he believed Dan was going to go. Ivor Jones was already a director and I asked him if he was interested but he said he didn't think the time was right for him. I told him to think about it because he was already there, he was a pal of mine and we wanted some Plymouth-based people involved. Peter Jones had Michael Foot lined up, we had Nic Warren and I did say to Dan that he could stay. I said it would be democratic and asked him if he knew what democratic meant. He said he did.

"I also spoke to John McNulty, who wasn't on the board at that stage because he'd already fallen out with Dan, and a few other people around

the city. Nothing came out. Dan was really impressed with that. It's the first thing to do with Argyle that's ever been kept quiet. While I was away in Turkey on holiday, I was in contact with Peter every day. It probably spoilt the family holiday, but my wife, Kim, understood what we were trying to achieve and was right behind me.

"When Peter was in Scotland on the tour, he said he'd met a chap called Phill Gill, who might be interested. He said: 'I don't know much about him – I met him in a bar – but he lives near me in Chiswick.' I said: 'Keep him on your back-burner, but I've still got Ivor and Peter.' I was looking at maybe seven directors, including Dan.

"I rang Ivor again and asked him whether he was interested. He said he wasn't sure. I told him I had someone else and he would have to resign. Peter Bloom still wasn't sure. I said I wanted him to have the opportunity. I don't think Peter or Ivor really thought it would happen. To be honest, we didn't really mind because we wanted new brooms. Peter met Phill and I said I'd leave it up to him whether he came on board. I didn't know him, but I trusted Peter's judgement. If he said he was alright, we'd have him. He rang me up and said he'd be okay. That was six. So I rang Dan and told him we were ready, we'd clear the club's overdraft and sort him out for his money. He said: 'Okay.'

"On the Monday before the season started, we went to the council and signed a 125-year lease on the ground. On the Thursday, Dan said: 'I'm coming down – let's go to the solicitors. I've done a draft agreement.' We went in there for two hours, agreed the draft, came out and Dan said: 'That's okay, we haven't signed it but we can announce it tomorrow.' He wanted to do it before the start of the season, although we weren't sure. We hadn't signed the agreement although I was happy for the new broom to start the new season. He said: 'Just do it.'

"He called the manager down – he looked stunned – and called a Press conference for Friday. Until that Thursday night, it hadn't been decided to do it. Peter, Sean, Paul Sturrock and I all went out for a meal to Chambers. Dan was invited, but I could see he wanted to go home because next day was the day he was stepping down.
"Paul's initial shock lessened and he warmed to it quite a bit, I think. We had a good meal and Sean and Peter stayed with Paul, which was good, in some respects. Next day, we had the big Press conference, although nothing had been signed officially.

"On the morning of the Press conference, I rang [director] Ken Jones – I felt quite guilty about Ken, because I'd got quite close to him when we worked together for the Development Trust – and asked him round to my house. I told him we were going to take over and that it meant he would have to resign. He was happy that Dan was going, I think.

"We had a board meeting before the Press conference, which was so amazing. We actually went through the normal business – apologies, what's happening, and all the rest. About a quarter of an hour before the scheduled start of the Press conference, I said to Dan: 'We'd better move on.' He said: 'Oh yes, as you know, I'm stepping down so I'd like you three to resign.' It was surreal.

"During the previous week or so, Dan had asked who was going to be the new chairman. I hadn't even thought about it – all I'd been thinking about was to get the deal done with Dan and Rotolok. I said it would be decided on a vote and he said he'd vote for me anyway. Peter Jones said I was the obvious choice and that he would vote for me and recommend to Michael Foot that he did the same. I said I was quite happy and it did make sense because I was in Plymouth. We're all equal; it's just that I'm in situ."

PETER JONES: "As far as I'm personally concerned, everything hinged on an impulse. I was in Plymouth in February, 2001 with Michael Foot. Because I'd been bringing Michael for years, I'd got to know the McCauleys and they were always very kind.

"I came into the boardroom, just after he'd put Ivor Jones back on the board. I looked at him and thought: 'I'm going to go for it.' I hadn't planned it. I said to Dan: 'Could I have word with you? I don't think you've got enough Joneses on the board. He said: 'Well, we've got two.' I said: 'I think you could do with a third.' If I hadn't done that, I don't think I would have been involved with the club.
"When Dan hinted that he might be thinking of selling the club, it was a bit unnerving, thinking that, if he did sell out, we'd be out on our rears the next day. We'd really worked hard for the club. Paul had done ten times what I'd done – he's really worked his tail off for the club over the past two years.

"I told Michael we were putting together a consortium, just to let him know. He said: 'Can I do it too?' He really wanted to do it. I asked him

if he had the available cash. The next day, we had a meeting at his bank in Holborn and it was absolutely clear he could do it.

"Phill was on the tour and he cornered me in a pub in Dundee and said he'd love to get involved with the club one day. So I took him to one side, swore him to secrecy, and said maybe he could.

"We had a Plymouth filter. I had informal conversations with people with loads of cash but we weren't interested unless they were Argyle people. I think that was the right decision. I had people who I knew from Deutsche Bank who wanted to do it, thought it would be a good crack but they weren't considered."

PHILL GILL: "In Dundee, I just got chatting to Peter, talking about all the things that had been wrong with the club for years, how it lacked vision, and, because he was fairly new on the board, I asked him how he got on. He told me and then asked whether it was anything I'd ever been interested in. I said it was an ambition of mine long-term, if I could effect a change. He said it might be sooner than I thought.

"His aunt has a got a big house in Knightsbridge – the sort of thing that never comes on the market and he said she may sell it at some point. The day after Mick Heathcote's Testimonial, I got a call about 11am. Before I took the call, I said to the guys in my office: 'This is my friend, the Argyle director; his aunt must have decided she's going to sell the house.' So we were all really excited, because these houses come on the market once every 30 years. Peter said he had important business and could we have lunch?

"He said: 'Do you remember what we said in Dundee?' I said 'Yes', thinking where's all this leading? And he got out a big wad of paperwork and said: 'Here's your opportunity', which obviously completely threw me. Luckily, I had some funds available that I wouldn't normally have had because, the day before the Scotland tour, I'd been gazumped on a house I'd been chasing for eight months."

CHAPTER EIGHT

TO add to the rebuilding in the board-room and on the terraces, Paul Sturrock undertook a little construction work himself on the eve of the new season, adding striker Dean Crowe to his small squad. Crowe, 22, was borrowed from Second Division Stoke City to supplement the Argyle strike-force of Michael Evans, Ian Stonebridge and Martin Gritton for their opening match of the season against Shrewsbury Town at Home Park.

"I didn't feel comfortable about going into the new season with only three strikers," said Sturrock, and the not-quite-ready feel of the place was enhanced by the non-appearance of midfielder Miguel Reisinho's work-permit.

"It's a strange scenario," said Sturrock. "The restructuring of the club is going ahead, the restructuring of the stadium is going ahead, and now the restructuring of the board is going ahead. It's a freshness, a positiveness, and you should try to be optimistic, but, although expectations are high, we are not the finished article.

"I can feel it in the air. I can taste the expectation levels of fans that have been disappointed for ten years. I'm telling you now, those hopes will be dented this year. The black days are not over, not by a long haul."

Not by 4.50pm the following afternoon, certainly. The match facts might have suggested that Argyle lost 1-0 to 10 men after Shrewsbury midfielder Karl Murray was sent off ten minutes before half-time, but Sturrock was convinced the Pilgrims were beaten by 11 men, all of who wore green.

"We shot ourselves in the foot, big time," he said, after Shrewsbury captain Nigel Jemson's 73rd-minute opportunist strike had proved decisive. "This defeat is totally Plymouth-based."

Like McCauley had before him, Stapleton did not see Argyle win in his first game as chairman, although he must have entertained his guests in the board-room at half-time believing that he would. With Brian McGlinchey and Buster Phillips buzzing down the flanks, and David Friio and Kevin Wills bossing midfield, Argyle might have been three up before Stapleton's visit to the drinks' cabinet, and any three of Evans, Stonebridge or Friio might have had a hat-trick.

Unfortunately, Evans and Stonebridge appeared to be engaged in some bizarre private game to see who could be most profligate, and Friio's headers packed as much power as a blown lightbulb. Sturrock said: "To dictate the game as much as that and not take the chances we had in the first half is nothing short of a

scandal. It was easier for Mickey Evans to score than miss the chances he's had; and David Friio..." Words failed him, but not for long. "Stonebridge looked so out of it – it was quite scary the chances he could have had today."

There was also criticism of his defence, after debutant centre-back Graham Coughlan and goalkeeper Romain Larrieu combined in Keystone Kops-like fashion to allow Steve Jagielka a free shot on goal. Although Jagielka proved more useful as a high score in Scrabble than a finisher, the subsequent corner conceded from his shot led to the game's only goal.

"It was a disaster waiting to happen," conceded Sturrock, "and one poor piece of communication and one defensive lapse at a corner and we ended up losing.

"If we're going to be positive, that first half was as good as we played for most of last season. If we can create the chances we created today, we're going to win a lot more games than we will lose."

Saturday, August 11, 2001, Nationwide League

Plymouth Argyle 0
Shrewsbury Town 1
Jemson 73

Plymouth Argyle (4-4-2): R Larrieu; S Adams, P Wotton, G Coughlan, J Beswetherick (S Evers 76); M Phillips, K Wills, D Friio, B McGlinchey; M Evans (M Gritton 76), I Stonebridge (D Crowe 66). **Substitutes** (not used): L McCormick (gk), P Connolly.
Booking: Beswetherick 38.

Shrewsbury Town (4-4-2): M Cartwright; I Jenkins, M Redmile, M Heathcote, G Rioch; S Jagielka, K Murray, M Atkins, P Wilding (A Tretton 82); L Rodgers (J Walker half-time), N Jemson (C Freestone 90). **Substitutes** (not used): I Dunbavin (gk), D Moss.
Sending-off: Murray 35 (second bookable offence).
Bookings: Murray 31, Jemson 78.
Referee: C Penton (E Sussex). **Attendance:** 5,087.

PAUL STURROCK: "A change of board isn't something you want to be going into your first game of the season with. All of sudden, the players are having this big news flashed through. I think it would be unsettling for anybody. It was for me. Thankfully, I was quite friendly with the new board members, but it was still not a great situation. I've seen other managers lose their job because of a change on the board. That wasn't an issue, because obviously I'd talked to people on the Thursday night and they'd made that plain.

"It wasn't the best start to a season, and then we walked away with a 1-0 defeat. It was the biggest one-sided 1-0 defeat I've ever seen in my life. We

Graham Coughlan and Brian McGlinchey celebrate, v Rushden (A)

Exeter 0, Argyle 1 (Phillips)

Exeter 2, Argyle 3 (Phillips, Evans, Stonebridge)

Michael Evans is sent off, v Luton (H)

Time problem, v Cheltenham (A)

Defeat, v Bristol Rovers, FA Cup (A)

Lee Hodges wins a penalty, v Scunthorpe (H)

Paul Wotton scores, v Scunthorpe (H)

Steve Adams scores, v Exeter (H)

Sean McCarthy's red card, v Exeter (H)

Virus-hit Paul Sturrock, v Shrewsbury (A)

Ian Stonebridge, v Luton (A)

Lincoln (A)

The Penalty That Never Was, v Southend (H)

Paul Stapleton and
Peter Jones

Was he watching?

had done all that work in Scotland, and, to be fair, we had brought it all to the game, although probably we hadn't done enough crossing and finishing. We'd packed in as much as we could. The chances we created were unbelievable.

"Everything was swirling round in my mind so, on the Saturday night, when I went out with the coaches for a meal, it was like eating cardboard. After an hour, I had to leave, I just couldn't face it.

"The result stuck in my craw near enough all season, and, what's worse, they were the one team to beat us twice. Sometimes you get a team you just can't handle."

KEVIN SUMMERFIELD: "It was the first time I'd been involved with the first team since I'd left Shrewsbury. Everybody was optimistic and to come off losing was mega-depressing. We lost our way in last ten or 15 minutes, but before that we created chance after chance after chance. It was some of the best football we played at home during the entire season. If that was a sign of the season, it was going to be a long hard season. I took the video home because Paul didn't want to look at it. I got up at 4am and watched it and we didn't play badly. I was okay afterwards, and went back to bed. I thought: 'We ain't far away here.' If Evo had taken a couple of headers, it could have been five or six. We pulled the players up on Monday over the goal we conceded. It didn't happen again."

Sturrock's own reconstruction work continued the following week, with one arrival, one non-arrival and two departures. On their way out of Home Park were Portuguese midfielder Reisinho, who returned home to his family after failing to agree details of the short-term contract Sturrock had offered him. His only contribution to Argyle's season was an appearance on the traditional pre-campaign team photo that is bound to have fans from future generations scratching their heads.

Of marginally more significance than Reisinho's brief flirtation with the Greens was Dean Crowe's fling. At least he managed to play some football while in Devon, although his 24-minute appearance as a substitute against Shrewsbury was entirely unmemorable, before "family problems" saw him return to the Potteries with three weeks of his one-month loan outstanding. Fortunately for Crowe, those problems subsided sufficiently for him to join Luton Town a couple of months later, and he proved to be a striker of some quality at Kenilworth Road.

There was further frustration for Sturrock when he failed to land Dundee United's 22-year-old former West Ham defender David Partridge. The clubs had

agreed a £40,000 fee for the Londoner, but, despite a full day's negotiations between the player, his agent, Sturrock and Stapleton, the Partridge deal went pear-shaped over personal terms. "We are a Third Division club," said Sturrock. "We have a wage-structure in place. The laddie was very keen to come here but it's not all about the player any longer, which I find is a strange scenario."

Partridge ended the season struggling to get a game on loan at Leyton Orient, which might have been handy for home, but hardly represented an upward move on the career graph.

Consolation for the Argyle manager came in the familiar form of Lee Hodges, who agreed a one-year deal which saw him return to Home Park eight years after a seven-game, two-goal loan spell under Peter Shilton in 1993. Hodges, 27, was then a Tottenham hot-shot teenager and in the intervening eight years had played for Barnet and Reading, who had released him at the end of the previous season. He had hoped to join Northampton before the Second Division club's finances dictated otherwise, and had also trialed at Luton.

"The good thing about him," said Sturrock, after adding Hodges to the Pilgrims' squad for their visit to Hull, "is that he's a three or four-position man and you need one or two of those in your team to fill holes that occur through injuries and suspensions."

Sturrock admitted that "all of a sudden, that bus is under pressure, going up the motorway: we don't know what we're going to be like away from home; we've got a fan-base whose expectations were shattered in 90 minutes last weekend; and players who are apprehensive. When it comes to man-management, I don't know whether my magic wand will work, but I won't be afraid and I'll convey that to the players."

The wand worked. With Hodges debuting at Hull on the left side of midfield in a 4-5-1 line-up that was to become more than a little familiar away from home over the coming months, the Pilgrims drew 0-0 at Boothferry Park to snaffle a point away from hosts who began the campaign as one of the favourites for promotion, having spent close on £1 million on players during the close season. Evans was the lone front man, and his contribution was hailed as "absolutely immense" by Sturrock, who used precisely the same phrase to describe Coughlan's performance in the heart of the defence. "He was a colossus," said Sturrock. "We battled hard and were definitely worth the point." It might have been all three if referee George Cain had seen the handball against Mike Edwards that Evans vehemently claimed.

One point. One step on the ladder.

Saturday, August 18 2001, Nationwide League

Hull City 0
Plymouth Argyle 0

Hull City (4-4-2): M Glennon; M Edwards, J Whittle, N Mohan, I Goodison; T Whitmore (R Matthews 69), M Greaves, J Johnsson, D Beresford; G Alexander, L Dudfield (R Rowe 86). **Substitutes (not used):** P Musselwhite (gk), D Lee, L Philpott.

Plymouth Argyle (4-5-1): R Larrieu; S Adams, P Wotton, G Coughlan, J Beswetherick; M Phillips, S Evers (J Broad 81), D Friio, B McGlinchey, L Hodges; M Evans (I Stonebridge 90). **Substitutes (not used):** L McCormick (gk), M Gritton, P Connolly.
Referee: G Cain (Bootle). **Attendance:** 10,755.

PAUL STURROCK: "I felt I'd made it plain that we would be in transition until Christmas. I knew there were holes in the team – big gaps – and that was something I was going to have to address as we went along. I knew I needed a left-sided player. I felt Brian was too defensive. He gave us balance but he didn't give us a goal-threat, so I was looking for competition for that place.

"Lee Hodges came and played against Bridgwater – showed fantastic pace, a great touch, and great in the air, but he'd been in the wilderness. He also had a couple of clubs who were interested in him and he was waiting on. They were going to pay more than we were going to pay. Eventually, we made him an offer and he signed.

"The problem was that he was half-fit because he'd missed pre-season. I was worried about that, but we made up our minds we'd get him fit through training and playing, so he came right into the side and played an awful lot of games. He's a manager's player. He still has a problem with his positional sense, though.

"The problem I had with Miguel was that he came on a three-month contract but very quickly all sorts of other things needed to be added to his contract – a car, a house, that sort of thing – and, when I weighed it all up, it looked as though he had played 3-5-2 all his life and I just couldn't see him fitting into the team. So I talked to the agent and quickly moved him on.

"The problem was that, with Craig Taylor really struggling to find his feet, the worrying aspect was that I didn't have any coverage at centre-half. I wasn't prepared to move Stevie Adams there, so I wanted to make sure there was enough coverage in the squad as far as defenders were concerned. I'd taken David Partridge up to Dundee United when he was a young player and he still had a naivete in his game.

"His personal terms were just too high. What I just don't understand about agents is that they sign contracts with players, and then take agents' fees from clubs. That isn't logical to me. If they did it properly and took the percentage off the player, I could see the point of that.

"I felt we were still short of strikers. I felt that I needed some coverage. Somebody had recommended Dean Crowe to me and I'd seen him once, I think, on my travels. Three or four people said: 'He's a player, have him'. He came down, but he had a lot of family problems at home, and I think he read the script when he was sitting on the bench for the first game. I think he thought he was going to start. He walked out on us; there was nothing I could do. I didn't feel he would become a regular for us from the performances I saw in training, although he's turned out to have done well for Luton.

"I remember sitting in the hotel at Hull and saying to them: 'Footballers have to believe in themselves and, last season, you didn't believe in yourselves. Now we can believe we are losers and lose a whole lot of games or we can we believe we are winners. This season will transpire the way it will, but take attitude, work-rate, commitment and will to win to the table with you, and if we lose, walk away and say that the better team beat you.'

"I changed the system that day as well and there was a belief that they could win the game or draw it. Hull were one of the favourites for the title and the crowd was 10,000-plus. I don't think we had a heart-stopping moment all game and came away with a 0-0. Nobody could believe we could lose to Shrewsbury at home and then go to Hull and get a draw.

"I think the whole pattern of the team, and all the work we had done, just started to groove into people's psyche: where they should be, what they should be doing, playing for each other, working for each other. It all started coming together."

KEVIN SUMMERFIELD: "Monday, August 13 was very important day in the season. We arranged a game at Bridgwater and managed to persuade Lee Hodges to come down from London. At half-time, you knew he would do for us. He was exactly what we were after.

"He was a brilliant shape player; he had one or two headers and a couple of shots, but his work-rate in that sort of game on that poor pitch made you think 'Great'. Even though, at the time, he was hoping to go to other clubs, we thought if we could get him, he'd be a big plus for us.
"If we'd have played Carlisle instead of Hull, it would have been a long

time before we saw what we were capable of. [Scout] Ken Trace had been to watch Hull at Exeter and he said they were the best team in the division that he'd seen for a long time – pace everywhere, very direct; they ripped Exeter to pieces. We looked at it and that's where the 4-5-1 came from. If we'd lost then, nil points from two games, we'd be staring down the barrel, so to walk off with a point then was good. The players played the system really, really well."

Sturrock persisted with the basic 4-5-1 formation for the Pilgrims' next match, a midweek Worthington Cup tie at First Division Watford.

"I played that system a long time in Scotland away from home," he said, "so I appreciated it could work. But you've got to have the personnel for it. Lee Hodges has come in and, all of a sudden, the pieces of the jigsaw fit."

Argyle lost 1-0 to an 82nd-minute free-kick from Jamaican international Marcus Gayle, after Brian McGlinchey had conceded ten yards' ground for backchatting the referee, but Sturrock was delighted with his team's determined defending and crisp passing and was later to admit that it was on that Tuesday in Hertfordshire that he first entertained the belief that the Pilgrims were capable of achieving promotion.

The small squad was stretched to the limit, with defenders Jon Beswetherick, David Worrell and Taylor missing and influential French midfielder Friio – the defensive 'sitter' in the five-man midfield – limping off with a tweaked hamstring after a dominant half-an-hour. Friio's replacement, 18-year-old Joe Broad, acquitted himself well, though, and Sturrock said: "I think we have shown tonight that we are going in the right direction. As I have said all along, progression is the name of the game.

"The manager and the players have got to make sure the fans go home happy, either with the performance or the result. Tonight, they will be disappointed with the result, but I'm sure they will be happy with the performance."

Tuesday, August 21 2001, Worthington Cup, first round

Watford 1
Gayle 82
Plymouth Argyle 0

Watford (4-4-2): E Baardsen; P Blondeau, R Vega, D Ward, P Robinson (J Panayi 64); N Wooter (H Helguson 84), P Vernazza, S Hughes, D Foley (A Neilsen 55); G Noel-Williams, M Gayle.
Substitutes (not used): A Chamberlain (gk), D Noble.
Plymouth Argyle (4-1-4-1): R Larrieu; S Adams, P Wotton, G Coughlan, B McGlinchey; D Friio (J Broad 31); M Phillips, S Evers, K Wills (I Stonebridge 84), L Hodges; M Evans (M Gritton 84).
Substitutes (not used): L McCormick (gk), P Connolly.
Booking: McGlinchey 81.
Referee: P Armstrong (Berkshire). **Attendance:** 9,230.

PAUL STURROCK: "I think the key to the season was Watford. We were written off. There was no chance of us getting a result. When we went to Magaluf at the end of the season, we were in the bar having a few drinks when this bloke, a Cockney over there on his holidays, came over and said: 'I want to thank you'. I said: 'Thank me for what?' He said: 'I'm very friendly with Luca Vialli and a lot of footballers in London, and my mate dragged me to see the Watford-Plymouth game. After the game, I put two bets on: one that Watford would be relegated, which was a bit of fun, and one that you would win the championship. After your performance, I could not see anyone touching you. You matched, if not bettered, a First Division team that night, with football, with a will to win. I knew, if you took that to most Third Division games, you would win.' We won him £27,000.

"Up at Forfar, I really started to think that, if we played like that when the season started, I couldn't see many teams beating us. The problem was that the standard had improved and four teams had come down that I didn't really know much about, so I wasn't sure. But the Watford game showed to me we were on the right track."

KEVIN SUMMERFIELD: "We can perhaps count ourselves fortunate that we played at Vicarage Road next. There was something about playing at Hull, Watford and then Rushden – all nice grounds, our support was fantastic, the pitches were great, 4-5-1 was made for it. It made us play."

WHILE a debate about whether the rebuilt Home Park should be re-Christened had started, football followers already believed Sturrock's men were playing under a new name: Plymouth Argylenil. An old joke, but a good one, rather like Argyle's defence (good, rather than an old joke) which had conceded two goals to set-pieces in three league and cup matches.

The problem was at the other end, where the Pilgrims had failed to score since

returning from their pre-season tour of Scotland – five games, including the full-scale first-team friendlies against Sunderland and Bournemouth. Hence Sturrock's next signing, on a three-month contract, of well-travelled forward Nicky Banger, whose previous clubs included Southampton, Oldham, Swindon and Dundee, where former Dundee United manager Sturrock noted him as one to keep an eye on.

"He's got a wee bit of guile," said Sturrock, of Banger (pronounced to rhyme with 'danger', rather than 'goal-hanger'). "He knows how to play the game; he knows where to sit and stand; he's thoughtful."

Sturrock also admitted that his strikers' failure to...well, strike was his one concern of the opening weeks of the campaign. "It's starting to play on players' minds," he said, in the run-up to the home match with Rochdale for which right-back Worrell was inked in for a return after a six-month lay-off with a broken ankle. "The sooner we get a goal or two and a couple of wins, the better."

Again no Argyle player managed to find the net as Dale left Devon with three points following a 2-1 victory. The Pilgrims' goal, after 12 minutes, was contributed by opposition centre-back Simon Coleman, after which a defensive loss of concentration a minute later allowed Gary Jones to equalise and a schoolboy error from substitute Broad (who *was* little more than a schoolboy) gave Kevin Townson the opportunity to set Paul Connor up for the 78th-minute winner.

"All the team seems to be doing at the moment is kicking ourselves in the teeth," said Sturrock afterwards. With his best laid plans ganging agley a wee bit too often in the early part of the season, one could only draw the conclusion that was because they were supposed to be aiming at the nose.

"Cardinal sins, like not being solid for five minutes after you score, and from a young, inexperienced player playing a square pass across the back four, have cost us dear."

Sturrock's assessment was as unforgiving as the Third Division table, in which Argyle were placed 22nd – already eight points behind leaders Bristol Rovers, who were about to go into a season-long tailspin – but still just the top team in Devon: Exeter were 23rd and Torquay bottom.

Saturday, August 25 2001, Nationwide League

Plymouth Argyle 1
Coleman og 12
Rochdale 2
Jones 13, Connor 78

Plymouth Argyle (4-4-2): R Larrieu; D Worrell (J Broad 75), P Wotton, G Coughlan, B McGlinchey; M Phillips, S Adams, S Evers (J Beswetherick 23), L Hodges; M Evans, I Stonebridge (N Banger 55).
Substitutes (not used): L McCormick (gk), M Gritton.
Bookings: McGlinchey 29, Larrieu 78.
Rochdale (4-5-1): N Edwards; W Evans, S Coleman, D Bayliss, S McAuley; T Ford (K Townson 73), D Flitcroft, G Jones, M Oliver, K Durkan (P Ware 85); C Platt (P Connor 65).
Substitutes (not used): M Gilks (gk), M Doughty.
Booking: Ford 40.
Referee: R Harris (Oxford). **Attendance:** 4,198. **League position:** 22nd.

PAUL STURROCK: "I honestly believe the Rochdale game was a hiccup. I thought we were as good as them, if not better than them. But for a naive pass from a young laddie we put on late on, we'd be sitting there with a draw.

"For the first half, we played quite well. We scored an own goal, so we still hadn't scored a goal in battle conditions. I still felt that the finishing and crossing wasn't coming together. Then we lost a zany goal at the end. Everybody was looking at it and thinking: 'What a disastrous start to the season – out of the cup and one draw from three games.' Everyone was thinking it was going to be much the same as any other year."

KEVIN SUMMERFIELD: "Poor pitch, poor referee, poor performance; the shape was not right; the back four had a bad day. They were not really better than us. We arranged a staff night out and we shouldn't have gone, because it was all doom and gloom."

CHAPTER NINE

IF there was one, single instance on which Argyle's season turned, it came in the 55th minute of their August Bank Holiday Monday fixture at Irthlingborough, home of the previous season's Nationwide Conference champions Rushden and Diamonds.

That the Pilgrims were underdogs to the Football League's newest members demonstrated how low ambition and expectations had fallen at Home Park, but Rushden justified their favouritism by taking a 2-0 lead, with former Torquay United striker Duane Darby netting both goals, in the 30th and 42nd minutes.

Michael Evans reduced the deficit seconds before half-time, heading home Paul Wotton's free-kick at close range and becoming the first Pilgrim to score in the 2001-02 campaign. Having fixed the radar, Argyle quickly located the opposition goal again after the interval, and another header, this time by Graham Coughlan from Jon Beswetherick's corner, levelled the scores in the 51st minute.

Then came the moment. Argyle were rampant and Rushden needed to stop them in their tracks. What better way than with another goal? Diamonds defender Mark Peters thought he had it when he headed powerfully towards goal. Such was his conviction that the ball was destined for the back of the net, that he began to raise his arms in anticipation of celebration.

Peters had reckoned without Argyle goalkeeper Romain Larrieu, however. Larrieu had already been in fine form, making some outstanding saves to keep the Pilgrims in the hunt. Now, he excelled himself to claw Peters' header away through exceptional athleticism and anticipation.

Who knows what might have become of Argyle's season had Larrieu not sprung to the rescue when he did? All that is certain is that Brian McGlinchey's 71st-minute half-volley would not have been the match-winner. As it was, the left-footer's right-footed shot gave the Pilgrims their first three-point haul of the season.

After the game, McGlinchey turned the spotlight away from himself and his 'keeper. "It wasn't my goal or Romain's saves that made the difference today," he said. "It was real team effort. We are all relieved to get three points. I don't think we deserve to be in the position we are in, because we have done reasonably well."

The irony that all Argyle's points had come away from home was not lost on the manager. "To be unbeaten away and not to have won a game at home – when we

only won two games away from home last season – is scary," he said. "If we can put our home form back on its usual standards, then it's onwards and upwards."

Or, as Steve Nicholson, editor of Argyle fanzine Rub of the Greens was later to observe: Diamonds were Argyle's best friends.

Monday, August 27 2001, Nationwide League

Rushden & Diamonds 2
Darby 30, 42
Plymouth Argyle 3
Evans 45, Coughlan 51, McGlinchey 71

Rushden & Diamonds (4-4-2): B Turley; T Mustafa, M Peters, J Rodwell, P Underwood; J Brady, S Carey, G Butterworth, S Gray (G Setchell 63); J Jackson (J-M Sigere 72), D Darby. **Substitutes (not used):** G Mills, T Pennock (gk), B Solkhorn.
Plymouth Argyle (4-5-1): R Larrieu; S Adams, P Wotton, G Coughlan, J Beswetherick; M Phillips, K Wills, J Broad, B McGlinchey, L Hodges; M Evans (M Gritton 82). Substitutes (not used): L McCormick (gk), I Stonebridge, N Banger, P Connolly.
Referee: G Hegley (Bishops Stortford). **Attendance:** 4,414. **League position:** 18th.

PAUL STURROCK: "To the 44th minute, it looked as though our season was going down the toilet. Then we scored a goal and, intentionally, I had one of my rare flippies at half-time. I was annoyed, but I probably went over the top. Certain people were verbally abused, cups were chucked about, things were kicked for the whole 15 minutes. A couple of players turned to me and said: 'I'll prove you wrong'. I said: 'Go and do it'. They went out and basically ran over Rushden, although later on we got a wee bit worried and Romain had to make one or two saves.

"They got both barrels; home truths were told to two or three players. From then on, for the whole second half, there was big lift to the team. To be fair, I think Wottsie got most of it. For one of the goals, he had been bullied into giving the ball away by one of their players. It bugged me rotten that my centre-halves were getting bullied. Coughlan had been second-rate, second best to everything as well – those two really, really got it. I didn't think we won enough tackles in midfield as well, so they got it. Mickey was very, very slack early on, so he got it; and Romain was a disgrace for one of the goals, so he got it. The goals had been a comedy of errors.

"I'd given them the talk at Hull about belief and team-spirit, and there was no belief and no team-spirit in that first 40 minutes. We got the response, got back in the game very quickly, and got the result. Cocko headed a corner and Brian got his only goal of this season."

KEVIN SUMMERFIELD: "It was hiding-to-nothing trip. No Friio, no Worrell, no Taylor. The centre midfield was Kevin Wills, Joe Broad and

Brian McGlinchey. It was a go-and-play pitch. We had 25 attempts on goal, which is phenomenal in any form of football. I picked out Mickey Evans, and Larrieu was absolutely awesome on the day. This was the first game when Paul offered odds to the players on them scoring or keeping clean-sheets. It became something of a ritual. It could have been the best thing he ever did; it was certainly the worse thing as far as his bank balance was concerned. And I had the problem of trying to sort it all out."

PAUL STAPLETON: "We should have won the Shrewsbury game by a hat-ful but we lost and I went to the theatre that night to see Sunset Boulevard, which is a depressing show anyway. I sat there thinking: 'I don't believe all this. We've just lost and I'm watching this depressing crap.' My wife Kim said to me: 'If you're going to be like this and wear it on your sleeve all the time, you may as well pack up now.'

"Then we lost the next home game and only 4,000 came, which was even worse – I had done all my forecasts on 5,000-5,200. The Rushden was the best experience I had. Watford was really good from the performance point of view, but Rushden was the one. We were 2-0 down; it was me, Peter, Dan, Ann and Ken Jones. I was sat between Ann and Ken Jones. We were 2-0 down but we had played well. I thought we could be bottom of the league going into our next game at Torquay, it'd be doom and gloom and we'd be labelled worse than Dan. Dan said: 'You shouldn't have taken over, yet. You should have let me lose a few, then you'd have been the white knights.'

"Anyway, we scored the one before half-time, came out for the second half all buoyed up and got the equaliser. I said to Peter: 'We're going to win this, you know. If we win, I don't know who to kiss, Ann McCauley or you.' He said: 'You think you've got a problem – I've got you or Ken Jones.'

"We came up together by car, but we flew back. We were so ecstatic we'd won. Nic Warren and his wife were there, too, because his wife's from that area and they had sponsored the game for Rushden. We had a fantastic buzz because, for us, that was the start of it. We never looked back from that day. Someone had lit the touchpaper and we were on our way."

Argyle were denied an immediate opportunity of building on their first victory of the season by the postponement of the following Saturday's home match against Swansea, due to international calls on the Welsh club's players.

The 'onwards and upwards' momentum was maintained off the field, however. First, Canadian international Jason Bent agreed to join the Pilgrims, subject to the club obtaining a work-permit from the government's Department of

Employment and Education for the 24-year-old, 25-times-capped midfielder. Given that First Division Preston North End had previously become entangled in red tape while trying to sign Bent, that was not a forgone conclusion.

Manager Paul Sturrock had tried to sign Bent twice before, for St Johnstone and Dundee United, and knew what he would be getting from the dreadlocked Ontario-based international whose career had already seen him play in Denmark, Germany and the USA. "He's a very versatile player and would bring a lot of positions to the table," said Sturrock. "You can't have enough of those type of people when injuries and suspensions start to bite."

Next on the Home Park agenda was the unveiling by the new board of their five-year plan for the club. Living up to their promise to support their manager financially and emotionally, the main plank of the Greenprint was an extension of Sturrock's contract to cover the five years, at the end of which, it was envisaged, the club would be established as a leading Second Division side.

Chairman Paul Stapleton said: "Like a new stand, if you don't get the foundations right, it will fall down. We don't want to be a yo-yo club. We want to be strong enough to push ourselves into Division One – that's got to be our aim. We've got to make sure that when we go up, we stay up."

"I am a long-term manager," said Sturrock. "If I do a job, it has to be organised and methodical, with the ultimate aim of improving the club. When I first came down here, I made it clear there would be no quick-fix solutions. The five-year offer appeals to me because it enables me to sit down, study the whole thing and get my teeth into this job. I'm very pleased the board have confidence in me."

Argyle's next match was a noon kick-off at Plainmoor, home of their nearest and dearest local rivals, Torquay United. For pessimists among the travelling Green Army, this was bad news, for it was more than five years since the Pilgrims had won consecutive matches away from home: for optimists, it was good news as Argyle had not been defeated in the previous 18 Devon derbies – since April, 1993.

The optimists were proved right by David Friio's 58th-minute header from Buster Phillips' cross that secured a 1-0 win in a nervy match. Coughlan was Argyle's man of the match, however, standing firm among Torquay's late onslaught during which Sturrock gave a more than passable impersonation of a pressure-cooker with a faulty valve.

"We looked tired; we looked stodgy; we looked like a side that hadn't played for 12 days," he said. "We were out of sorts but, obviously, we will take the result. There have been times when we have gone away from home and played very well and got nothing."

Saturday, September 8 2001, Nationwide League

Torquay United 0
Plymouth Argyle 1
Friio 58

Torquay United (3-5-2): K Dearden; M McNeil, S Woods (R Herrera 53), D Woozley; S Tully, C Brandon, J Rees, A Russell, K Hill (M Nicholls 82); D Graham, N Roach (E Williams 58). **Substitutes (not used):** R Northmore (gk), A Greyling.
Booking: Hill 20.
Plymouth Argyle (4-4-1-1): R Larrieu; D Worrell, P Wotton, G Coughlan, J Beswetherick; M Phillips, S Adams, D Friio, L Hodges; I Stonebridge (B McGlinchey 72); M Evans (N Banger 90). **Substitutes (not used):** L McCormick (gk), K Wills, J Broad.
Bookings: Worrell 5, Friio 38.
Referee: J Brandwood (Lichfield). **Attendance:** 4,217. **League position:** 14th.

PAUL STURROCK: "We changed the system for the derby. It was a poor, poor game; poor fare. I don't believe that Torquay's pitch is a benefit to a football team. It was dry and bumpy on the day and it isn't big enough. It's always a battle there, always a war, but we were up for a war. For 20 minutes of the second half, we ran over the top of Torquay. We got the 1-0, laid back as usual, and brought Torquay right back on top of us. We hung on for the result. It wasn't pretty, but it was good enough on the day."

KEVIN SUMMERFIELD: "With Swansea being off, I went to watch Luton play at Exeter and wrote: 'We'll beat both of these.' It was poor game. Exeter should have won. Luton looked like they were waiting for players to come in. Jason had come down by this time. Even though we'd done okay, other people were coming into the equation to keep everybody ticking over. He was a big part of the puzzle.

"The game at Torquay was a struggle but we still had enough to win, even though we didn't play particularly well. Friio's ability to score goals was beginning to show and it was a massive win to get two away on the trot."

PETER JONES: "The five-year plan was part of our thinking and it was something that Paul Sturrock bought into totally. He always thought the club would be so much stronger if it spelt out what it wanted to do and put a realistic time-scale on it. It was important to us as an agenda, and I personally think the community elements of it, the transparency elements of it, and the internal culture elements of it are every bit as important as the stuff relating to where we want to be in five years' time.

"When we're not wearing our directors' suits, we are fans. I'm going to Rub of the Green website to have a look, not as a director, but as a fan. £15 is a huge chunk of your walking about money. If they are prepared to invest

financially and emotionally in us, we're going to respond by investing as much was we can in their comfort, etc."

Given that Argyle had already matched the number of away wins that they recorded in the previous season before they had won at Home Park, some fans were wondering whether Sturrock was taking their advice on his appointment – "All you've got to do to succeed at Plymouth Argyle is turn the away form around" – a little too literally. Should they have mentioned to keep the home form going, too?

Sturrock was keen to rectify the situation, which he saw being partly caused by the closure of three sides of Home Park while the rebuilding work gathered pace.

"Our season starts here, as far as our home results are concerned," he said, on the eve of the rearranged midweek game against Swansea. "It can't be coincidence we have lost our opening two games with only one stand open – it has to be a factor – but, if we worry about it, it will get ten times worse."

The date of Swansea's visit tells you all you need to know about the atmosphere at Home Park as Argyle opened their 2001-02 home account with a 3-1 win which took them into the top half of the Third Division: September 11, 2001 will be remembered for many things, but a Football League match in Devon is not one of them. There were calls for the game to be postponed in the wake of the terrorist attacks on the Pentagon and the World Trade Centre buildings in America earlier in the day, and only 3,850 people tore themselves away from the endless news bulletins devoted to the tragedies to indulge in what seemed an even more trivial pursuit than usual.

Captain Wotton led the way, becoming the first Pilgrim to score at home since the previous Spring with a 24th-minute penalty after Evans had toppled like a Saturday night drunk under Kris O'Leary's challenge. Nicky Banger marked his debut with the second just before half-time, with a looping header from a cross by Buster Phillips, who rounded off the scoring himself in the 61st minute with a kung-fu kick finish after Evans had flicked on Wotton's free-kick. A mistake ten minutes before time by Steve Adams allowed Mamady Sidibe to pull a goal back. After three games without a win, Argyle had now won three in a row, but Sturrock was not about to become carried away. He said: "As I've said, we're still in transition, but I was delighted we passed the ball as well as we have been away from home, although I still think we can improve on that."

Tuesday, September 11 2001, Nationwide League

Plymouth Argyle 3
Wotton pen 24, Banger 45, Phillips 61
Swansea City 1
Sidibe 79

Plymouth Argyle (4-4-2): R Larrieu; D Worrell, P Wotton, G Coughlan, J Beswetherick; M Phillips, S Adams, D Friio, B McGlinchey; N Banger (L Hodges 83), M Evans.
Substitutes (not used): L McCormick (gk), K Wills, J Broad, I Stonebridge.
Booking: McGlinchey 90.
Swansea City (4-4-2): R Freestone; L Jenkins, K O'Leary, M Bound, M Howards; S Roberts (N Cusack 71), G Phillips, N Mezzina (C Todd 51), J Coates; M Sidibe, N Tyson (J Williams 45).
Substitutes (not used): J Jones (gk), R Appleby.
Booking: Todd 67.
Referee: P Prosser (Gloucester). **Attendance:** 3,850. **League position:** 8th.

PAUL STURROCK: "We didn't know if the game was going to be played or not because they were humming and hawing at lunchtime that day that everything should be cancelled, but it went ahead. I think everybody had watched all day what was happening in America so maybe, in a way, it helped, because it took people's minds off it.

"Swansea were a Second Division team the season before, so we'd not had any gauge on them and they'd just won a big game, 5-1 or 5-2. We were worried about their big strike force. It wasn't a great game to play in, but the players were very professional in their approach, very strong on the night, and never looked back from the first whistle. There was only going to be one winner from start to finish.

"We hadn't won at home, which was another thing that was playing on my mind. To put three wins in a row together puts you in the right direction. Unfortunately, their manager lost his job that night, one of many that went around that time of the year. It's scary.

"Nicky had played two unbelievable games for Dundee against St Johnstone – one reserve, one first team – when he had created mayhem down the left. Since then, he had been injured long-term but I just felt that he brought a bit of experience, and could play wide left, wide right or centre-forward. He came in and did a very good job, but the problem was that he couldn't get rid of a hamstring problem he had. He trained indifferently because of it. It was always a worry to me.

"He made a goal and scored one that night and he definitely contributed to the season. His whole nature is to play; he doesn't like to play second fid-

dle. I felt it could only benefit him by moving him on later because I couldn't promise him a regular game."

KEVIN SUMMERFIELD: "Obviously there was a lot of talk and discussion about what had happened in America in the dressing-room but, once they went out, I thought we played very well. Bezzie had one of his best games of the season and Buster was firing on all cylinders.

"The only disappointing thing about that game was that we conceded a goal when we didn't deserve to. I think Stevie gave the ball away in midfield."

A measure of the transition Sturrock talked about in the wake of the defeat of Swansea which cost the Welsh side's manager John Hollins his job could be gauged by comparing the Pilgrims' line-up against the Swans to that which had been humbled 3-0 by Kidderminster the previous April: only Wotton, Evans, Phillips and Friio played in both games. It was no coincidence that Phillips and Evans had combined with Banger to deconstruct Swansea in a game in which Wotton had opened the scoring, and that Friio had been the match-winner at Plainmoor the previous Saturday.

The defeat at Aggborough rankled Sturrock and he was grateful of the early opportunity to put things right the following Saturday. "Kidderminster left a bad taste in my mouth last year," he said. "It was our poorest performance of the whole season. It would be nice to turn that around this year. There were certain games last year that even Cesar Menotti could not have turned around."

A 0-0 draw against Jan Molby's side kept the Pilgrims' unbeaten away record going and represented the progress that Sturrock had hoped for, although he declared himself disappointed with a lethargic display that relied on the defensive prowess of goalkeeper Larrieu and centre-backs Wotton and Coughlan.

He said: "There was a lot of days last year when we would come to places like this and let ourselves get turned over, but there's a bit of character in the team now and they appreciate what hard work's done for them.

'To be fair, we dug a result out. The only pleasing things to take out of the game is that we have come away with a result and the team's shown character."

Saturday, September 15 2001, Nationwide League

Kidderminster Harriers 0
Plymouth Argyle 0

Kidderminster Harriers (4-4-2): S Brock; I Joy, A Smith, M Shail, I Clarkson; S Shilton (S Stamps 67), D Williams, M Blake, T Bird (A Ducros 82); D Bennett, C Larkin (D Broughton half-time). **Substitutes (not used):** B Murphy (gk), B Davies.
Plymouth Argyle (4-1-4-1): R Larrieu; D Worrell, P Wotton, G Coughlan, J Beswetherick; D Friio; M Phillips, K Wills (N Banger half-time), S Adams, L Hodges (B McGlinchey 77); M Evans (I Stonebridge 81). **Substitutes (not used):** L McCormick (gk), J Broad.
Referee: S Baines (Chesterfield). **Attendance:** 2,801. **League position:** 9th.

PAUL STURROCK: "This was another key game. It was afterwards that I felt we had the potential to do something. We were so bad and, in the olden days, we would have capitulated like we did the season before, maybe 2-0 or 3-0, but this lot rolled their sleeves up and gave it everything and, by the way, could have snatched it late on in the game. We were absolutely hopeless but came away with a 0-0. I thought if we could keep this resilience away from home, and win a few games at home, we might have a chance of promotion through the play-offs. To get to the play-offs would have been a great season.

"Managers see 0-0 differently than fans. To me, it was a clean-sheet, it meant we'd played shape. They never really had many clear-cut chances. I think 0-0 to a fan is disappointing – they think it's been a horrible game – but, to a coach, it's a result."

KEVIN SUMMERFIELD: "It was a nightmare trip. We were very lucky. We sat on the bench and after half an hour, we couldn't wait for the whistle to go.

"We were in on the Sunday. If we had a midweek game, we always came in on a Sunday. What that would enable us to do was to have a better training session on the Monday, rather than come in stiff as board and take forever and a day to get up to work-rate, like everyone else does on a Monday morning. To the players, it wasn't Monday morning.

"We started doing a lot of things that would benefit the players, so that they were ready for the next game. I could possibly count games on one hand when any player would go and have any sort of alcoholic drink after a game. They just didn't do it. They are not allowed to drink alcohol for an hour and half, two hours, after a game. It's got to be water, pasta. That was really important. We always had jelly babies and drinks before a game.

Little things like that, thanks to Maxie [physiotherapist Paul Maxwell], really made a difference."

Argyle's new-found and totally unexpected away resilience passed another severe examination the following Tuesday on an evening of high drama at St James' Park, home of deadly rivals Exeter City. For the second time in four away games, they won a match after conceding two goals and looking dead and buried.

Substitute Ian Stonebridge's unlikely 90th-minute winner extended the Pilgrims' unbeaten run in the Devon Expressway Derby to 12 matches and, to ice the cake for the travelling Green Army, put Exeter back to the bottom of the division.

City, though, had confounded their lowly position – and a ten-match winless streak – to hold a deserved 2-1 lead thanks to a superbly-executed finish by Christian Roberts after Phillips and Chris Curran had traded early goals against their former clubs. Evans headed home a cross from former Exeter favourite Phillips for a 65th-minute equaliser, before Stonebridge's late header – again, from a cross supplied by Phillips – settled matters.

Even Sturrock conceded his side did not deserve to win, after Exeter, whose endeavours were predictably spearheaded by Argyle Old Boys Martin Barlow and Sean McCarthy, dictated the first half. He said: "If I was an Exeter fan or on their staff, I'd be disappointed because I felt we didn't merit a win. But football's like that. There's many a day we've walked away saying 'how did we lose?' So we'll take it.

"My worry is that there were two teams on the pitch – one wanted to play and one wanted to win, and the team that wanted to win showed it. I wouldn't have argued if we'd been 3-1 down at half-time on the performance Exeter showed. There were strong words said at half-time."

Some of those words were directed at left-back Jon Beswetherick, who, having been mauled by Roberts and committing an error from which the City midfielder scored his goal, was substituted at the interval and was not to be seen in an Argyle starting line-up for weeks afterwards.

"Defensive errors like that will not be tolerated and that's why he was taken off," said Sturrock. "His performance was nowhere near the standard I would expect. To go from how he performed against Swansea last week, when he was the best player on the park, to how he performed last night defies logic."

Argyle's day of delight was completed by the news that the Department of Employment and Education had agreed to grant a work-permit to Bent, follow-

ing the club's appeal against the government's decision to turn down their original application.

Their appeal – presented at a meeting at the Immigration and Nationality Directorate in Sheffield by Sturrock and Argyle chief executive David Tall – had been supported by, amongst others, former England manager Bobby Robson, for whom Bent played at PSV Eindhoven, and Sunderland's Peter Reid, who trialed Bent the previous season. Sturrock said: "I have been chasing Jason for quite a long time for three different clubs and I am delighted it's come to fruition."

Tuesday, September 17 2001, Nationwide League

Exeter City 2
Curran 7, Roberts 18
Plymouth Argyle 3
Phillips 6, Evans 65, Stonebridge 90

Exeter City (4-4-2): M Gregg; B McConnell, A Watson, J Campbell, G Power; C Roberts (M Burrows 80), M Barlow, C Curran, G Breslan; S McCarthy (C Diallo 88), S Flack. **Substitutes (not used):** A van Heusden (gk), K Ampadu, G Birch.
Plymouth Argyle (4-4-2): R Larrieu; D Worrell, P Wotton, G Coughlan, J Beswetherick (L Hodges half-time); M Phillips, S Adams, D Friio, B McGlinchey; M Evans, N Banger (I Stonebridge 76). **Substitutes (not used):** L McCormick (gk), S Evers, J Broad.
Referee: D Gallagher (Banbury). **Attendance:** 6,756. **League position:** 8th.

PAUL STURROCK: "What can I say about Exeter? Stupidly, again, I went and played 4-4-2. I had been playing 4-5-1 away from home but I felt we'd been so bad at Kidderminster. The first half was the best I've ever seen Exeter play. They could have gone in 3-1 up. Things had to be said at half-time and were said. Bezzie had lost a bit of confidence after one or two indifferent performances and it came to a head at that game. It meant I took him off at half-time, put Brian on, and put Hodges on. I think the substitutions had a great influence. We looked far more comfortable. Barlow had gone and played in Friio's area, and Friio's the type who lets the other team's player play, as long as he is allowed to play himself. Barlow was getting the freedom of the park, so we put Adams on to Chopsy and he fell out of the game; they fell right out of the game. We had a few chances before Mickey scored. Buster then took over the show and the third goal was a great finish by Stonebridge.

"The euphoria that night was unbelievable. We very much played bit parts in games in the early part of the season – 20 minutes here, half an hour there. We'd run out and be magnificent one half and hopeless the next. We were that kind of team at the start of the season – we just couldn't seem to piece a whole 90 minutes together. Apart from Watford.

"When you win, you have got to make sure you appreciate there's a game the next week and it's only three points. Same as, if you lose, you have got to pick out the two or three things you've done well or the two or three players that have done well, factors in the game that have contributed to the result. I've been very negative about defeats in the past and it does you no good at all. If you do it that way, I think it keeps things on a level. This team could have easily gone Billy Bigtime. I think there were two or three teams in our league who would change like the wind because of one result; their psyche would be completely different one game to the next – who would have would believed Luton would have won 4-0 at Hull and then gone home and drew 0-0 with Macclesfield?

"My job was to make sure we didn't get excitable, because we had a fan-base that was getting excitable and if we all went that way, we would have become very disappointed very quickly. There were a couple of games where I'd point the finger at certain people who felt they just had to turn up. I think Torquay was like that. We were half-cock, and that's why we got that result that day."

KEVIN SUMMERFIELD: "We never seemed to get along with 4-4-2 away from home. Whether we let the other team get into the game too early, I don't know. When we played 4-5-1, teams found it difficult to start against us, because we denied them space; they had to play in front of us. For the first 45 minutes, they probably gave us as hard a game as we had all season. They were wellying into us; they were up for it and played really, really well. Once we changed, second half, we played well. Dermot Gallagher had a really good game, too. He's the sort of referee you need for that game."

Bent made his debut the following Saturday when he came on as a substitute five minutes from the end of an easy 2-0 home victory over Macclesfield that saw the Pilgrims move into the play-off positions for the first time. Striker Michael Evans was the man given a breather, meaning that one full international replaced another, which does not exactly happen every match day at Home Park.

Argyle's fifth win from six matches was achieved with goals from midfielders Lee Hodges, just before half-time, and Friio, in the 64th minute, and underlined the fact that Bent was going to do well simply to win a place in the Pilgrims' starting line-up. Who could Sturrock drop? Either one of the goalscorers? Difficult to justify. The ever-present and omnipresent Adams? Harsh. Certainly not Phillips, who was in the form of his life and the architect of much that had been good about the Pilgrims.

Hodges, who had himself been dropped for the previous match at Exeter, opened the scoring with a skilful left-footed lob over goalkeeper Steve Wilson, and Friio profited from Wilson's inability to hold on to a shot by Phillips, who later rattled the crossbar as the confidence continued to flow through his frail, but beautifully balanced, frame.

Sturrock urged what he called his increasingly expectant fan-base to still expect some dark days ahead but there was little to dissuade them that the squad he was gradually putting together was emerging as the best since Neil Warnock's Wembley warriors had won promotion six seasons previously. Like Warnock's winners, Sturrock's men had rallied after an uncertain start to the season, and facing them was becoming an occupational hazard for managers: after Hollins' sacking earlier in the month, Noel Blake left Exeter at the end of a week in which he lost a Devon derby on his own turf.

Saturday, September 21 2001, Nationwide League

Plymouth Argyle 2
Hodges 45, Friio 64
Macclesfield Town 0

Plymouth Argyle (4-4-2): R Larrieu; D Worrell, P Wotton, G Coughlan, B McGlinchey; M Phillips, S Adams, D Friio, L Hodges; M Evans (J Bent 85), I Stonebridge.
Substitutes (not used): L McCormick (gk), M Gritton, J Beswetherick, S Evers.
Macclesfield Town (4-4-2): S Wilson; G Abbey, D Ridler, D Tinson, S Hitchen (P O'Neill 65); R Tracy, C Priest, K Munroe (C Byrne 73), K Keen; K Lightbourne (J Askey 73), L Glover.
Substitutes (not used): L Martin (gk), R Eyre.
Bookings: Munroe 69, Priest 70, Tracy 89.
Referee: J Ross (London). **Attendance:** 4,227. **League position:** 5th.

PAUL STURROCK: "Macclesfield gave us a right torrid time. It was never 2-0 in the game. We were very lucky to get a couple of goals. They caused us a lot of concern without having the icing on the cake of scoring goals. They paid the penalty that day.

"Jason had been one I had been chasing for years. I had a wee sniff at him for St Johnstone and agreed a fee for him, but the problem was the work-permit. When I got here, I thought there was no chance of getting him for Argyle, but we looked into it. An agent came along and a friend of mine, who used to be company secretary at Dundee United and who is very influential with work-permits, took a hand in it, and we put a great show on as far as the committee was concerned. They were very impressed with it. I was very pleased they allowed Jason in. Jason was pleased because he'd been at Preston near enough four months, twiddling his thumbs, so he came to me very lacking in match-practice – he'd not played for anyone for that season – but I knew I was getting a player.

"Expectations are like a train – if the carriages, which are the fans, go ahead of the engine, which is the club, you've got a real problem. All of a sudden, the train will start to turn. I'm driving the train and seeing fans go past me with their expectation levels. It was a worry to me. It was basically 'here we go, we're off; we're up already' and it was still only September. The fans had been brought to the heights and slapped down so many times, I didn't want to raise them again and smash them down. They are very fragile as it is."

KEVIN SUMMERFIELD: "I wrote: 'Pleasing signs of a good team coming through.' There was a belief that they'll only get when they are winning. Some of the games we could have played really well, lost 1-0 and they wouldn't have believed in themselves – but the dividing line was so narrow in some games we played – like Kidderminster, when we hung on for 0-0. We managed to scramble a 0-0, so what we were trying to do as a team was 50 per cent working, because your defensive side was working."

The most notable thing about Argyle's subsequent visit to York City the following Tuesday was that the point they gained from a 0-0 draw with, which Sturrock pronounced himself happy, was their 12th from their travels – a haul which equalled their entire away output of the previous season.

Their growing reputation preceded them to Bootham Crescent. York manager Terry Dolan said: "You can see why they haven't been beaten away from home this season. They are very well organised and get a lot of men behind the ball."

Sturrock concurred, although he regretted not introducing substitute Ian Stonebridge earlier after the striker twice went close to winning all three points with long-range shots. "I probably should have gone 4-4-2 quicker than I did," he admitted. "Stonebridge looked lively and could have had the match-winner in him, but we are happy to go down the road with a draw."

Tuesday, September 24 2001, Nationwide League

York City 0
Plymouth Argyle 0

York City (4-4-2): A Fettis; D Edmondson, M Hocking, M Basham, G Potter; R Cooper, L Bullock, C Brass, C Fox (M Salvati 80); L Nogan, M Proctor.
Substitutes (not used): A Mathie, R Howarth (gk), N Richardson, N Stamp.
Bookings: Basham 45, Bullock 90.
Plymouth Argyle (4-1-4-1): R Larrieu; D Worrell, P Wotton, G Coughlan, B McGlinchey; S Adams; M Phillips, K Wills (I Stonebridge 78), D Friio, L Hodges; M Evans.
Substitutes (not used): L McCormick (gk), J Beswetherick, J Bent, S Evers.
Bookings: McGlinchey 44, Friio 72.
Referee: M Cowburn (Blackpool). **Attendance:** 2,282. **League position:** 7th.

PAUL STURROCK: "York was a game in which we played very, very well. We deserved to win the game quite convincingly but couldn't score on the day. We had umpteen chances and, the way we played our system, it never looked like York were going to hurt us. They couldn't handle us. Their manager said afterwards they couldn't cope with our system – 'The play-maker [Friio] causes all sorts of concerns, but, if you pick him up, there's easy balls available for Mickey Evans.' I was disappointed we didn't come away with three points, but, again, not losing was the key for us.

"I was pleased with the system. Management is all about having the experience to make these decisions. From my playing career, coaching career and management career, there are certain things I know, certain principles that can influence games. Having your finger on the pulse and knowing how the other team is playing and their manager's thoughts on how the game should be played, sometimes you are able to steal a march on them.

"As I said to my players: 'You play shape, organisation and tactical awareness for me, I'll win you games.'

"I was 17 years old when I started coaching teams – boys' clubs. I always knew I was going to be a manager. I read a lot of books about it, through the years, listened to Jim McLean, Walter Smith and Archie Knox at Dundee United, sat down with the players afterwards when we had lost, asking what we had done wrong, what we could have done.

"I'm not scared of making a mistake. That's probably the focus of it all. I've changed things and it's cost us, but there's been other games when I've changed things and we've won. That'll always happen.

"As a manager, the first thing you look at is your players – what they can achieve, what sort of systems of play they can play, whether they can pass the ball or whether we have to play long-ball. Then you look at the opposition."

KEVIN SUMMERFIELD: "This was a good game to get something from. They were not bad. We left 6.30am, stopped at Rotherham, back on the coach, travelled the other hour and a half, played the game. Then back at about 5am. A 24-hour trip for a point. We played well. Willsy had chance after chance, hit the bar, shot just wide. We came off; we'd got something, so you aren't going down the road with your tail between your legs."

CHAPTER TEN

THE draw at York was a calm precursor to a stormy meeting between the Third Division's two in-form sides, although there barely seemed any point in one of them turning up, according to the other. If talk was an ability that counted towards the destination of the title, Joe Kinnear's Luton Town would have been even shorter-priced favourites than they were when they came to Home Park on Saturday, September 29.

The confidence engendered by two admittedly impressive victories that had taken Bedfordshire's only league side to the top of the division was something to behold. "We're well clear of anybody in the league," Kinnear had claimed after a 3-1 victory which had left those giants of lower league football, Shrewsbury and Rochdale, trailing by as much as a whole point, and Argyle a massive three points behind.

That gap was bound to increase at Home Park, too, according to the club's equally gung-ho website. "Joe Kinnear will probably tell his players that Argyle can beat average sides in the Third," it surmised, "but, as soon as they come up against top sides, they do not do so well."

Neither were the players backward in coming forward. Striker Steve Howard summed up their feelings when he said: "I don't think there will be too many problems in us beating Plymouth. The whole team is playing well at the moment and the spirit is better than ever."

Sturrock was not persuaded to give his side the afternoon off, however. "They're a good side," he said. "Everyone's waxing lyrical about them. I've heard it all before – let's see who comes out on top. We don't hype ourselves up too much for this one."

Thanks to the remarks from Kinnear and the website somehow finding their way into the home dressing-room, Sturrock's team-talk had been taken care of for him.

Argyle achieved better victories than their subsequent 2-1 triumph which knocked Luton off the top and advanced their own claims for promotion, and bigger ones, too, but none – not even the promotion-clincher at Rochdale and the championship-winner at Darlington – was as satisfying as the comeuppance they served on Kinnear's cocky Hatters.

The Luton manager and his players surfed into the South West on such a wave of self-adoration and swell-headed confidence that it was a pleasure to see the team

"well clear of anybody in the league" made to look anything but that – despite them having the advantage of an extra man for the best part of an hour after Michael Evans was sent off, erroneously as it later turned out.

If you are going to talk the talk, you have to have the players to walk the walk, and Luton just did not have them. French winger Jean-Louis Valois had been heralded as the best player in the division but he was hunted down and expelled to the margins by Jason Bent, finally making his full debut. He could not even claim to be the best player on the pitch and, in fact, just scraped in as third-best Frenchman on show behind Argyle's increasingly impressive goalkeeper Larrieu and match-winner Friio.

Centre-backs Chris Coyne and Russell Perrett, previously "a solid unit", were unhinged by Ian Stonebridge, a strip of a lad just out of his teens who revelled in the lone attacking role thrust upon him by Evans' dismissal. Midfielder Kevin Nicholls was apparently "worth two normal players" but, judging from (a) his lack of marking for Friio's winner, (b) the altercation he had with Argyle physio Paul Maxwell during the second half, and (c) the spat he had with one of his own team-mates after the final whistle, two heads were not better than one.

Given the opposition's attitude, it was entirely appropriate that their newest signing should be called Crowe – Dean of that ilk, who had the briefest of loan spells at Home Park earlier in the season. Inevitably, it was Crowe who opened the scoring, hooking the ball home in the 14th minute after Larrieu had brilliantly stopped Howard's point-blank header.

Argyle sides of previous seasons would not have recovered from such a blow, but Sturrock's men levelled seven minutes later. Bent's astute header released Ian Stonebridge to run on goal from halfway and his pass to Buster Phillips, switched from right wing to left for the day to accommodate Bent's policing of Valois, was timed precisely enough for the Pilgrims' midfielder to slot home his third goal of the campaign.

David Friio joined him as the club's joint-top scorer with a stooping near-post header from Wotton's corner in first-half stoppage time, added on in part for a rash of bookings by referee Andy Hall, who yellow-carded six players between the ninth and 37th minutes, as well as dismissing Evans.
Valois hit the bar direct from a free-kick, but that was about as close as Luton came to living up to their pre-match pomposity. The numerical advantage handed Luton by Hall forced Argyle into disciplined defence, from Stonebridge back to Larrieu, whose flying save to tip Matt Taylor's shot over the bar was the pick of an impressive bunch of stops.

The back four was superb and the whole squad heroic in victory. They didn't

claim to be world-beaters, nor even the best in the division, but they showed they were on the right track and going about their business quietly and efficiently.

Unlike Kinnear, whose ungraciousness in defeat was as unbecoming as his pre-match remarks. Asked by Plymouth reporters if he thought his comments might have inspired Argyle, whose players he described as "odds and sods", to prove a point, he replied: "I don't really care. I couldn't give a **** what they think. What position are you in the league?"

He denied rumours that he had a heated exchange with Argyle defender Graham Coughlan after the final whistle. "Who's Graham Coughlan?" he asked. "Never heard of him. Was he playing? I don't even know where he comes from. He's just an average Joe Soap centre-half, isn't he?"

Sturrock declined to comment on Kinnear's comments, but praised Bent and David Worrell for their containment of Valois and left-back Matt Taylor. He said: "Bent had a very good full debut. That's him without playing a game in a year, so it will be scary to see him when he's played several games. Valois never got himself involved in the game because he was well mastered by the two boys on that side. That cut down the ammunition that was coming in the box.

"Buster has been magnificent on the right, but the problem was their left-back was meant to be very offensive as well. We didn't want Buster doing his work in the wrong areas, so we tied up their more constructive area of the pitch. I think it worked well."

Saturday, September 29 2001, Nationwide League

Plymouth Argyle 2
Phillips 21, Friio 45
Luton Town 1
Crowe 14

Plymouth Argyle (4-4-2): R Larrieu; D Worrell, P Wotton, G Coughlan, B McGlinchey; J Bent (K Wills 85), S Adams, D Friio, M Phillips (L Hodges 53); M Evans, I Stonebridge.
Substitutes (not used): L McCormick (gk), J Beswetherick, N Banger.
Sending-off: Evans 37 (violent conduct).
Bookings: Bent 15, Friio 16, Wotton 26.
Luton Town (4-4-2): M Ovendale; E Boyce, R Perrett, C Coyne, M Taylor; P Holmes (A Forbes 52), M Spring (L Mansell 90), K Nicholls, J-L Valois (S Douglas 85); D Crowe, S Howard.
Substitutes (not used): C Emberson (gk), R Dryden.
Bookings: Holmes 9, Perrett, 27, Taylor 32, Howard 73, Valois 76.
Referee: A Hall (Birmingham). **Attendance:** 5,782. **League position:** 4th.

PAUL STURROCK: "If there was one game when the noise was a key factor – even with the thousands we had towards the end of the season – it

was this one. I have never heard our supporters shout and bawl and support a team like they did that day. It was unbelievable. You felt the whole stadium was full, even though there was nobody in three of the sides. The injustice of those remarks had got to the Plymouth people; then the remarks afterwards kept them going.

"In fact, for part of the season, Joe was my best player. I don't say that in an unkind way – all I did was use his comments. I like Joe – I think he's had a very successful career as a very good manager – but he did my team-talk for me that day. We pinned up his comments on the board in the dressing-room. It definitely was a factor. He was a huge influence to our team over the season.

"His track record with Wimbledon is second to none. You can't do what he's done and not deserve some accolades, but I do feel that he was a great benefit to our cause, because he kept coming out with things, which were probably played up by our Press, which were a great benefit to our cause.

"The game was another building-block for us. It was a difficult game. They battered us for 20 minutes. They scored, we got it back to 1-1, then Mickey was sent off. I thought Stonebridge was fantastic – he bossed the game at times because he was really content at holding the ball up and taking it for runs. Romain really came of age that day, with two or three valuable saves at the right times in the game, and the result revamped everybody, what with the ref's sending-off of Mickey and Joe's comments after the game.

"We knew we had fighting spirit after that. Although we'd had tussles at Rushden and Exeter, this one was the belief game. Walking out of this when everything seemed to be geared against us made the players believe in themselves. After that, there was a lot of banter on fans' websites, so it fuelled everything up for the game at their place."

KEVIN SUMMERFIELD: "Cocko wasn't well on the Friday. He couldn't head the ball; he was really struggling, feeling ill, getting headaches. It was a worry. He was a key player. This was the most exciting game of the season for me – everything about the game, all the banter before. We showed spirit. We didn't want to lose. We'd been away and not lost and you see yourself getting there.

"They were getting into the mentality where we probably weren't scoring enough goals but, as a team, we were doing great. The defensive side of the game was rock solid and we were nicking goals, which we needed to do. If we drew, we'd be disappointed.

"We didn't know how good Luton were. They thought they were better than us. We thought we'd show them we were better than them and that's what made the game. I still wrote that I thought Luton would go up."

The victory over Luton – which extended Argyle's unbeaten run to eight matches – helped Sturrock win the Third Division manager of the month award for September from Football League sponsors Nationwide.

Argyle had won five of their seven games during the month, and drawn the other two, to move from 18th place in the divisional table to fourth. That run made Nationwide's decision simple, according to the building society's media manager Chris Hull.

He said: "Paul won the award by a country mile. It was an easy decision because his nearest challengers were four or five points away from him.

"It has been a remarkable climb up the table. Paul and Plymouth Argyle's record speaks volumes for the effort and commitment shown at Home Park at the moment. Everyone who knows anything about professional football knows the passion for football in Plymouth. Let's hope this is the start of something of a renaissance."

Sturrock, who became the first Argyle manager since Peter Shilton eight years previously to be so honoured, celebrated the award by taking his squad to Exeter races and was generous enough to share the plaudits. "It's not about one man," he said. "It's about everybody involved with the club. The players deserve everything they have achieved."

However, he made sure that the players' feet remained firmly on the turf. "The problem is," he said, "players are getting their backs slapped. It causes complacency to creep in. It's a terrible word 'complacency' and it can kick you in the teeth very, very quickly.

"We've got to keep churning, churning, churning – be workmanlike and show good attitude. If we start listening to what people are saying, those games where we've done well because we've had an extra edge will go against us. Everyone loves praise, but when you start believing it, that extra yard, that extra challenge – all of sudden they are not there."

Nationwide were not the only ones to recognise Sturrock's success. St Johnstone, the club where he began his managerial career, and Motherwell both sounded out whether he would consider a return to Scotland, but Pilgrims' chairman Paul Stapleton said: "We had a chat with Paul and he's very settled. He's committed

to doing a job for Plymouth Argyle. He knows he's at the start of a journey with us. You can never say 'never' in football, but we are confident he will be staying here, which is good news."

The Exeter races outing was another visible manifestation of something Sturrock had made a priority: team-bonding. Another was the players' on-field huddle immediately prior to kick-off. No-one, least of all Sturrock was clear how it evolved, although the finger of suspicion pointed firmly at Graham Coughlan, Argyle's centre-back and supporter of Celtic, who had introduced the increasingly popular concept to British football.

"You want the team-spirit to be good," said Sturrock, on the eve of the team's visit to Oxford United. "In the past, we've had a lot of people who floated in and floated out again. I've got 21 players who live in each other's pockets, enjoy golf together, enjoy nights out together, who will eventually turn into friends.

"I knew, when I was with Dundee United, if you take that on to the pitch – if you have to play with your mate – you play ten per cent harder, ten per cent better, because you don't want to let your mate down."

Argyle needed that extra ten per cent at the Kassam Stadium to ensure that the so-called manager-of-the-month jinx, whereby recipients of the honour lose their subsequent match, was foiled by substitute Nicky Banger.

Banger scored within two minutes of his introduction as a 78th-minute substitute to earn the Pilgrims' a 1-1 draw against one of his former clubs, finishing off a sprightly 20-yard run with low shot past goalkeeper Ian McCaldon as Argyle came back from a goal down away from home and extended their record on their travels to seven matches without defeat.

"The script was written for Nicky," said Sturrock, who admitted pleasure at the character his side showed after falling behind to Paul Moody's disputed penalty 16 minutes from time.

"I thought it was a reasonable performance and we passed the ball well in spells. When we do that, we look a good side and seem to be going in the right direction."

Saturday, October 6 2001, Nationwide League

Oxford United 1
Moody pen 74
Plymouth Argyle 1
Banger 80

Oxford United (5-3-2): I McCaldon; S Stockley, S Guyett, P Bolland, W Hatswell, S Ricketts; P Tait (M Thomas 63), D Savage, D Whitehead; P Moody, M Omoyinmi. **Substitutes (not used):** R Knight (gk), J Richardson, J Brooks, R Folland. **Bookings:** Omoyinmi 44, Moody 48.

Plymouth Argyle (4-1-4-1): R Larrieu; D Worrell, P Wotton, G Coughlan, B McGlinchey; M Phillips (K Wills 83), S Adams, D Friio, J Bent (N Banger 78); L Hodges; M Evans (I Stonebridge 78). **Substitutes (not used):** L McCormick (gk), J Beswetherick. **Booking:** Friio 48.

Referee: P Alcock (Halstead). **Attendance:** 6,071. **League position:** 5th.

PAUL STURROCK: "We were starting to have trouble against teams that played 3-5-2: it is okay to play 4-5-1 but, against 3-5-2, you can get yourself set back and they can dictate the game from their three at the back. We started the game very well and never looked out of their league. Games against teams that had come down the previous season were difficult for me because I had no foreknowledge of them. We lost a goal with about 20 minutes to go and it looked as though we had run our race, but we put Stoney and Banger on and we turned things. I was very pleased with the way subs were used this year; they were very influential to our progress. Banger came on, got involved and scored a very good goal against one of his old clubs. The result was a fair result on the day,

"A lot of times, subs come on and destroy the rhythm of the team, but our ones would just come right into the pace of the game and would fit straight in because they knew their job.

"The first manager of the month award was very pleasing. We'd worked so hard. People will not appreciate what that pre-season build-up was like. It was hectic, methodical, intense, and we filled people's heads with an awful lot over a short period of time. This award was the icing on the cake for everyone at the football club, and the big decision a new board had taken to spend their money on it.

"I was worried about complacency. I've seen it so may times in football clubs. I knew we would have some dark days, so I tried to emphasise to the players that attitude and work-rate, with shape and organisation, would take us through."

KEVIN SUMMERFIELD: "We had an overnight for Oxford because of an

early kick-off. England were playing Greece in the World Cup. We played well. It was reasonable game. They were never a threat, apart from Moody battering everybody. We got back on the coach and everybody wanted to know how England were getting on. Paul went back with the chairman, but had to come to the coach to get his gear and found out England were 1-0 down; he was well chuffed. The Irish lads were well chuffed and singing all the time England were behind.

"The day at the races at Exeter was funny. Most of us had not a clue what we doing. Exeter were there. Sean [McCarthy] brought the Exeter boys over – if there was racing, Sean was going to be there. It was a good few hours, then we went back to town and had a few beers. We were thoroughly unprofessional, but when the boys came back in the next day, they'd switched back to professional mode."

Sturrock celebrated his 45th birthday on October 10 by putting pen to paper on the extension to the contract offered him the previous month as part of the board's five-year plan for the club.

Chairman Paul Stapleton declared himself 'elated' by the formal completion of a deal which was not due to expire until the end of the 2005-06 season and which could see Sturrock become the longest-serving Pilgrims' manager for half a century.

The manager endorsed his board's motives. He said: "I think their objectives are very much the same as mine. They feel that, too many times, this club has been pressurised into quick-fixes and quick decisions – panicky decisions – and they have tried to stabilise it.

"There's big, big teams with big support who've chucked millions after millions at manager after manager and are floundering in the lower leagues at the moment due to the pressure of trying to put their club in the right position in the league. I think Plymouth comes into that category, the way some managers have had money chucked at them. Now we're going to do it the right way. I've always been a long-term man, who organises things, beds things down slowly, and takes my time."

Stapleton said: "We're elated that Paul has shown the same faith in us that we have shown in him. We believe he is the man who can take Plymouth Argyle back to where it belongs."

Should Sturrock remain at Home Park for the duration of his contract, he will become the longest-serving Argyle manager since Jimmy Rae, who was in charge between 1948-1955. Rae, who won promotion from the Third Division (South) in

his fourth season, was a Scot, like Sturrock, who said that his migration to the Westcountry, with wife Barbara and the two youngest of his four children, Aaron and Kirk, had been a boon.

"I feel that my family life has benefited big time from being down here, because I'm a bit out of the road from all the pressures," he said. "Our port of call now is Plymouth, not Dundee. There's also not a staleness I probably had when I was north of the border, and there's a big challenge here and I seem to be the type of manager who loves these type of challenges. So everything augured well for me to sign this contract."

The sense that nothing could burst the Argyle bubble after Sturrock's agreement, his manager of the month award, the successful Bent appeal, their best league placing for four seasons and an unbeaten run away from home was further endorsed when the Football Association rescinded Evans' red card against Luton.

An FA panel decided that referee Andy Hall had been wrong to judge Evans' challenge on Hatters' central defender Chris Coyne that led to his dismissal as deliberate use of the elbow and, after hearing depositions from Pilgrims' director Phill Gill at their Soho headquarters as to Evans' good character and exemplary disciplinary record, upheld Argyle's appeal.

The same day, Paul Sturrock's 20-year-old son Blair was released by Dundee United and immediately joined two-thirds of his family in Plymouth to begin a six-week trial with Argyle. Sturrock fils, who played 20 times for Brechin on loan the previous season, scoring six times, was told to expect no favours from Sturrock pere.

Paul Sturrock said: "He's been told he fends for himself over the next six weeks, then we'll make a judgment whether he's up to standards. My coaching staff will have a big influence on that decision. If he does well down here, he could progress in football. I'm left in no doubt after his loan spell at Brechin that he will be a professional footballer.

"In most manager-son relationships, the son gets it twice as hard as the other players and I don't envisage it will be any different with me."

Of more pressing concern to Sturrock was the visit of low-lying Halifax to Home Park for a game which, given the feelgood factor at Home Park, carried expectations of an easy three points. He said: "Things are going well, but it could start to deteriorate very quickly if we're not careful. It is a difficult game and I would like people to appreciate that. If somebody told me it was going to be 1-0, I would be highly delighted, because I feel there is danger in this game."

He need not have worried. Argyle won 3-0 to extend their unbeaten run to 10 matches – the best by an Argyle side since Neil Warnock's promotion-winners won six and drew four during February and March, 1996 – with all three goals coming in a half-hour first-half spell during which Argyle were so superior to their opponents in most departments that you almost felt sorry for Halifax in their shadow-chasing.

Crisp, visionary passing through the French-Canadian midfield fulcrum of Friio and Bent, surging wing-play from twin Irish full-backs Worrell and McGlinchey, creation and denouement from Phillips, and sharp movement in all areas of the field made it seem Halifax were playing in lead studs on a treacle surface.

When right centre-back Paul Wotton, a man who had not trained all week because of a sore groin that was to be a feature of his season, started making sprints down the left wing, you knew you were watching an extraordinary performance. Either that or you were dreaming, and there was precious little chance of falling asleep at Home Park during such a game.

The score was only 3-0 because Argyle started toying with their opponents, working them over, showboating, taking the mickey royally; and because the crossbar kept out an outrageously cheeky dipping 20-yard shot from Phillips, who became the club's leading scorer when he shot across goalkeeper Lee Butler for the Pilgrims' second after 23 minutes. Who you gonna call? Goal Buster.

Phillips also made the first, Coughlan heading home his 15th-minute corner at the far post, and another header, from Lee Hodges in the 25th minute following Worrell's right-wing cross, completed the scoring.

Nevertheless, even after witnessing a tenth straight game unbeaten, a fourth successive home win, and a sixth clean-sheet in 13 matches; after winning the September manager of the month award by the length of Armada Way; after assembling what was the indisputably Third Division's most in-form side; and after watching that side disdainfully dispose of Halifax, something still rankled with Sturrock. It went back to the opening day of the season, when Shrewsbury pricked Home Park's highly-inflated bubble of expectation, and not even a Halifax's demolition – as surgical as anything Barr Construction had achieved beyond the sidelines – could fully make amends.

Sturrock said: "The disappointment for me is that Shrewsbury has still been our best performance at home, and we came out of that game with nothing."

The man is clearly a perfectionist, or was trying to keep those quickly reflating expectations within boundaries. Or, one suspected, both.

Saturday, October 13 2001, Nationwide League

Plymouth Argyle 3
Coughlan 15, Phillips 23, Hodges 25
Halifax Town 0

Plymouth Argyle (4-4-2): R Larrieu; D Worrell, P Wotton, G Coughlan, B McGlinchey; M Phillips (S Adams 70), J Bent, D Friio, L Hodges; N Banger (M Evans 67), I Stonebridge.
Substitutes (not used): L McCormick (gk), J Beswetherick, K Wills.
Halifax Town (3-5-2): L Butler; P Stoneman, G Mitchell, M Clarke; S Swales, P Harsley, N Redfearn (C Middleton 56), G Smith, M Jules (C Midgely 53); G Jones, S Kerrigan (J Wood 56). **Substitutes (not used):** P Crookes (gk), P Herbert.
Bookings: Redfearn 55, Mitchell 77, Swales 85.
Referee: M Warren (Walsall). **Attendance:** 5,065. **League position:** 4th.

PAUL STURROCK: "I think it's difficult for us to play at home. It's difficult for any team to play at home. You are the offensive team. The onus is on you. As the season went on, more and more teams didn't come here to play. We had a half-hour spell in the first half when we looked very good but Halifax had a half-hour spell in the second half when they could have nipped a couple of goals. I always felt we were going to be patchy at home this season for the simple reason that it's harder to build a house than it is to knock it down. We were on the knock-it-down stage away from home – it was easier for us to play – whereas, to be more offensive, we left the back door open for other teams. We got the goal seasily enough; there were some good passing movements, some great crosses, and we were getting on the end of things. It was probably the first time we had shown that kind of rhythm at home."

KEVIN SUMMERFIELD: "It was like watching a training session. Halifax were that poor. Some teams would only handle the way we were playing for so long and then do something about it. But it just carried on. It was total domination. After the first goal, you knew we were going to win.

"I didn't feel any pressure regarding Blair. Either he was going to be good enough or not. There's no room for sentiment. He trained badly, every Thursday afternoon he seemed to have the yellow jersey reserved for the week's worst trainer. Only Mickey Evans came close.

"The pressure was on Blair as well and the biggest thing that helped him out was that we were going so well. When anyone came in, the lads took to them, which showed a lot about their character; they weren't worried about the new face taking their place and cause problems for him. If the players went out and showed their worth on the field, there would be no comebacks on them, which was good."

The Pilgrims' unbeaten run came to an end the following Tuesday at Whaddon Road, when they exited the LDV Vans Trophy at the hands of Cheltenham, 2-1. Friio gave them the lead after 16 minutes of a first half they dominated, but the appropriately-named Jamie Victory and Julian Alsop ensured a third successive home win against Argyle for Cheltenham since their elevation to the Nationwide League in 1999.

Cheltenham's winning goal came in the 63rd minute, after Larrieu came charging off his line for a cross but failed to make any contact with the ball, leaving Alsop to head home.

Sturrock forgave his French number one for the rare error of judgment. He said: "Romain has saved us two or three times this year. This is the first game he has cost us, so I won't be too hard on him. I would rather he comes for crosses, than stays on his line."

Tuesday, October 16 2001, LDV Vans Trophy, first round

Cheltenham Town 2
Victory 53, Alsop 63
Plymouth Argyle 1
Friio 16

Cheltenham Town (4-4-2): S Book; N Howarth, M Duff, C Banks, J Victory; L Williams, L Howells, R Milton, H McAuley; T Naylor, J Alsop. Substitutes (not used): J Brough, A Griffin, M Devaney, M Jackson, C Muggleton (gk).
Plymouth Argyle (4-4-2): R Larrieu; D Worrell, P Wotton, G Coughlan, J Beswetherick; J Bent, S Adams (K Wills 81), D Friio, L Hodges; I Stonebridge (M Evans 72), N Banger (B McGlinchey 72). **Substitutes (not used):** L McCormick (gk), M Malonga.
Booking: Wotton 64.
Referee: P Rejer (Leamington Spa). **Attendance:** 1,310.

PAUL STURROCK: "I would have liked to have a run in the LDV but I changed the team that day as I wanted to have a look at 4-4-2 away from home. I thought Bent, for half an hour, was flying and, to be fair, our first-half performance that night was probably our best away from home – how we came in only 1-0 up, I don't know. Again we allowed ourselves to fall back on a 1-0 lead and you can't do that. We paid the penalty and lost. I was disappointed, because I don't like losing, but it gave me food for thought on systems of play and personnel.

"The boys were really gutted that night. They were disappointed with losing and how we lost. Every time we lost, the players seemed to use the defeat as a catalyst to pushing on again. Every time it happened, we seemed to bounce back. That's testament to good character, good attitude and having a belief they can win games."

KEVIN SUMMERFIELD: "We went 4-4-2 to have a look at a strong midfield. Plus we definitely had the objective in mind that we were going to play them in a league game, which was far more important, and we were going to go 4-5-1 against them. Larrieu got done for the goal. Alsop got above him and nodded it in and Romain came out and hit him when the ball was already in the net. Someone was having a go at Romain later in the season, because they were always winding each other up. Someone said: 'Alsop sorted you out' and Romain replied: 'But don't forget, in the LDV, I smashed him and he was on the ground for ages.' The lads cracked up – 'Yeah, but the ball was in the back of the net."

Argyle could not have asked for a stiffer test of their new-found resolve away from home following their LDV Vans Trophy exit than a trip to Mansfield, who had won five straight league games at Field Mill, scoring 15 goals, since an opening day 0-0 draw against visiting Southend. Ignoring the cup blip at Whaddon Road, Argyle were undefeated in seven Nationwide games, and had kept cleansheets in four of them.

Sturrock, though, was happy for Argyle's credentials to go on the line in what was his 50th game in charge of the Pilgrims' progress since being appointed the previous year. He admitted Christmas had arrived early for the team, which had blended more easily than he had imagined when he was mapping out their future on his arrival.

"Everything's come about a bit quicker than I'd expected," he said. "I'd have thought we'd be in transition and I expected we'd start making a move around about Christmas – but we're not going to knock it and long may it last.

"It's psychologically a big game for us because of our defeat on Tuesday. We are playing a very good side. People are saying it's a match between the two most improved teams in the league and you couldn't argue with that – but any game was going to be a question-maker after a defeat."

As it turned out, Argyle had all the answers. A 3-0 victory was testament to the Pilgrims' extraordinary change in fortunes on their travels and lifted them into second place in the Third Division, behind Rochdale. Even the most optimistic Argyle fan cannot have expected them to fall no lower for the remainder of the season.

Evans, who would have been suspended had it not been for the FA overturning his red card against Luton, opened the scoring in the 54th minute and Argyle were clinging on to that lead before the introduction of Stonebridge as an 87th-minute substitute. Stonebridge's run down the right in stoppage-time set up Friio for his fourth goal of the season, and the former England Under-18 interna-

tional then claimed the third when he strolled through and calmly slotted home past goalkeeper Kevin Pilkington.

Sturrock was angry that it had taken until the dying moments for Argyle to put the result beyond a doubt that was brought into focus when Lee Williamson's curling 30-yard shot had clattered Larrieu's left-hand post. "We just seem to clutch on to what we have when we've got on top," he said, introducing a theme to which he was to return time and again, "instead of going and getting the killer punch.

"Today, it went the right way, but, if we keep doing what we did in the second half, we are going to pay for it sooner or later. There hasn't been a team so far which has frightened the living daylights out of me, so I did feel we could get a result, but 3-0 maybe flatters us."

He was not the only one happy to see the Pilgrims win. Former chairman Dan McCauley and his wife Ann survived a 70mph crash on the M42 on his way to Nottinghamshire for the game, when his Jaguar span out of control and hit a crash-barrier next to the hard shoulder.

"As soon as I put my foot on the brake, I lost complete control of the car," said McCauley. "I slewed to the left, I slewed to the right and I went into a spin. There were cars and lorries all round me." McCauley coaxed the Jaguar to the team hotel and admitted: "When we got out, we were both shaking. I think it's because we realised how lucky we were."

Saturday, October 20 2001, Nationwide League

Mansfield Town 0
Plymouth Argyle 3
Evans 54, Friio 90, Stonebridge 90

Mansfield Town (4-4-2): K Pilkington; B Hassell (R Harris 87), L Robinson, S Reddington, M Pemberton; L Lawrence, L Williamson, C Disley, W Corden; J White (S Bradley 61), C Greenacre. **Substitutes (not used):** A Asher, M Bingham (gk), A Tankard. **Bookings:** Reddington 31, Pemberton 90.
Plymouth Argyle (4-1-4-1): R Larrieu; D Worrell, P Wotton, G Coughlan, B McGlinchey; D Friio; M Phillips (J Beswetherick 64), S Adams, K Wills (J Broad 87), L Hodges; M Evans (I Stonebridge 87). **Substitutes (not used):** L McCormick (gk), N Banger. **Booking:** Coughlan 18.
Referee: G Frankland (Middlesbrough). **Attendance:** 4,621. **League position:** 2nd.

PAUL STURROCK: "Mansfield probably epitomised our style away from home and it was probably the best we got out of the system. For an hour, they could not handle Friio playing in the free role, and our two full-backs dictated the game to the stage where the home team had to change their

system to try and handle us. They couldn't get a grip on the game. We got a goal, maybe out of nothing – Mickey put a big presence on a boy, the boy made a bad mistake and Mickey went through and scored. Then they forgot to put a marker on Friio and he ran the show – we got two more goals, but it could have been four or five apart from a wee spell when it was 1-0 and they had a couple of half-chances. They were a very good side, very attack-minded with good wide players, and their strikers looked pretty cute, too. Had they had a good solid back four, they would have gained promotion much more easily. It was a fantastic win because they were flying.

"Again I was worried about complacency because they were very buoyant, coming home on the bus. Even our directors had painted their faces. I was doing an interview and Nic Warren wandered by, daubed in green and white. It was that kind of atmosphere. That was the theme for me all season – to try and keep things level. Our fans were always a worry because they hadn't tasted success for such a long time and all of a sudden they were getting that bit of joy and talking about this, that and the next.

"The letters I received had us winning the league already. There were also a few times that I thought one or two of the directors were getting a little bit too excited about things, so I had to go into board-meetings and slap them about a bit, too. I tried to temper things in the media, to make sure the players were okay, and every time I spoke to a fan, to make sure they were okay as well, so it was a difficult job.

"People would say 'why not go with the flow?' but I've seen too many times people go with the flow and fall on their arse. I had to bring some negativity to all the positiveness that was happening. I genuinely felt that complacency and overconfidence is as big a sin as lack of confidence and I feel it could kick us in the teeth. I've been complacent many times and it's actually one of 25 rules that I wrote down when I left Dundee United. There have been times when I have been overconfident and let my standards slip and my training slip because we were on Easy Street, and I've finished up getting a thump from somewhere and having to start all over again.

"I didn't want that to happen, so I was very conscious I was on the ball as far as training was concerned, and the players were also on the ball. There's been a few players I've nipped over the season because their training standards were not what I would have expected."

KEVIN SUMMERFIELD: "I spoke to Danny Begera at Mansfield. He came to see me before the game and wanted to know the team and the formation. He said he was working for the Press. I ended up giving him the team, nearly. I was still very dubious. After the game, he was very, very compli-

mentary. He said we played like England. At the end of the season at the League Managers' Association do, he came over to me and said: 'I thought you'd do it.' I wrote after the game they were the best team we'd played and we'd won 3-0. The question was whether their youngsters would last."

Luck was to the fore for Argyle the following Tuesday, when a 2-0 home victory over Lincoln City at Home Park, coupled with Rochdale being held to a 2-2 draw at Spotland by Cheltenham, saw the Pilgrims reach the top of the Third Division in only the 15th match of their first full season under Sturrock.

The manager, though, was dismissive of both victory and achievement, in public at least. "This was our worst performance of the season," he said. "I'm pleased for some of them. Paul Wotton did say it is the first time he's ever been top of a league, so it's a nice feeling, but we have got to get back to reality and appreciate we didn't play to the standards we have achieved so far this year."

As for being top of the division – "It means nothing. If I'm in this position in April, I'll be a happy camper. Until that time, I know there's plenty of bridges to cross. We've got four huge games coming up now: Bristol Rovers on Sunday, Hartlepool, Cheltenham and Southend, who all finished above us last year, and three of them are away, so we've got to go and churn out results."

Goals from Friio and Coughlan, midway through each half, gave Argyle their victory, while Victory – Jamie, of that ilk – earned Cheltenham a point in Rochdale as the Pilgrims extended their unbeaten league run to 12 games after Sturrock had continued to employ one of the hallmarks of his management by "freshening things up" and dropping Kevin Wills and Steve Adams from the starting line-up of the team that had carved up Mansfield at Field Mill.

Phillips set up the first in the 28th minute for Friio, whose sly push on his marker saw the Frenchman create a small space within which to power home Phillips' curling cross from the right wing with a trademark header. Another header in the 75th minute saw the off-colour Greens finally kill off tidy Lincoln, Coughlan striding in unmarked at the far post to convert Brian McGlinchey's corner.

Tuesday, October 23 2001, Nationwide League

Plymouth Argyle 2
Friio 28, Coughlan 75
Lincoln City 0

Plymouth Argyle (4-4-2): R Larrieu; D Worrell, P Wotton, G Coughlan, B McGlinchey; M Phillips (S Adams 74), J Bent, D Friio, L Hodges; M Evans, I Stonebridge (N Banger 83).
Substitutes (not used): L McCormick (gk), J Beswetherick, K Wills.
Booking: Evans 53.
Lincoln City (4-4-2): A Marriott; M Bailey, S Holmes, G Brown, S Bimson; J Barnett (T Battersby half-time), J Walker, B Sedgemore (R Betts 81), P Gain (A Buckley 81); K Black, D Cameron.
Substitutes (not used): P Morgan, P Pettinger (gk).
Booking: Walker 80.
Referee: M Fletcher (Warley). **Attendance:** 6,572. **League position:** 1st.

PAUL STURROCK: "Lincoln was our worst performance of the season. Lincoln were very unlucky not to come away with a draw, minimum, that night. They battered us early on. We got a goal and, from then on, it was nip and tuck. Alan Buckley had done his homework and that was the first game that I realised that the jungle drums had been beating with other managers. From then on, everyone pressurised our two full-backs very high up the pitch, which meant we couldn't get a flow to our game and that we had to go from back to front a lot more direct than we wanted. We were having to shovel things down channels and up to our strikers' feet much earlier than we would have liked to.

"There were a couple of games later in the season when we told the goalkeeper to kick everything because the opposition wouldn't let us play at all. We decided we might just as well go and play for scraps.

"The disappointment for me was that the Lincoln crowd was very poor one after the results we'd come off. I was expecting much more than 5,000. The whole game was low key."

KEVIN SUMMERFIELD: "They always seem to play well at Home Park. It was hard. We hit the post three times. Wottsie was on TV that week. He always put himself out. He never shied away from the fact that the club needed taking out and, as the captain, he was the representative of the players."

CHAPTER 11

ARGYLE immediately relinquished top spot, although there was precious little they could do about it. With their visit to Westcountry rivals Bristol Rovers postponed until Sunday, October 28, to allow the game to be shown live on regional television, Luton advanced to the head of the table following a 3-0 home defeat of Swansea City.

They held the position for less than 24 hours as goals from Phillips and Hodges in a 2-1 victory at the Memorial Ground secured the Pilgrims their 10th win since the by now distant 2-1 home reversal against Rochdale, although Paul Sturrock considered his team had not done themselves full justice in front of the couch potatoes.

"The result in a derby is normally more important than the performance," said the veteran of many a Tayside spat, who blamed Phillips' second-minute strike for "putting a relaxation into the performance. We stumbled through the first half after that and never really got any flow into our game. In the second half, we started to get the ball down and do the things we are good at, but Bristol made it very hard for us and we're just pleased to come away with the three points."

Nevertheless, Sturrock was prepared to commit himself to mentioning the prospects of promotion for the first time. "We aim to get ourselves promoted this year," he said, "but it's only 16 games gone, it's a tight league and everybody's cutting each other's throats. We've just got to keep plugging away."

With Evans leading the line excellently against his former club in a now-familiar basic 4-5-1 away formation, the Pilgrims took the lead when Wills got enough on Wotton's early corner to force goalkeeper Scott Howie into parrying the ball straight to Phillips, who lashed it home from unmissable range.

Argyle retreated as they had done at Mansfield, but Rovers, without a goal in five previous matches, could make little headway in the space afforded them by the Pilgrims' generous defence. Argyle regrouped at the interval and another Wotton set-piece in the 58th minute, a free-kick this time, saw Coughlan flick the ball on to Hodges, who found the net with a powerful low shot.

Rovers set up an unexpected nerve-wracking climax for Argyle when substitute Martin Cameron glanced home a header with five minutes to go, but the Pilgrims held out to maintain a 100 per cent record for matches in which they have featured on live television.

Neither of Argyle's goalscorers caught the eye as much as Evans, however, leaving Sturrock in awe of the former Rover. "I thought he was outstanding," he said. "He held things up, ran the line and got himself in the right areas. I thought he was magnificent near enough the whole game."

The day was completed by the draw for the first round of the FA Cup, which handed the Pilgrims an unenviable journey to north Yorkshire for a fixture against Unibond Premier League part-timers Whitby Town. "If we are going to progress in the cup, we are going to have to go wherever we are drawn," said Sturrock philosophically. "It will be a difficult game – it's the David and Goliath scenario."

Sunday, October 28 2001, Nationwide League

Bristol Rovers 1
Cameron 85
Plymouth Argyle 2
Phillips 2, Hodges 58

Bristol Rovers (5-3-2): S Howie; C Wilson, A Thomson, S Foster, M Foran, T Challis (S Jones 64); K Gall, D Plummer, M Walters (A Bubb 87); D Gilroy (M Cameron 60), N Ross. **Substitutes (not used):** S Bryant, R Clarke (gk). **Bookings:** Foran 54, Thomson 57, Plummer 64, Gall 73.
Plymouth Argyle (4-1-4-1): R Larrieu; D Worrell, P Wotton, G Coughlan, B McGlinchey; S Adams; M Phillips (J Bent 86), K Wills (J Beswetherick 90), D Friio, L Hodges; M Evans (I Stonebridge 78). **Substitutes (not used):** L McCormick (gk), N Banger. **Booking:** McGlinchey 27.
Referee: M Halsey (Bolton). **Attendance:** 6,889. **League position:** 1st.

PAUL STURROCK: "If you looked at our fixtures, we never had an easy spell, like four successive fixtures against teams in the bottom half of the table. We always seemed to have a big spicy game on the horizon. We got an early goal, which settled us down, and there were spells in the game when we were very methodical and tactically aware and very solid. They huffed and puffed, but never looked like they were going to do anything to us.

"We dictated the game from the first goal, had several half-chances but never looked like we were going to score, but they never looked up for the cause, either. Then Hodgy got one and they battered us a little bit late on as we did our usual fall back and hang on stuff. It was a very testy last five minutes, but we never looked like we were going to lose.

"Our two centre-halves probably didn't realise they were doing it, but they kept taking the team back and letting people play in front of us. It's human nature. Which meant our midfield came back to support, which, in turn,

meant that, when we did have the ball and play things up to Mickey, there was no real support coming and we would play half an hour spells when we couldn't get out of our box and would rely very much defensively on the team. It worked, but our goalie had to be top-notch and our defence had to know what it was doing. All you did was create crosses into your box, which shouldn't have happened. What they didn't realise was that, if they defended further up the pitch, the crosses wouldn't have come in.

"Our set-pieces the season before were in the shambolic stage and I can't remember a goal we scored off a corner, but we didn't have time to address that. When we went on the pre-season tours, we put a couple of hours aside for them. Wottsie didn't take them last season, either. At the start of the season, we tried five or six different people and Wottsie came up and said he'd have a wee go at it and they looked good when they came.

"We scored a high percentage from set-pieces. We're not a big side, but the service into the box has been very, very good. We had five routines; we probably didn't use them all.

"I thought it was a difficult game for Mickey, because he had come from that club and had taken a lot of stick from the fans. Even their chairman had said he was the worst signing he had ever made. So it was always going to be a difficult game for him, but he went in there and ran the show for an hour before he ran out of legs. He did exceptional things on the day that they just couldn't handle. Mickey probably wouldn't admit this, but he probably prefers to play alone, rather than have someone else to worry about. I think he's a better player as an individual, rather than having to play with a partner, whereas I think Stoney, Marino and Blair are more appreciative of a pairing."

KEVIN SUMMERFIELD: "I don't think that Luton having gone ahead of us on the Saturday was a factor before the game. No-one talked about it. They did afterwards. I think we again showed our resilience but we had too much for them on the day."

A rare week without a Tuesday night match allowed Paul Sturrock the luxury of being able to reflect on his first year as manager of Plymouth Argyle in which he had taken them from near bottom of the Third Division to the top of the table, thanks largely to a complete transfusion of his playing staff.

"There is a belief about the team and the players have shown their character," he said. "When we go through bad spells, we don't just cave in. They keep battling.

"I also think we are passing the ball much better than we did last year. The

essence is to take the sting out of the opposition. The longer you have the ball, the more chances you have and the fewer opportunities they have. I just felt we kicked the ball from one end of the park to the other last year. We never really had any confidence we could get results. We also have some reasonable passers now, which I didn't feel we had."

Sturrock also warned that Argyle's emergence as genuine promotion contenders could have a detrimental affect on their ambitions. He said: "A lot of teams are going to give us respect at home and it's going to be much more difficult. I think we could lose some games on the break.

"There is a banana-skin waiting for us and it's not a case of 'if', but 'when'. It's how we react to that banana-skin that will show me how good a side we are. The dangers to us are complacency and over-confidence," he added, with the air of a man who would stamp out either or both should he get a whiff of one or the other on the training-ground.

The figures bore out Argyle supporters' beliefs that Sturrock was building a side to compare favourably with Green Dream Teams of the past. Of the six other Pilgrims' sides to win promotion, only Robert Jack's Division Three (South) champions of 1929-30 and Tony Waiters' Division Three runners-up of 1974-75 had put together longer unbeaten sequences than Sturrock's side's run of 13.

The victory at Bristol Rovers also established a new club record for successive away league matches without defeat, surpassing the eight in a row during one season by Jack's side, which also won their final away game of the previous campaign. Avoiding defeat at Cheltenham the following Friday would set another record.

Before that, however, Sturrock had two important engagements. The first was another convivial luncheon on the Football League's sponsors as he picked up a second successive Nationwide Third Division manager of the month award at Chambers restaurant on Plymouth's historic Barbican.

Nationwide media manager Chris Hull said Sturrock won the award in the face of stiff opposition from Luton's Joe Kinnear, Rushden and Diamonds' Brian Talbot and Exeter's John Cornforth – in his first full month in charge of Argyle's rivals – because the Pilgrims had again won more points than any of their rivals during October. "Argyle are still flying high and the consistency of the club is remarkable," he said. "Since the end of August, Plymouth have not looked back. Their record is phenomenal. It made it difficult to give the award elsewhere."

Never mind manager of the month – Sturrock made a great claim for poet of the week prior to picking up his champagne on the eve of the visit of Hartlepool to

Home Park when he addressed the Pilgrims' 13-game unbeaten run that helped earn the spicy prawns in filo pastry and fresh turbot.

"The thing about tidal waves," he said, reaching effortlessly for a metaphor to explain his concerns, "is that they always end up crashing against the rocks."

Sturrock would not have been surprised if Argyle's fortunes ebbed against fourth-from-bottom Hartlepool, believing that the recognition earnt – and deserved – for himself, his staff and his team could be a double-edged sword. "I honestly think Hartlepool could be our most difficult game of the season," he said. "Luton came down with a cavalier attitude, but Hartlepool will be more cautious and work hard.

"They are in a false position – I fully expect them to finish in the top ten – and it is a difficult game and one that calls for patience from our fans, myself and my staff and the players."

Right on both counts. Hartlepool did indeed rally later in the season, qualifying for the end-of-season play-offs, and did require Argyle to show plenty of patience in a 1-0 win from a match that did not please the committed, the casual or the connoisseur, for whom the greatest joy of the afternoon was reserved for Luton's demise at Mansfield.

Hartlepool manager Chris Turner employed a defensive 4-5-1 formation for the first time during the season, but his attempts to out-Sturrock Sturrock were thwarted by David Friio's seventh goal of the campaign four minutes before the end of a first-half dominated by the number of chances that fell to Michael Evans.

Evans made hay against centre-back James Sharp, whose surname served as a thoroughly inappropriate description of his abilities. The Argyle forward pulled out saves from goalkeeper Anthony Williams after a neat link with full-back David Worrell, and with a flying header following an extended one-two with Lee Hodges. He wasted a cross from Buster Phillips by heading wide, and shot into the side-netting after a weaving run that left three defenders flailing.

Just when it seemed the breakthrough would not come, it, like Friio himself, came late with good effect. Worrell took the ball unhindered into the penalty area and squared for the late-arriving Friio to slot the ball home. C'est simple comme bonjour.

Sturrock recognised Hartlepool's attempts at containment and said he believed they would be just the first of many teams that would come to Home Park intent on spoiling and frustrating. "A lot of jungle drums are going as far as managers are concerned," he said. "They know our game-plan."

Saturday, November 3 2001, Nationwide League

Plymouth Argyle 1
Friio 41
Hartlepool United 0

Plymouth Argyle (4-4-2): R Larrieu; D Worrell, P Wotton, G Coughlan, B McGlinchey; M Phillips (S Adams 81), J Bent, D Friio, L Hodges; I Stonebridge (N Banger 81), M Evans. **Substitutes (not used):** L McCormick (gk), J Beswetherick, K Wills.
Booking: Evans 80.
Hartlepool United (4-5-1): A Williams; J Bass, J Sharp (G Simms half-time), C Westwood, M Robinson; D Clarke, P Stephenson (P Smith 58), M Barron, M Tinkler, R Humphreys (T Lormor 58); G Watson. **Substitutes (not used):** A Boyd, M Hollund (gk).
Bookings: Barron 72 Williams 76, Simms 87.
Referee: B Jordan (Tring). **Attendance:** 5,723. **League position:** 1st.

PAUL STURROCK: "This was a difficult game. They had lost a lot of games – after I had hyped them to do well in the league. They'd come down here the previous year and absolutely battered us. They had the same players. They came out and changed their system, which I was very surprised about, and their team never seemed settled with it. We took full advantage. Although it was only 1-0, we had an awful lot of the ball and an awful lot of chances we didn't take.

"The team that let me down this year was Scunthorpe. I thought they were racing certainties to be in the top three, or at least the play-offs. Hartlepool were very good last year and I gauged my opinions on what I saw then. I had a very good six months watching.

"I could understand the psyche of the manger. It was rumoured he was going to get the sack. He was looking to stifle.

"Friio and Phillips were very influential players at the start of the season, and scored a lot of goals, but both had run their race before Christmas as far as that was concerned.

"Dundee United were third-top one season before Christmas and flying and Billy Dodds had scored near enough all our goals. Then he was sold and we didn't score again and ended up finishing eighth. So I can see the point of strikers influencing but I normally find, when you have a goalscorer, no-one else scores and I think sharing the load is a much better option. We finished the season as fifth or sixth goalscorers in the division. We weren't shy of goals. People pointed the finger and said we needed a 20-goal merchant. But where are you going to find them? Can you guarantee me they are going to do it?

"Normally you find it affects the others in the team. You find they rely on him too much."

KEVIN SUMMERFIELD: "This was another struggle. The key was the defence. People knew what we were all about now. The way that they looked at games was wrong – they looked to stop us playing. But they weren't going to get anything out of the game if they stopped us playing, because we aren't going to give anything away. They didn't think 'how can we beat them?' There weren't many teams who came to Home Park and overran us and caused us problems going forward – even the good teams didn't do it. It might have been that our success was putting negatives in the minds of other teams. You've earnt the right for teams to look at you that way."

Sturrock continued to juggle his options the following week. Having already transfer-listed one striker, Martin Gritton, a few months into a new two-year contract, he signed another, picking up Marino Keith on a Bosman free-transfer after the 27-year-old was released by Livingston.

Keith became Sturrock's first Scottish signing – the exotic first name is due to having a French grandmother with Italian blood – having been born in Peterhead, and he played for Dundee United and Falkirk as well as Livingston, where he was a team-mate of Graham Coughlan. He had suffered injuries in the previous two seasons, but, when healthy, scored at a healthy rate.

"He's the type of striker that will fit very well into the mix," said Sturrock. "He has definite attributes that I have been looking for: he holds the ball up quite well and wants to run down the channels. His goalscoring ratio is very good, too. I don't need to remould him, because I know he will fit into the way I want to play.

"It's taken a while to get him, but the important thing is that you get the right people. If you have to wait for them, you have to wait."

Keith became Sturrock's 10th long-term signing on the same day he announced he would not stand in the way of midfielder Sean Evers leaving Home Park, despite announcing that the former Luton and Reading man had been the player around who he wanted to build his side when he signed him the previous season.

Sturrock said: "The football club has moved on and people have jumped ahead of Sean. He's down the pecking-order because injuries have prevented him putting forward a solid case. I don't want anybody who is unhappy involved with the club."

Keith was not considered for Argyle's visit to Cheltenham, brought forward to a Friday night because of England's international friendly against Sweden, where the Pilgrims would seek to lay the Whaddon Road bogey and equal the club record for consecutive undefeated away league matches.

Gloucestershire's ancient spa town might have plenty to recommend it, but there is little doubt Argyle supporters approached a trip there with the same degree of apprehensiveness as a Sunday afternoon jaunt to the in-laws. The previous September, a 5-2 thrashing contributed to the dismissal of Kevin Hodges as manager and, even though his successor could do little wrong, Sturrock was not immune from the curse of the Robins, who had been the only Third Division side to beat Argyle away from home since the beginning of the season.

That LDV Vans Trophy defeat came in a match in which Sturrock, an enthusiastic small-stakes poker player, did not reveal his full hand: no Phillips, McGlinchey or Evans, and 4-4-2, rather than 4-5-1. His line-up on the night was a different one: slightly different from the earlier meeting between the two sides, and hugely different from the one that earnt Hodges his P45: only one of the starting XI that ran up the white flag 13 months previously – Jon Beswetherick – was still employed by the club, and he was an unused substitute.

Jon Sheffield, Wayne O'Sullivan, Chris Leadbitter, Adam Barrett, Paul Mardon, Martin Barlow, Terry Fleming, Sean McCarthy, Paul McGregor and Jason Peake had all departed the club and, of the five substitutes, two – John Hodges and Kevin Nancekivell – had also gone; two more – Steve Guinan and Gritton – were on borrowed time; and only Paul Wotton was a regular on the 2001-02 team-sheet.

As someone once said: "There are 0-0 draws and 0-0 draws and this one was certainly in the latter category." Well, you knew what he meant. What the encounter lacked in goals, it certainly made up for in incidents.

A bruising, bad-tempered encounter exploded acrimoniously when referee Brian Curson finally blew his whistle to signify half-time after mistakenly adding 10 minutes stoppage-time to a first half in which, despite the near freezing conditions, both sides increasingly got hot under the collar.

When Curson finally signalled a halt to the first 45 – actually 55 – minutes, players and officials from both sides scuffled by the dug-outs following a spat between Wotton and Cheltenham manager Steve Cotterill. The arguments continued down the tunnel and Sturrock's later throwaway dismissal of the incident as "handbags at dawn" glossed over what in reality was an ugly situation.

It could be argued that Curson's tolerance of some red-blooded Cheltenham

The Huddle

Paul Wotton after victory at Lincoln

**Rochdale 1
Argyle 1
(Keith)**

Rochdale 1
Argyle 3
(Hodges)

Lee Hodges goes to ground after scoring against Rochdale

The Argyle players celebrate at Rochdale

Steve Adams

Jason Bent

Jon Beswetherick

Joe Broad

Graham Coughlan

Michael Evans

David Friio

Neil Heaney

Lee Hodges

Marino Keith

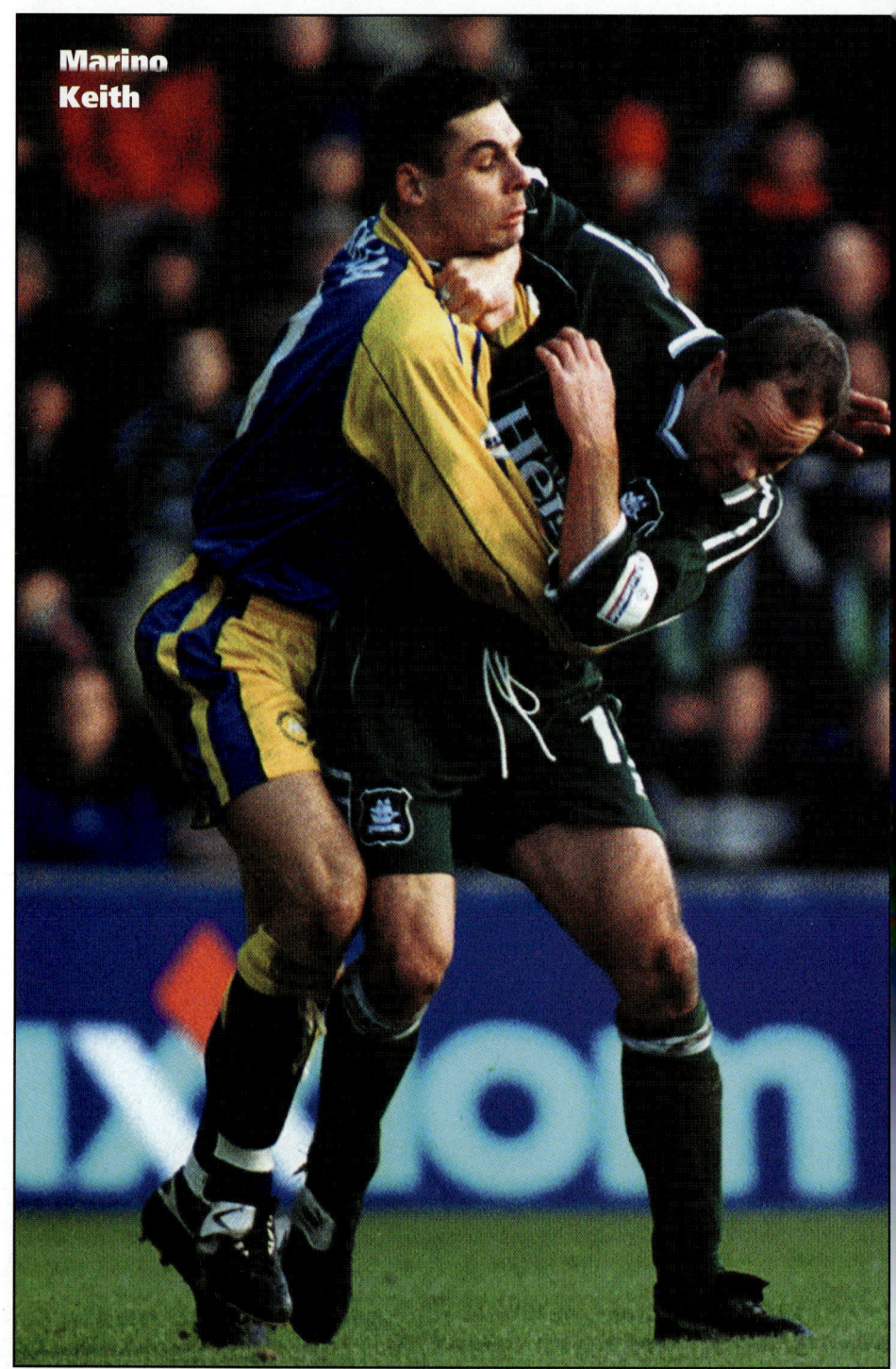

Romain Larrieu

Brian McGlinchey

Martin Phillips

Ian Stonebridge

Blair Sturrock

Kevin Wills

David Worrell

Paul Wotton

The Gaffer

Kevin Summerfield

Michael Evans celebrates scoring the opener at Darlington

Marino Keith (centre) heads home at Darlington

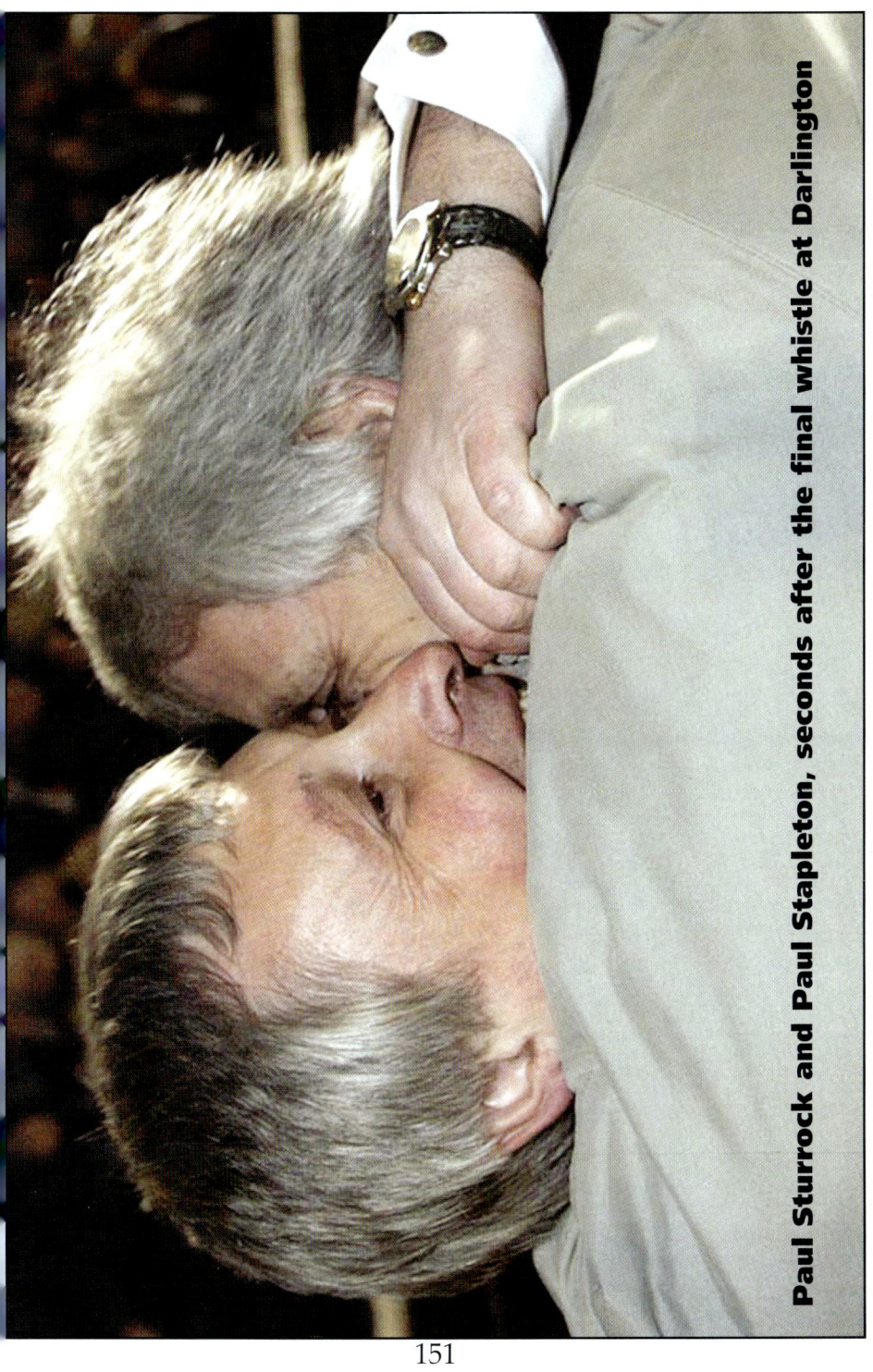

Paul Sturrock and Paul Stapleton, seconds after the final whistle at Darlington

Invasion of the Darlington Directors' Box

The away dressing-room at Darlington

Blair and Paul Sturrock celebrate at Rochdale

154

tackles had not helped the situation, as neither had his booking of Argyle midfielder Jason Bent for 'diving' when it was obvious to most people in the ground that the Canadian international had merely lost his footing on the slippery Whaddon Road surface.

Given the heated nature of the contest, if not the environment, it was no surprise when someone was sent off. Cheltenham's Mark Yates went after, having already been booked for an off-the-ball tackle on David Friio, he was red-carded for leaving a set of stud marks on the chest of Friio's compatriot, Romain Larrieu.

Cheltenham worked hard to secure a home point after being reduced to ten men, but almost undeservingly lost it in the final minute, when substitute Ian Stonebridge headed Lee Hodges' overhit left-wing cross wide at the far post.

Sturrock described Argyle's performance as their worst away from home of the season. He said: "I think the word to use is 'sloppy'. We never really got started and you have got to give Cheltenham credit – they worked very hard to make sure we couldn't get a rhythm to our passing.

"We will just take the draw and get down the road. If you draw your games away from home and win your home ones, you are going to be there or thereabouts."

Friday, November 9 2001, Nationwide League

Cheltenham Town 0
Plymouth Argyle 0

Cheltenham Town (4-4-2): S Book; N Howarth, M Duff, C Banks, J Victory; H McAuley (L Williams half-time), M Yates, L Howells, R Milton; T Naylor (M Devaney 55), J Alsop.
Substitutes (not used): N Grayson, A Griffin, C Muggleton (gk).
Sending-off: M Yates 53 (second bookable offence).
Booking: Yates 40.
Plymouth Argyle (4-1-4-1): R Larrieu; D Worrell, P Wotton, G Coughlan, B McGlinchey; S Adams (I Stonebridge 62); M Phillips (N Banger 85), J Bent (K Wills 85), D Friio, L Hodges; M Evans. **Substitutes (not used):** L McCormick (gk), J Beswetherick.
Booking: Bent 17.
Referee: B Curson (Burbage). **Attendance:** 5,035. **League position:** 1st.

PAUL STURROCK: "This was a nice catalyst to the season. During the ten minutes injury-time at the end of the first half, there was a bit of jabbering that went on between their manager and a couple of my players, which I got a little bit upset about. There is a rule is that you don't get involved with the other team's players. He said something that I took umbrage to. Thankfully, as I got to him, my physio flew past me because I'm not the bravest person in the world. I'd sort of veered to the side because the refer-

ee had blown the whistle and I was now looking to abuse him. When I turned back, there was my team and their team weighing into each other going up the tunnel.

"When I got round the corner, two of my boys were trying to get into their changing-room. It showed there was a bit of team-spirit and a bit of rallying to the cause, though we didn't play well, it was a poor performance. They never looked as they were going to break us down, but we huffed and puffed and really it was a disappointing performance.

"It was Friday night, it was cold, the pitch was going a bit crusty and we never hit the heights but, at the end of the day, we bored them to death and came away with a point.

"I told the players at half-time that I thought there would be a few of them looking to excite the referee so I was relatively pleased our players calmed down at half-time and were very professional in the second half. It was poor, but we'd been to Cheltenham the year before and got absolutely whitewashed so, as I said to the players: 'When you play badly and come out with something, it's a huge benefit to the team.'

"I think we didn't get many cards because our boys are more content in trying to do the things to get the team to play well than they are thinking about the opposition. We have players who are footballers and a management team that is interested in playing. We stop other teams, but we don't stop them at all costs. We play the game the proper way.

"For Wottsie and Cocko to go through the season playing every game was incredible, but they knew Craig Taylor was lying in wait. They'd seen what had happened to Bezzie and they knew I'm a great believer in whoever has the shirt keeps the shirt in a winning streak. They realised they might not get back in.

"The secret of football is to have a small squad. People don't realise that. With loans, you can cover yourself. You might be overextended for a game but you'll be able to cover yourselves. I'm a great believer in a small squad. Everybody knows the situation, everybody knows their own job; it's a team game.

"Marino came and played trial game with Blair at Torquay and I thought the pair of them were very exciting together. It's one of the pairings I never used very much but, when they did come together, they influenced a lot of games. It was probably our best pairing. I'd left Summers and Stuart Gibson to make a decision on Blair, which I thought was fair, but Marino had a goalscoring knack. I did feel that he was never fully match-fit for us

until the last two weeks of the season. He went through a real torrid spell when he felt tired all the time and he had a couple of poor performances because of it, but I did feel his goalscoring would be a benefit to us and he got something like nine goals in 13 starts. He wasn't one of the targets I had – Connolly was always the one I wanted – but I thought he and Coughlan might be an influence, they seemed to get on and he was up for the challenge because he had been in the wilderness for a couple of years. I like those types of players. These boys always have a hunger and I thought he brought a hunger to us.

"David Worrell was out of things at Dundee United; Brian had been a schoolboy at Manchester United and lost his way; Graham Coughlan was on the scrapheap; Marino and Mickey Evans too; Lee Hodges was going nowhere.

"You'll always have a failure rate on that – I think Sean's proved that – but I always feel they're on payback. They have a hunger to do well. They know it's the Last Chance Saloon on a lot of occasions and normally we get the best out of them; rehab them as footballers and give them the confidence of being wanted. St Johnstone was the same – Dundee United was different and that part of my career I've blanked out – I took and awful lot of people who were going nowhere and moulded an extremely good side out of them. They went on to play in Europe as well.

"Marino and Coughlan had also tasted success on a regular basis. Those two players were sorely missed by the Livingston fans. They couldn't believe Coughlan was going and were very surprised Marino hadn't been given his chance."

KEVIN SUMMERFIELD: "This was always going to be a game. There were bits of niggle going on. Lots of mouthing. Steve Cotterill gets his team wound up. They were a very organised team; good players. He was the only one who came out to beat us. He knew his team could beat us. Instead of being all us, he went the other way, like 'we're going to beat you; we deserve to be as good as or better than you.' That might have added an edge to the game. There was little bit of nastiness and mouthing going on. The referee mucked it up by adding the ten minutes on. Everyone was getting heated when really we needed everybody off as quickly as possible, calm down, get back out. We possibly would have taken 0-0 before the game because we knew what sort of game it was going to be.

"My first impression of Marino was that he had something. He had been injured, but he was so willing; he never stopped running; was as honest as the day is long, which is fits into exactly what we expect of players on a Saturday."

Nicky Banger's five-minute cameo as substitute at Whaddon Road was his last appearance in a green shirt. Having signed Marino Keith the previous week, Sturrock was reluctant to extend his three-month contract.

"He's done really well for us," he said, "but I've got to be aware of having an experienced player who would be down the pecking-order. All of a sudden, Marino Keith became available and so the timing of things has been a bit disappointing to Nicky. He needs to play in somebody's line-up. I didn't think it was appropriate to have another six months when he's playing a bit-part."

Argyle enjoyed a break from league action the following Saturday, and a break from routine, when they flew up to north Yorkshire intent on improving Sturrock's FA Cup record at non-league Whitby. Sturrock (played two, won none, drawn one, lost to Chester City) played down the perception of his side as favourites against the Unibond Premier League side, but stressed he still expected to be involved in the second round draw and did not intend to follow in the footsteps of Bram Stoker.

Stoker was so spooked by his experience of Whitby that he wrote the seminal vampire novel 'Dracula' after a visit to St Mary's Churchyard adjacent to the remains of Whitby Abbey, but Sturrock believed the seaside resort should hold no terrors for his Pilgrims, despite the classic ingredients for a cup upset: a pocket-handkerchief sized pitch, winds gusting in off the North Sea, and expectant 'Match of the Day' cameras.

"We're going to be methodical and professional in our approach," he said, "and match them in work-rate, attitude and commitment because one thing's for sure – tiredness will not be a problem for Whitby: adrenaline will keep them going.

"If we are going to be successful, we are going to have to adapt to every situation. If we do that, I'm confident, but we are on a hiding to nothing."
Argyle, starting without the suspended McGlinchey and Bent, who had endured a horrendous journey back from Cyprus in midweek after winning his 26th Canadian cap in a friendly international, just about escaped with their hides intact. Phillips scored in the 72nd minute to cancel out Alex Gildea's 43rd-minute opener and earn a 1-1 draw to spare the Third Division leaders' blushes.

On the subject of embarrassing moments, Phillips' goal came two minutes after Coughlan had nearly scored the own goal of the decade. Thirty yards from goal, the Argyle centre-back tried to play a square pass to defensive colleague Wotton only for the ball to hit him on the shinpad and slice elegantly towards his own net, with Larrieu stretching to keep it out. All lovingly caught on 'Match of the Day' cameras, too.

As he had done in their previous cup-tie, Sturrock experimented with a 4-4-2 starting line-up and saw his side struggle. "You can't put your finger on it," he said. "We allowed ourselves to get in a rut of slow play, slow build-up, and caused our own concern. We were very slack, but it's Whitby's day and they should reap the accolades for their performance. We live to fight another day and that's all I really want to say."

Saturday, November 17 2001, FA Cup, first round

Whitby Town 1
Gildea 43
Plymouth Argyle 1
Phillips 72

Whitby Town (4-4-2): P Naisbett; G Rennison, D Goodchild, B Dixon, D Logan; L Ure (S Ingram 90), I Williams, G Williams, A Gildea (C Veart 72); G Robinson, J Burt (D Key 89).
Substitutes (not used): K Graham, J Mohan (gk).
Booking: Rennison 85.
Plymouth Argyle (4-4-2): R Larrieu; D Worrell, P Wotton, G Coughlan, J Beswetherick; M Phillips (J Bent 85), S Adams (K Wills 54), D Friio, L Hodges; M Evans (M Keith 72), I Stonebridge. **Substitutes (not used):** L McCormick (gk), C Taylor.
Bookings: Friio 41, Wotton 50, Keith 80.
Referee: N Barry (Scunthorpe). **Attendance:** 2,202.

PAUL STURROCK: "Although the club made a loss on the flight, it was made up for ten-fold on the next two or three games, especially on the following Tuesday night.

"We had a real torrid time in cups. We lost a whole load of goals in cups and I could never put my finger on why that was. We didn't seem to play cup games the way we played league games. We went out and tried to play teams. We didn't seem to do things right.

"I didn't believe Whitby should be given the courtesy of a 4-5-1. They were a couple of leagues down from us. The pitch was in absolutely scandalous condition – you couldn't pass the ball 10 yards. We had to revert to a lot of things that were alien to us. The pitch was tight; they had a boy running about up front who was as good a player as I saw all season [Jamie Burt]. I had a lot of debate about him but I didn't come close to signing him. The problem was his off-field activities. I could not bring him into our environment. It was never a real debate. Had he not had that background, he might have been a big benefit. He's a player. He scored six or seven goals for Chesterfield after he signed for them at the end of the season.

"We scored late on although we had an unbelievable amount if chances in

the game which we did not take. We were on a hiding to nothing, conditions were not the best, they were all up for it. They played well. It was very scary.

"There was so much emphasis on the league, I think we found the cups a hindrance, rather than a benefit. We were very open, very slack."

KEVIN SUMMERFIELD: "It was a different experience. We weren't playing for points. Everybody was focused on the league and the way it was all panning out. People maybe thought we could not worry; if we lost, we were not going to lose any points. It was an unconscious thing."

Argyle were back on the road – in both senses of the expression – the following Tuesday, seeking to extend their unbeaten away league record into a fifth month. From Hull in August, through September and October, to Cheltenham, Argyle had not suffered defeat away from Home Park and avoiding a nil-pointer at Southend on their final travels in November would see them take the run to Leyton Orient on December 1.

Southend's record was not the most consistent in the division, but they faced Argyle straight after knocking Luton out of the FA Cup to demonstrate they remained a potent force when everything clicked. Sturrock, though, was on the look-out for his potential banana-skin (although, if he found one, it would immediately cease to be one, since the quintessential nature of a banana-skin is its ability to surprise) and was wary of a pratfall at Roots Hall.

"We have not been playing that well – to the standards I have come to expect – for the last two or three matches," he cautioned. "Of course, there will be troughs during a season and it would be nice if those troughs were draws, rather than defeats." He must, then, have been delighted that the Pilgrims opened up a four-point lead at the top of the Third Division as they maintained their hugely impressive away form with a first success at Roots Hall for 45 seasons.
Not half as delighted, though, as midfielder Steve Adams, whose first ever Argyle goal three minutes before the half-time interval earned a 1-0 win and preserved their record as the only unbeaten team away from home in the entire Nationwide League.

Adams' perfectly placed header after an equally perfectly timed run into the penalty area to meet recalled left-back McGlinchey's cross proved the difference between the two sides and meant Argyle had picked up 40 points out of a possible 48 from their last 16 matches. Adams joked: "I've taken plenty of stick for not scoring but I showed them: one attempt, one goal – I'm happy with that."

Otherwise, Adams' defensive capabilities were very much to the fore as the

Pilgrims protected Larrieu's goal so effectively that the Frenchman did not really have a save of note to make. Sturrock said: "The lads have done well at the back all season and Romain has kept a lot of clean-sheets, but it's a team effort – everyone is defending well, starting from the front."

Tuesday, November 20 2001, Nationwide League

**Southend United 0
Plymouth Argyle 1**
Adams 42

Southend United (4-4-2): D Flahavan; D McSweeney, P Whelan (D Webb 87), L Cort, D Searle; S Clark, S Thurgood, K Maher, L Johnson (R D'Sane 71); M Rawle, T Bramble. **Substitutes (not used):** D Kerrigan, D Gay (gk), B Belgrave.
Bookings: Whelan 37, Rawle 54, Clark 63.
Plymouth Argyle (4-5-1): R Larrieu; D Worrell, P Wotton, G Coughlan, B McGlinchey; J Bent, S Adams, K Wills, D Friio, L Hodges; M Evans. **Substitutes (not used):** L McCormick (gk), I Stonebridge, M Phillips, M Keith, J Beswetherick.
Referee: P Taylor (Cheshunt). **Attendance:** 3,716. **League position:** 1st.

PAUL STURROCK: "Our shape won us the game. We played shape very well. Although they had a lot of possession, apart from the first couple of minutes, when there was a boy right through and Romain made a great save, they never really pressurised us. For a lot of people, it was probably our best performance of the season away from home.

"It was Stevie Adams' first goal for the club. Mickey Evans had a great second-half performance. They could not handle him, in the air or on the floor, and even running down channels. It was very methodical, very thoughtful and they couldn't break us down.

"It's nice to know you're not going to get totally nipped. There will be a game or two that somebody gets two goals against you because you've dropped a gear or two, but we never really had that problem. You're still apprehensive. You know you've got a long time to go and they've got to be offensive and to chase the game."

KEVIN SUMMERFIELD: "This, to me, was one of the key wins. They were going well at the time. We'd left at 7am and done a lot of travelling. It was a long, long day. How would get over not playing well at Whitby? We played really, really well. There were some great individual performances – Brian, Mickey Evans, Stevie Adams. We sat on the bus after the game, and thought we now had a right chance of doing something. We were totally professional; we played well and created a lot of chances. A massive game."

The players that had taken Argyle to the top of the Third Division had the opportunity to further enshrine themselves in Home Park folklore the following Saturday by what looked the fairly simple task of avoiding defeat by Carlisle United, one of three teams equal on 16 points at the bottom of the table.

Sturrock's men had already set one club record during the campaign, with their then 11-game unbeaten away run two better than the previous record established 71 years previously by Robert Jack's Third Division (South) champions. That away form had contributed to a 16-game undefeated streak which matched the post-war record set by Tony Waiters' side that won promotion to the Second Division in 1975 and was equalled five years later by Bobby Saxton's teams at the end of the 1979-80 season and beginning of the 1980-81 campaign.

Sturrock was playing little heed to history, however, although it is impossible to imagine he was getting no satisfaction out of what had happened – it was his job, after all – and that some future Sturrock grandchildren are not going to get a proud lugholeful 25 years hence. He was, he insisted, more interested in the immediate future.

"It's three points to be played for," he said. "That's the way I look at it because, in 30 or 40 years time, someone will be telling another manager he's beaten such and such a record. The important thing for us is to be appreciative it's going to be a hard game."

Sturrock drummed home a familiar message in the days leading up to the Carlisle game, his 50th league match in charge of the Pilgrims: passing, patience and perseverance. It was directed, not just to his players, but also to Argyle supporters who believed all that their team had to do to claim their 13th victory from 20 games was to show a face and shake a leg.

The prima facie evidence for such a feeling was admittedly compelling – Carlisle were the only Nationwide Third Division team without an away victory – from nine attempts – and had scored just three goals in their previous seven matches – but Sturrock was quick to point out that, in their last eight matches, they had either kept a clean-sheet or conceded a single goal. Nuff respect.
He said: "Tell all the supporters they could be caught unawares. If the expectation is that we will go charging down their end from the first whistle and batter them, and people will be turning up expecting us to win 4-0 or 5-0, and that's just not going to happen."

He was right, but only just. Argyle's 3-0 victory was a cakewalk. Goals from Evans, Bent and Phillips extended the Pilgrims' lead at the top of the Third Division to a comfortable six points and, less importantly in the record-eschewing Sturrock's eyes, set a post-war best benchmark for consecutive games with-

out defeat. Jack's 1929 heroes that went 22 games without being beaten (18 in one season after four the preceding campaign) remained the only previous Pilgrims to have bested this effort 72 years later.

The superstitious Argyle manager might abhor the very mention of records – and search for wood to furiously tap every time someone brings one up – but even he must have conceded that they were merely a reflection of the long overdue success which he had brought to Home Park.

These were halcyon days to be Green and worth cherishing while they lasted. When before had Argyle boasted the longest run of undefeated matches by any club in England (17); or most points (44) in the country; or the most wins (13); or the most clean-sheets (12); or the best goal-difference (+20); or the longest winning sequence at home (7); or the longest undefeated streak away from home (11); or the fewest goals conceded per game (0.55)? Reading that should have brought about a few splinters Chez Sturrock.

The success had been achieved by a lot of hard work on and off the pitch, by players, management and the non-footballing staff, of course, but even events over which Sturrock had no control were conspiring to help the cause. The benign weather had kept pitches flat and firm, to the benefit of the passing game he espouses, long after frost and rain would have reduced them to a quagmire; Argyle's rivals for promotion were all faltering (Mansfield, Luton, Hull and Rochdale all had matches they should have won while Argyle were beating Carlisle – none of them did); suspensions and injuries had been mercifully light; and the new-board-new-ground-new-approach feeling had reinforced the optimistic outlook generated by the results.

Bent's goal – his first for Argyle – was the pick of the three, coming in the dying seconds of an explosive first half, between Evans' 17th-minute opener and Phillips' 88th-minute coup de grace. The ball reached him on the right edge of the penalty area following a short-corner routine involving Phillips and McGlinchey, and he struck it powerfully across goalkeeper Peter Keen into the opposite corner of the net.

Bent's goal effectively sealed a match which Argyle did not so much win as allow the highly-combustible Carlisle to lose. A goal down to Evans' capitalisation on Friio's break, they imploded on the half-hour mark, when Steve Soley was sent off for hauling Friio down from behind.

Soley exited swinging punches at Friio which fortunately were as accurate as his earlier attempts to win the ball cleanly, and, when he eventually left the pitch, flourished a v-sign at the crowd. Accusations of spitting were later made by both sides. Mark Birch was booked, then immediately substituted to prevent him out-

Soleying Soley, which was an amazingly clear-headed piece of management by Carlisle's Roddy Collins, given that he had been acting like a man with a red-hot poker down his trousers since the sending-off.

Evans continued to work his socks off (although closer inspection revealed that might just have been his current fashion) but otherwise Argyle went into their showboating routine, flicking, nudging, overlapping, one-twoing and generally overelaborating until Phillips applied the finishing touch to a Wotton corner that had been headed on by Evans.

Saturday, November 24 2001, Nationwide League

Plymouth Argyle 3
Evans 17, Bent 45, Phillips 88
Carlisle United 0

Plymouth Argyle (4-4-2): R Larrieu; D Worrell, P Wotton, G Coughlan, B McGlinchey; M Phillips, J Bent, D Friio (S Adams 86), L Hodges (J Beswetherick 77); M Evans, I Stonebridge (M Keith 80). **Substitutes (not used):** L McCormick (gk), K Wills.
Booking: Friio 55.
Carlisle United (4-1-4-1): P Keen; M Birch (D Morley 38), L Andrews, M Winstanley, P Murphy (J Allan 26); S Whitehead; B McGill, S Soley, T Hopper (M Jack 58), P Hadland; S Halliday.
Substitutes (not used): I Stevens, C McAughtrie.
Sending-off: Soley 33 (second bookable offence).
Bookings: Soley 19, Whitehead 29, Birch 37.
Referee: R Harris (Isle of Wight). **Attendance:** 5,870. **League position:** 1st.

PAUL STURROCK: "This was a teethy game. They finished with ten men. We ran over the top of them for about 25 minutes and let them back in it in the second half. They had a couple of chances in the second half. We knew that it was going to be an aggressive game, because of the manager's style and the way he wants his teams to play. They didn't let us down. There were a couple of teethy tackles, they had a boy sent off and had to take another one off very quickly before he got sent off."

KEVIN SUMMERFIELD: "It was always going to be a tough game. With Roddy Collins in charge, they were never going to not come out and give it a right go. We'd heard a lot about that, so we it was important we stressed before the game keep the discipline. We got a three and a nil, so both parts of our game were coming together."

Sturrock confessed he did not know whether reaching the Third Division summit and gazing down on the rest of the division would go to his players' heads as they prepared for their FA Cup first-round replay against Whitby. He did, however, make it clear that if they did become giddy on their success, it would be the first and last time that 'Billy Bigtime' appeared on a team-sheet of his.

"I think there will come a time where the position we are looking down from will affect them," he said, "and that's dangerous. It would last for one game and it could cost us dear but, after that, they would be well warned."

As expected, Argyle duly ended Whitby's cup adventure although the battle of the ports was anything but a cruise for the Pilgrims, who earned a second-round home tie against Bristol Rovers with a 3-2 victory, their eighth straight win at Home Park.

From bossing the game through Friio and Bent and taking a 3-0 interval lead despite the 37th-minute sending-off of Michael Evans for a piece of entirely avoidable stupidity, they fell asleep and were given a rude wake-up call when the Yorkshire side hit two goals inside three minutes. Goals from Bent, Stonebridge and leading scorer Phillips appeared to have eased Argyle's passage but they lost their way badly – "We played mind-games with ourselves," said Sturrock afterwards – and Whitby became only the fifth side in the season to score more than a single goal against the Pilgrims' parsimonious defence when Burt and Graham Robinson netted.

Sturrock, who achieved his first FA Cup win from his fourth game in the competition, was always convinced his side was going to win, however. "This lot," he said, referring to his players, "are a strange breed. They seem to live off those kinds of problems. I knew they would have dug deep. Even if Whitby had got a third goal, our lot would have lifted it."

Sturrock was sharply critical of Evans, who raised an arm towards Dave Goodchild after the Whitby player prevented him from taking a quick free-kick, and was sent-off. "I'm not paying wages to people who are not giving us service," he said. "The most he can get taken off him under FA rules, he will get taken off him."

Argyle led by Bent's 16th-minute strike, set up by Evans, and the Pilgrims were initially unfazed by their team-mate's absence. Stonebridge side-footed a left-foot shot home in the 39th minute for number two, and Phillips ended an end-to-end move which had begun with Larrieu's raking throw, went through Friio and Bent, and finished with the right-winger slotting home a left-footer off the post.

Burt was the biggest thorn in Argyle's side and he reduced the arrears in the 69th minute before Robinson's 20-yarder from nowhere three minutes later put a different gloss on the result.

"We played some really, really good football," said Sturrock, "but when you drop gears, like we did in the second half, it is very difficult to raise them again."

Tuesday, November 27 2001, FA Cup, first round replay

Plymouth Argyle 3
Bent 16, Stonebridge 39, Phillips 45
Whitby Town 2
Burt 69, Robinson 72

Plymouth Argyle (4-4-2): R Larrieu; D Worrell, P Wotton, G Coughlan, B McGlinchey; M Phillips, J Bent (S Adams 61), D Friio, L Hodges (J Beswetherick 84); M Evans, I Stonebridge.
Substitutes (not used): L McCormick (gk), K Wills, M Keith.
Sending-off: Evans 37 (violent conduct).
Whitby Town (5-3-2): P Naisbett; G Rennison, D Goodchild, D Logan, B Dixon, A Gildea (R Allen 51); G Williams, D Key, G Robinson; L Ure (A Anderson 76), J Burt.
Substitutes (not used): J Mohan (gk), K Graham, R Dunning.
Bookings: Goodchild 38, Key 79.
Referee: P Durkin (Portland). **Attendance:** 5,914.

PAUL STURROCK: "For about 20 minutes we played very well, ran right over the top of them. We got complacent, had Mickey sent off, a couple of crosses come in, and all of a sudden, we're sitting at 3-2, but never looked like losing. There was no way you could put your finger on the way we performed in cup-ties. That was the strangest scenario of the season."

KEVIN SUMMERFIELD: "We were lucky. We had a great first half, then we struggled. Mickey caused all the problems. There was no need to get wound up by a young kid like that. At the end of the night, we got through and that was all that mattered about the evening. We conceded two goals and possibly the lackadaisical defending on that night knocked on."

A second Sturrock joined the Home Park pay-roll at the end of November, with the manager's 20-year-old son Blair signing a one-year deal after coming through a six-week trial at Argyle that must have been as nerve-wracking for dad as it was for his offspring.

The signing was made on the recommendation of Sturrock's assistant Kevin Summerfield and director of youth Stuart Gibson, who had monitored Blair's progress in reserve games and training since his arrival from Dundee United the previous month. Sturrock senior was happy that they had made the right decision. "He plays the way I want my strikers to play," said dad, of son, "and, to be fair, I think he merits a contract. Had he not been my son, I would have signed him straight away after the way he played in reserve games against Saltash and Torquay.

"There are several Scottish clubs he could have gone to, but I feel there is something for me to work on for the benefit of Plymouth Argyle. Kevin Wills and Joe Broad are still developing as players and I would put him in the same category.

It will be doubly hard for him because he is the manager's son, but he has been there before and will be judged on his own merits."

Argyle's incredible record-breaking season rolled on to Brisbane Road, where they drew 0-0 with Leyton Orient. This was truly a case of getting something out of nothing: Larrieu added another zero to his value by keeping another zero on the scoresheet and chalking up a fifth consecutive league shut-out – a post-war club record and one shy of the all-time best of 77 seasons previously.

Staying unbeaten left the Pilgrims one league victory short of beating the previous one-season best of 1929-30, although the performance that got them their point was gritty, rather than spectacular. Without Friio (suspended) and Bent (injured), Sturrock was forced to play Hodges in central midfield and Beswetherick on the flank, which unsettled the Pilgrims.

Afterwards, Sturrock again expressed his concern that other teams had worked out how Argyle played away from home and adapted specifically to nullify their threat. He said: "Six wins and six draws away from home – anybody would be happy with that, but I think we're going to have to sit down and have a wee think about our style of play. I think people have latched on to us and maybe it's about time we tampered a wee bit."

Saturday, December 1 2001, Nationwide League

Leyton Orient 0
Plymouth Argyle 0

Leyton Orient (4-4-2): S Barrett; M Joseph, D Smith, D McGhee, M Leigertwood; A Harris, S Houghton (D Hatcher 84), J Martin, B Jones (M Lockwood 66); S Watts (S Gray 72), J Ibehre.
Substitutes (not used): S Canham, G Morris (gk).
Plymouth Argyle (4-5-1): R Larrieu; D Worrell, P Wotton, G Coughlan, B McGlinchey; M Phillips (S Evers 83), S Adams, L Hodges, K Wills, J Beswetherick; M Evans.
Substitutes (not used): L McCormick (gk), I Stonebridge, B Sturrock, P Connolly.
Referee: S Dunn (Bristol). **Attendance:** 6,342. **League position:** 1st.

PAUL STURROCK: "It's been difficult for Blair. At Dundee United, he had a real stiff task. He'd have to have been Maradona. He had a confidence thing about that. When he came down here, nobody knew him – nobody knew my history – and he was judged on his own merits. He seemed to gain confidence. He maybe should have had more games than he did because of his influence. To be fair, there's been times when he's been an easy option to leave out. You are a bit harsh. When he doesn't do things, you get annoyed as a parent and as a coach. I think he's found his feet very well here. Once or twice, when I'd not been really strong, I could have left Blair out and that is because he is your son – that's something you've got to

be strong about and get it out of your mind. I think he's merited his selection; the goals he's laid on and the goal he scored have been a big influence for us.

"My wife gives me a hard time at times. She feels Marino and Blair are the best pairing. She seems to think whenever they've come together in games, they influenced it, but I've never given them a chance to start together. The two of them don't get on that well – it's like giving whisky to the Indians when they are in a room together – but her motherly instincts come out and a couple of times, sitting up in bed, has mooted her thoughts.

"We felt Blair wasn't out of sorts with anybody and he brought a wee bit more pace to the mixture of front players. And his linkage was very good, which is what we were trying to achieve. There was about a month and a half when he was influential in every game that he played.

"I never pushed Blair and I won't push the other two. The oldest, Kirk, plays for a team but he doesn't seem that interested, but Arran, the younger one, has always got a ball in his hands and, whenever I've seen him, he looks very useful. But you never can tell. My dad never once pushed me in any direction. Blair was left to his own devices and was a hell of a late developer. He looked out of sorts with football until he was 16. Barbara used to take him to games and stand on the touchline because I knew I would start to get grumpy and make comments and would end up having a bad relationship with him, rather than an open relationship."

KEVIN SUMMERFIELD: "You could tell in Blair's first game over at Saltash that he'd got something. Paul wouldn't have even thought about bringing him down if he didn't think he was good enough. That's immense pressure on both of them. Blair showed throughout the rest of the season that he justified his contract. I think everybody was wanting him to do well. There was no sense of him coming here for an easy ride because of Paul. The lads took to him. To me, that epitomises the strength of the group; if they can see someone who's going to be a benefit for the team, they took to him. Chris Adamson was only here for five minutes, but they took to him straight away.

"Blair was under pressure because of his father, but he did his talking on the pitch. You cannot fool the supporters. If they saw that he was detrimental to the team, they would let you know, whatever reverence they held Paul in. That never happened. It went the other way."

PAUL STURROCK: "I thought we'd played badly at Cheltenham and Kidderminster in 0-0 draws, but Orient took the biscuit. We were so out of

sorts, it was unbelievable. But there are 46 games in a season and you can't play well in every game. We never looked content, until the last ten minutes, when we nearly nicked a goal. Had we shown that influence well before that, I think we would have sneaked it because they had been in a rocky spell."

KEVIN SUMMERFIELD: "We had no Friio, Marino, Benty; we had to reshuffle. Orient and Kidderminster were the real poor games. Orient was the best support we had away from home and we served up a right bunch of garbage. But they kept on singing right to the end. The lads knew it and all went over after the game. It was a big thing for us, but it was dire. Then we had six and half hours on the bus away from home. It wasn't a happy dressing-room after the game; there were bits of arguments going on. But, at the end of the day, we hadn't lost. We could have easily got turned over, but we came away with a point.

"We wanted to up training that week; we felt we were getting a little bit sluggish. But it was impossible because of the pitches."

Sturrock made his final signing of the season as early as the first week of December when he landed long-time target Neil Heaney. Sturrock had to wait until the 30-year-old former Arsenal and Southampton midfielder was released from his contract at Dundee United so he could sign him on a Bosman free transfer and, when Heaney settled up at Tannadice, Sturrock dived in.

Sturrock, who had taken Heaney to United from Darlington for £200,000 just prior to leaving Dundee United, said: "I said all along that there were three or four targets and Neil is one of them.

"I think Neil has got to the stage where he has got to find a home. He wants to settle down, get concentrating on his football, and be where he is wanted. He has come here to put severe pressure on people to take their places. Plymouth will benefit from that type of competition."

Heaney was ineligible for the FA Cup second-round tie against Bristol Rovers as the Pilgrims went for the league and cup double against their rapidly faltering West of England rivals. The match saw the return of Ronnie Maugé, the pivotal figure in the singularly most important moment in Argyle's recent history, for the first time since leaving the club three years earlier – a return to Home Park, though not to Plymouth, where he regularly visited his young son Daniel.

If Maugé will forever be a part of Plymouth Argyle, then Argyle will always be a part of Maugé. The bond he formed with supporters remained mutually strong and the man whose spring-heeled header at Wembley in the Spring of 1996 won Argyle promotion to the Second Division was delighted at the club's success.

"I am so happy for the fans," he said. "They deserve it. The club is flying. They have a good manager, a board with good ideas, and everything that I thought could happen for them is happening. I'm looking forward to returning to my old stamping ground, although, the way Plymouth are going, it will be a hard game for us."

Not that hard, as it turned out. After weathering a storming start by the Pilgrims in which Ian Stonebridge hit the underside of the crossbar and Paul Wotton smashed one long-range free-kick against the post before scoring direct from a longer-range dead-ball, Rovers bounced back to earn a 1-1 draw and set up a third meeting between the two sides in less than a month.

The introduction of 37-year-old former England midfielder Mark Walters as a half-time substitute proved the turning point as he used his years of top-flight experience to haul the Pirates back into the competition. Walters levelled on the hour, leaving Sturrock to rue his team's early profligacy.

"We missed an awful lot of chances in the first half, which you just cannot afford to do in these type of cup-ties," he said. "Had we taken one, I think the game would have got easier. Bristol played well in the second half, we've dropped a couple of gears, lost our shape in midfield, and we have paid dear."

Saturday, December 8 2001, FA Cup, second round

Plymouth Argyle 1
Wotton 28
Bristol Rovers 1
Walters 60

Plymouth Argyle (4-4-2): R Larrieu; D Worrell, P Wotton, G Coughlan, B McGlinchey; M Phillips (S Adams 88), D Friio, J Bent, L Hodges (J Beswetherick 88); I Stonebridge, M Evans (B Sturrock 88). **Substitutes (not used):** L McCormick (gk), K Wills.
Bristol Rovers (5-3-2): S Howie; C Wilson, M Foran, A Thomson, M Trought, V Astafjevs (M Walters half-time); L Hogg, R Maugé, D Plummer (T Challis 20); M Cameron, N Ellington (K Gall 90). **Substitutes (not used):** R Clarke (gk), S Ommel.
Sending-off: Challis 90 (second bookable offence).
Bookings: Foran 30, Challis 45, Walters 90.
Referee: R Beeby (Northampton). **Attendance:** 6,141.

PAUL STURROCK: "This was a disappointment because we'd really played well in the first half and given them a torrid time. We went in only 1-0 up and if we'd finished them off early, they wouldn't have come back. They changed their system at half-time, we didn't adapt to it and, although we had a couple of half-chances, we never reached the first-half heights.
"Neil was one I'd signed at Dundee United. I saw him playing at

Darlington and he was a revelation in the Third Division. He caused mayhem to teams. He lost his way when I left Dundee United so quickly after he got there. When he got down here, the team was flying and he wasn't match-fit because of the lack of games he was getting at Dundee United, so I couldn't stick him in, the team kept winning, Buster kept doing well at home. He was brought in to put the pressure on Buster, they are both reasonably competent on both wings and we wanted competition in that area. His knee started to bother him and he never really hit the heights I would have expected."

KEVIN SUMMERFIELD: "We had a great first half against Bristol Rovers; could have been 4-1 up at half-time. Then we lost our way in the second half. It was two different halves, but we were still in the cup and were drawn to play Derby, which, with the history between the two clubs, meant there was something on it."

Argyle began a sequence of seven matches in 22 days over the Christmas and New Year period a bit short on the striking front. Michael Evans was suspended following his Whitby misdemeanour, Marino Keith was suffering from a sore Achilles, Neil Heaney had injured himself in a training-ground accident with former Manchester City team-mate Buster Phillips, Martin Gritton was on loan to Irish League champions Shelbourne, and Steve Guinan was Siberiaised.

Sturrock senior chose to ignore the claims of junior for the visit of Darlington to Home Park for the last match which would be played before a three-quarters empty ground, and instead pushed Lee Hodges into the role which he had occupied on his first spell with the Pilgrims eight years previously. Jon Beswetherick deputised for Hodges on the left side of midfield, and both players struggled in unfamiliar positions.

Beswetherick, in particular, was a fish out of water, but that was no excuse for the cheer that went up from the home supporters when he was substituted, nor for the understandable abuse dished out to those spectators by the player. "I was shocked by the reaction of the fans," said Sturrock afterwards. "I'm bitterly disillusioned with the whole scenario. Bezzie should not have become involved in the situation, but I was sitting in the dug-out and heard the abuse and I must confess that, as a player, I might have reacted exactly the same.

"I've got a small enough squad as it is, without players losing confidence. When supporters get on at their own players, it makes it much harder."

In a perverse way, though, the striking selection played its part in Argyle achieving the 1-0 victory which established the 2001-02 Pilgrims as record-breakers – never before had an Argyle team gone 19 matches unbeaten in one season. The disciplined Darlington defence had become so used to dealing with Hodges and

Stonebridge that the injection of pace from the bench in the shape of, first, Keith, and, later, Blair Sturrock, rattled them. The Scottish pair would not have been as effective had they been on from the start.

Sturrock arrived in the 80th minute (to the refrain of 'Ooh, Aah, Sturrock junior') and within 60 seconds had set up the Devonport End winner for David Friio. Keith and David Worrell began the build-up down the Lyndhurst side before Sturrock supplied the killer pass through the defence and Friio lifted the ball over goalkeeper Andy Collett.

Paul Sturrock probably issued a 'thanks, son' in private, but he understandably played a dead bat to reporters' questions afterwards. "He did alright," was dad's verdict.

Pilgrims' skipper Paul Wotton was at the other end of the emotional scale, delighted to have led his hometown team into the history books. "The boys are over the moon," he said. "We are absolutely buzzing with the result."

Wotton and his defensive colleagues had again laid the foundations of a result that saw Argyle extend their lead at the top of the Third Division to six points. No back-line in the country had conceded fewer goals (11 in 22 matches), or kept more clean sheets (14), and goalkeeper Romain Larrieu, who had had to fish the ball out of his net only once in 900 minutes of league football, was in danger of being charged an admission fee for spectating next time he turned up.

"It just goes to show," said Wotton, "that you only need one chance. You get one goal, you keep a clean-sheet, you win the game."

Saturday, December 15 2001, Nationwide League

Plymouth Argyle 1
Friio 81
Darlington 0

Plymouth Argyle (4-4-2): R Larrieu; D Worrell, P Wotton, G Coughlan, B McGlinchey; M Phillips (B Sturrock 80), J Bent, D Friio, J Beswetherick (M Keith 60); I Stonebridge (S Adams 80), L Hodges. **Substitutes (not used):** L McCormick (gk), K Wills.
Booking: Keith 65.
Darlington (4-4-2): A Collett; S Betts, G Caldwell, D Brightwell, P Heckingbottom; N Wainwright, P Brumwell, B Atkinson, I Clark; D Mellanby (N Maddison 72), D Chillingworth (P Campbell 74). **Substitutes (not used):** R Hodgson, F van der Geest (gk), B Healy.
Sending-off: Caldwell 85 (second bookable offence).
Bookings: Heckingbottom 12, Caldwell 33, Betts 55, Brumwell 68.
Referee: M Cooper (Walsall). **Attendance:** 5,041. **League position:** 1st.

PAUL STURROCK: "They gave us a torrid time. They caused a lot of concern. We deserved nothing out of the game, but Blair's come on and seen a pass and Friio's finishing takes us to the win. As I've said, managers had been talking about us and everybody was coming and defending high up the pitch, which was causing us a lot of concern because we couldn't break teams down and we couldn't get a flow to our game. I knew than it was going to be one of those difficult seasons at home, because we were going to have to have a lot of pressure to win games.

"Bezzie played wide left and he didn't look content, so we weren't blazing on all guns."

KEVIN SUMMERFIELD: "A lot of our more fluent games had been away from home and there were patches of Home Park that were proving difficult to play on. The boys commented on it before the game. It was very cold but we looked very lethargic. It was a shocking day. We got off the pitch, had a little go at the players, then the results came through, everybody else has lost, and we've won the lottery."

The dark days of which Sturrock had preached duly arrived over the Christmas period, although, in truth, they were not that gloomy.

First, the Pilgrims exited the FA Cup in a see-saw second-round replay at Bristol Rovers, a result made more annoying by the knowledge that a lucrative third-round trip to Premiership side Derby County awaited the winners.

Argyle rallied after going 2-0 down to goals by Dutchman Sergio Ommel and Lewis Hogg, and levelled the match through two strikes inside 11 minutes from Friio. Almost immediately, however, Nathan Ellington raced through and slotted past Larrieu to give Rovers a 3-2 lead. Even then, Argyle were not out of things entirely and nearly forced extra-time when Sturrock's cross was headed against a goalpost by Keith.

Paul Sturrock was keen to take some positives out of the cup exit. "For spells in the first half, we played as well as we have played away from home," he said. "Bristol caught us out with two good goals which meant we had to chase the game. All credit to the players, they got themselves back in it, but I think they got so excited about it, they left themselves open at the back."

Tuesday, December 18 2001, FA Cup, second round, replay

Bristol Rovers 3
Ommel 56, Hogg 71, Ellington 87
Plymouth Argyle 2
Friio 76, 86

Bristol Rovers (5-3-2): S Howie; C Wilson, M Foran, A Thomson, M Trought, T Challis; L Hogg, D Hillier (M Walters 27, M Smith 87), V Astafjevs; M Cameron (S Ommel half-time), N Ellington. **Substitutes (not used):** K Gall, R Clarke (gk).
Bookings: Wilson 42, Thomson 45.
Plymouth Argyle (4-5-1): R Larrieu; D Worrell, P Wotton, G Coughlan, B McGlinchey; M Phillips, K Wills (M Keith 70), S Adams, D Friio, L Hodges (S Evers 80); I Stonebridge (B Sturrock 70). **Substitutes (not used):** L McCormick (gk), J Beswetherick.
Bookings: Keith 83, Coughlan 90.
Referee: R Beeby (Northampton). **Attendance:** 5,763.

PAUL STURROCK: "Away from home, I have never seen a team dominate a game like that in my life, first half, and we walked in 0-0. There were things flashing across goal. We turned around and lost a goal straight away; lost another one and the game looked buried. The boys have dug deep and got us to 2-2. There's was a great photograph of every player walking off with their heads down and really it was the first time losing had really hurt them."

KEVIN SUMMERFIELD: "The first half was the best we played all season. We were fantastic. We absolutely killed them down the left-hand side. Crosses galore went in; we just never got on the end of anything. After that, we worked on that for the rest of the week. We went behind and came back to 2-2 before possibly the best individual player in the league won the game on his own."

The Pilgrims' cup exit was followed by their first league defeat since the second Saturday of the season, a 2-1 reversal at Scunthorpe bringing to an end their 19-game unbeaten league run and ending a 12-match streak of away league games without defeat that stretched back to the beginning of the campaign.

Inevitably, it was former Pilgrim Lee Hodges, the diminutive namesake of Argyle's current left-sided midfielder, who did the damage. Scunthorpe's Hodges, who played nine times for the Pilgrims under Mick Jones while on loan from West Ham United, scored both the home side's goals as the Iron flattened Argyle's hopes of going into Christmas with their records intact.

On a surface covered by a sprinkling of snow, Hodges scored in the sixth minute with a goal described as 'a comedy of errors' by Argyle manager Sturrock, and again in the 25th, again after some defending that Sturrock found 'zany'.

For Hodges' first, Coughlan miscued a clearance by the corner flag, sending the ball high into his own penalty area. Larrieu caught it, but succumbed to pressure from Steve Torpey and dropped it at Hodges' feet.

The second came after Worrell had made a mess of trying to clear Carl Bradshaw's right-wing cross. Worrell prevented a corner at the far greater cost of heading the ball to Hodges, who drilled it back with interest.

Coughlan atoned for his earlier error by heading the Pilgrims' back into the game from Wotton's corner, although Coughlan's former Livingston team-mate Keith looked to have legitimate claims for the vital final touch. Both sides traded blows after that and, although Argyle might have levelled had goalkeeper Tommy Evans not denied Keith in the dying minutes, so, too, might they have gone behind had not the woodwork and Larrieu intervened on several occasions.

"When you concede goals like we have done, it is difficult to come back against a good side," said Sturrock afterwards. "The first one was a comedy of errors and it cost us dear because we had to chase the game after that. An experienced player like Coughlan should kick the ball out for a throw-in and not muck about with it. He kicked it up in the air and then my goalie decided to try and catch the ball around a striker, instead of punching it.

"Romain's last two performances have been nowhere near the standards I would expect from him."

"For the second one, David Worrell should have cleared it for a corner, instead of heading it back into the middle of the goal area.

"It's quite zany that this back four has been exceptional all season and then this happens. I think we gave away a couple of Christmas presents today."

It was left to the embarrassed Coughlan to rally his team-mates and supporters for the Boxing Day derby against Torquay United, when the new-look all-seater Devonport and Barn Park ends of the Home Park would be open for the first time.

"We are still five points clear at the top," said Coughlan. "Let no-one forget that. We were not torn apart by Scunthorpe. It was an even game. I do feel that luck deserted us, whereas in previous games, it was with us. We have got a massive game on Boxing Day and we will bounce straight back. I have no doubt we will come out with all guns blazing."

Saturday, December 22 2001, Nationwide League

Scunthorpe United 2
Hodges 6, 25
Plymouth Argyle 1
Coughlan 51

Scunthorpe United (4-4-2): T Evans; N Stanton, J McCombe, M Jackson, A Dawson; S Brough, C Bradshaw (M Sparrow 76), A Calvo-Garcia, L Hodges; M Carruthers, S Torpey.
Substitutes (not used): T Barwick, B Quailey, L Ridley, C Bennion (gk).
Booking: Dawson 3.
Plymouth Argyle (4-5-1): R Larrieu; D Worrell, P Wotton, G Coughlan, B McGlinchey; M Phillips, K Wills (M Keith 37), S Adams, D Friio, L Hodges; I Stonebridge (B Sturrock 71).
Substitutes (not used): L McCormick (gk), S Evers, J Beswetherick.
Referee: G Laws (Whitley Bay). **Attendance:** 3,602. **League position:** 1st.

PAUL STURROCK: "The disappointing thing for me is that I thought the game should have been off and I took that attitude into the dressing-room. When I looked at the pitch, I wasn't happy. But it was playable and I didn't react properly. We lost to uncharacteristic goals and never looked in the game until we got it back to 2-1. Then we had three unbelievable chances to sneak something out of the game. There were games we didn't merit anything out of that we'd sneaked and that one probably merited a draw, so it's swings and roundabouts.

"David Worrell will never do the thing he did for the second goal again, and had never done it before. For the first goal, Brian's got the opportunity to clear it, Graham's got the opportunity to clear it twice, and doesn't do it.

"I'd heard rumours that Romain was a bit down because he'd split up with his girlfriend and he got well told from me on that scenario. No footballer should take outside influences into the match.

"I get mooted there's some boys that have personal problems at home but, when the whistle goes and they have the ball, I don't think anything should influence them. He was given short shrift as far as I was concerned, and I think the conversation definitely benefited him.

"We got word on the bus coming back that Mickey Evans' wife Tyra had been involved in a bad car accident. Mickey wasn't with us because he was suspended. The lads immediately forgot about the game. We didn't see Mickey for nearly three weeks and it kind of knocked us sideways, because I thought Torquay might have a weakness on crosses and he might have been an influence for us."

KEVIN SUMMERFIELD: "We came in the next day, which was unusual. It

was on our minds that we'd conceded two goals and three goals in recent matches. We had a spell when we worked on the defence and worked on crossing and finishing. The goals were that comical you can't say 'don't do it' because they are errors that they will never do again – one-offs in the season. Three individual errors gave them two goals. We started well – I watched the video after the game and Brian Laws was on the gantry next to the video operator and he's screaming down, trying to get them to sort the system out because we were mullering them through midfield. We conceded two bad goals but we played well and battered them second half. We got a goal back and should have at least drawn. The news about Tyra changed everything; we forgot about football."

CHAPTER 12

AS it turned out, Boxing Day at Home Park was probably similar to what went on all over the Westcountry: invite the neighbours round for lunch and then quietly seethe while they spoil your Christmas.

Torquay United became the first side to leave the new-look Home Park with as much as a point for four months. They deserved their end of a 2-2 draw – even Sturrock admitted as much – and a good case could have been made for them returning up the Devon Expressway with all three.

Argyle, who were experiencing what Sturrock described as 'a wee hiccup' (three games without a win, seven goals conceded), could not rise to the occasion as 13,677 people – the Third Division's largest crowd of the season at that point – packed into the impressive-looking ground. Some had queued round the block for a ticket; some had posted desperate appeals in the Internet; some were prepared to pay over the odds to witness the dawn of a new era; some even expressed the opinion that the anticipation of the game made Christmas pale by comparison.

That the game kicked off as scheduled at noon, was a triumph in itself for associate director John McNulty, who had lived and breathed Nou Home Park since the project was conceived and whose confident smiles during the previous week that there would be no problem on D-Day could easily have been mistaken for the grin of a lunatic.

The Pilgrims took the lead through a fluke goal from centre-back Graham Coughlan early in the second half and quickly added to the lead with Ian Stonebridge's brave header.

However, the Gulls did what gulls have a habit of doing to the unsuspecting and fought back to level in the last minute through Richard Logan's penalty, given for a foul on substitute Eifion Williams by Brian McGlinchey, the Argyle player having earlier started Torquay's comeback with a headed own goal.

McGlinchey was far from a lone culprit for Argyle's shortcomings, though, and had it not have been for two further interventions by the Irishman – clearing Alex Russell's long-range shot off the line, and coming between Logan and a shot on goal – Argyle would have lost the game.

They thought they had won it within a six-minute period after half-time. First, Paul Wotton's mishit free-kick from the left hit Coughlan on the shin and deflected past Torquay goalkeeper Kevin Dearden, to the delight of the Devonport End,

then McGlinchey's high curler from the right was met by Stonebridge, putting his body between Dearden and the goal, for a fine header.

Torquay responded positively, but Argyle appeared to have survived their onslaught when McGlinchey, under little opposition pressure, headed Greg Goodridge's right-wing cross past Romain Larrieu with a precision few of his attacking colleagues had managed.

Argyle had two chances to wrap the Christmas points up. Marino Keith, playing in place of Michael Evans, who was on compassionate leave (David Friio displayed a T-shirt with the message 'Trigger, We Love You' after Coughlan's goal), headed substitute Neil Heaney's cross into Dearden's hands, then fellow substitute Kevin Wills headed a cross from third benchman Blair Sturrock wide.

However, it was a Torquay replacement – Eifion Williams – who made a telling contribution, when he was hauled down, no arguments, by McGlinchey, in the final minute, leaving Logan to convert despite Romain Larrieu's best efforts, and ensure honours were even. Sturrock said: "I think Torquay merited a draw. We've scored five goals in three games and not won. The part of our game that has been rock-solid all season is now showing frailties that I would never have expected of them. We have to get a grip with it on the training-ground."

Wednesday, December 26 2001, Nationwide League

Plymouth Argyle 2
Coughlan 49, Stonebridge 51
Torquay United 2
McGlinchey og 65, Logan pen 90

Plymouth Argyle (4-4-2): R Larrieu; D Worrell, P Wotton, G Coughlan, B McGlinchey; M Phillips (N Heaney 79), S Adams, D Friio, L Hodges; I Stonebridge (B Sturrock 79), M Keith (K Wills 87). **Substitutes (not used):** L McCormick, J Beswetherick.
Booking: Friio 35.
Torquay United (4-4-2): K Dearden; S Tully, S Woods, S Hankin, C Hanson; G Goodridge, J Fowler, A Russell, K Hill (D Preece 84); R Logan, D Graham (E Williams 89). **Substitutes (not used):** J Rees, M McNeil, R Northmore (gk).
Referee: P Rejer (Worcestershire). **Attendance:** 13,677. **League position:** 1st.

PAUL STURROCK: "If there was one team that played well against us, it was Torquay. I was quite relieved to walk away with a point, because they had four of five chances more than other teams had done at Home Park. It was disappointing to go 2-0 up and let them back into it. After the errors at Scunthorpe, Brian's scored an own goal and given away a penalty. All of a sudden we've lost seven goals in three games and I think it was a turning-point. We went back on the training-ground and worked hard on our back four for a wee while. We had a team-meeting and they were very receptive to what was said.

"It was derby game, which always seems to throw the formbook out of the window. I don't think the fans got behind the team; it was more of a party atmosphere. I honestly believe there were an awful lot of people at the game who were not regular football fans. It was a day out for them. The crowd was much more of an influence on the team at the Rushden game which followed, although it was a smaller gate."

KEVIN SUMMERFIELD: "A great occasion, great crowd, poor performance. They were one of the few teams who outplayed us. They deserved the goals. Brian had an aberration that Dave and Graham had at Scunthorpe. He knew it. There was no point in saying to him: 'Brian, you shouldn't have done that.' We were very fortunate to get a draw. We sat down and the conclusion was that we had to get back to basics. Next day, we set ourselves a target of 83 points and worked on our back four."

Sturrock, normally the subject of media enquiries, was asking some of the questions at the traditionally Friday lunchtime Press call before Argyle's final game of 2001 – a first visit of Rushden & Diamonds to Home Park – as he sought to give some perspective to the Pilgrims' blip in form.

The previous week had seen Argyle surrender their FA Cup place, a club-record 19-match unbeaten run, and a healthy eight-game home winning streak in consecutive matches, but they were three points clear at the top of the division and would remain leaders whatever happened against Brian Talbot's side.

"Let's be a supporter at the start of the season," hypothesised Sturrock. "We start the season after the turmoil of last season and the personnel changes we had. Let's say we are now seventh in the league – would you be happy with that?"

The point was well made, as was Keith's 81st-minute winning goal in the 1-0 victory over Diamonds the following day.

More tends to divide Plymouth Argyle supporters than unites them, but there is one thing that most Pilgrims are agreed upon: the club has never replaced Tommy Tynan. Indeed, how could it? Strikers who have the potential to score 200-plus league goals do not stroll up to the Home Park gates every day and casually ask for a trial. Ten years since Scouser Tom left his spiritual home and still the search for his successor – an natural-born goalscorer – goes on.

Or had it just ended? Because the question being whispered down Outland Road was: is Marino Keith the new Tommy Tynan? The omens were auspicious. Keith's first goal since his October move from Livingston was straight out of the Tynan Goalpedia. Most observers thought that Mark Peters had turned substitute Blair Sturrock's wickedly placed cross into his own net, but

Keith claimed a final featherweight touch that redefined the meaning of the word 'deft'.

Fair enough. His performance merited some reward, he was 'robbed' of a strike by team-mate Coughlan at Scunthorpe, and, anyway, if he had not stuck his hand up for the goal, Tynan would have been straight up from Stoke Social in a taxi to claim it for himself.

The Argyle manager was among those hoping the 27-year-old Scot might be able to follow in Tynan's studmarks. "He could be a big player for us," said Sturrock, who knows a thing or two about the goalscorer's art himself. "He's very influential in the box and likes to get on the end of things. He's had a real torrid year with injuries, and I still think he's got a long way to go to get his total match-fitness and sharpness back."

Keith was on the end of plenty, especially during a second-half that Argyle dominated. Trouble was, Diamonds' goalkeeper Billy Turley was on the end of most that Keith was on the end of. "Their goalie had what you would call an exceptional performance," said Sturrock, "and I thought their team worked very hard. It was a difficult game."

The prize for the most original excuse by an opposition manager for a defeat at Home Park was won by Brian Talbot, who noted that Argyle's goal originated from a quickly-taken throw-in, and complained that the ball-boys and girls had been biased in favour of Argyle. "They have got that ploy here," he said. "They do it for the home team only, which I don't think is right."

Saturday, December 29 2001, Nationwide League

Plymouth Argyle 1
Keith 81
Rushden & Diamonds 0

Plymouth Argyle (4-4-2): R Larrieu; D Worrell, P Wotton, G Coughlan, B McGlinchey; M Phillips (S Evers 90), S Adams, D Friio, L Hodges; I Stonebridge (B Sturrock 76), M Keith. **Substitutes (not used):** L McCormick (gk), J Beswetherick, N Heaney.
Booking: Wotton 60.
Rushden & Diamonds (4-4-2): B Turley; A Sambrook (T Mustafa 89), M Peters, P Underwood, G Setchell; P Hall, M McElhatton (D Bell 85), G Butterworth, S Gray (D Darby 85); O Lowe, S Partridge. **Substitutes (not used):** T Pennock (gk), D Talbot.
Bookings: Setchell 34, Underwood 45.
Referee: L Cable (Woking). **Attendance:** 9,503. **League position:** 1st.

PAUL STURROCK: "This was the first time we'd changed to Stoney coming off the front and that was an influence to the game. We started to look more tight and more balanced. We cut down on our opportunities from

open play and worked much harder at set-pieces. It was the Blair-Marino partnership that opened things up late on. They were one of the top form teams at the time – absolutely flying – and I don't think Romain had a save to make. Their goalie made unbelievable saves all day.

"Marino still claims Scunthorpe was his first goal, although Cocko was never going to give it to him."

KEVIN SUMMERFIELD: "We were back to normal. Their goalkeeper had an absolute blinder. It was very comfortable. I thought we played very well. Unfortunately, we had Swansea and Rochdale off after that."

Argyles's first two matches of 2002 fell victim to the weather. The New Year's Day fixture at Swansea was frozen off 24 hours before the scheduled kick-off, allowing the Pilgrims' players the rare luxury of being able to celebrate the day before like the rest of us, while the following Saturday's proposed visit to Rochdale also fell victim to the sub-zero temperatures.

With Home Park perfectly playable – it's warmer in the South West, you know – Argyle manager Paul Sturrock arranged a game for his team against the only opposition he could find: Argyle. Sturrock organised a full-scale practice game involving his whole squad, to which spectators were invited. Entry was by programme only, and around 1,000 spectators, curious to witness the occasion and see the rapidly evolving ground, helped raise around £1,700 for the club's Youth Development Trust.

Only regular first-teamers Paul Wotton (injured) and Buster Phillips (ill) were absent as a team wearing green, captained by David Friio, beat a team wearing blue, captained by Blair Sturrock, 4-2. Friio netted a hat-trick for the Greens, who opened the scoring through Stewart Yetton, while the Blues' goals came from Evans, making a comeback after his wife's car accident, and Coughlan, who had earlier handled the ball to concede a penalty which formed the middle of Friio's triple.

Sturrock deemed the game, which also saw the return of Jason Bent after injury, a success, even though he lost reserve goalkeeper Luke McCormick to a thigh injury. He said: "I'm very pleased the way things have worked out. The crowd was unbelievable and helped give the match an edge these sort of games sometimes lack."

Saturday, January 5 2002, Friendly

Plymouth Argyle Blues 2
Evans 45, Coughlan 60
Plymouth Argyle Greens 4
Yetton 6, Friio 41, pen 53, 66

Plymouth Argyle Blues **(4-4-2):** L McCormick (K Schofield 23); D Worrell, P Connolly, G Coughlan, B McGlinchey; S Evers, J Bent, K Wills (R Fice 81), N Heaney; M Evans (I Stonebridge half-time), B Sturrock.
Plymouth Argyle Greens **(4-4-2):** R Larrieu; J McGowan, D Bance, C Taylor, J Beswetherick; S Yetton (J Barwick 31), S Adams, D Friio (M Martin 76), L Hodges (R Trudgian 66); I Stonebridge (M Evans half-time), M Keith.

McCormick's torn thigh meant Sturrock had to find a replacement for his replacement goalkeeper and turned to West Bromwich Albion's third-choice custodian Chris Adamson as cover for Larrieu, who had conceded only 15 goals in 25 league matches.

Adamson took McCormick's place on the bench for the visit of Hull City, who had been among the pre-season favourites to win the Third Division. Victory for Argyle, who remained divisional leaders despite not having played a league match for two weeks, against the Tigers would put 14 points between the two sides and effectively knock out a side still seen then as potential promotion rivals.

Sturrock viewed the match as the first in a sequence of six in 28 days that would determine Argyle's fate. "We want to get off on the right foot. The important thing is to still be in our position at the end of these games. We don't want a confidence-denter. It's important we start properly. I think there's no doubt this is our biggest game of the season so far."

If the game was big, then the 1-0 victory carved out by Stonebridge's 20th-minute header, after Lee Hodges and Coughlan had played head-tennis with McGlinchey's right-wing corner, was "massive."

Argyle remained on course for the title with their 16th league win from 26 starts after completely outplaying a Hull side that started the day in fifth position but was tactically and individually in an inferior league – 1-0, and, to parrot Bill Shankly, they were lucky to get nil. Some excellent goalkeeping by Paul Musselwhite, desperate goalmouth defending, and Argyle's inability to convert all but one of 17 clear-cut chances kept things interesting, however, and Larrieu prevented a dissatisfying draw with his only save, from Lawrie Dudfield, in the 84th minute.
"We exerted a lot of pressure and came away with only one goal," summarised Sturrock. "You start to worry, but the boys worked very hard in the second half. I'd like to win games more than 1-0 – it keeps you on tenterhooks – but the result was massive."

Sturrock had special words of praise for one of the unsung heroes of the campaign, Steve Adams, the 21-year-old midfielder who had played some part in all of Argyle's games and had emerged from most of them in the manager's personal top three.

Sturrock was assiduous in giving all his players a verbal pat on the back during his post-match Press debriefing. No-one was below standard, he rightly pointed out, declining to comment on individual names proffered by the probing scribes and microphone men. A team game today, he stressed, referring to shape, organisation and tactical awareness as proof of his assessment.

Finally, he could contain himself no longer. "I thought Stevie Adams was absolutely immense today," he said, and, in case the Press corps had missed it, he said it again. "Immense."

Argyle supporters held Adams in some affection, of course, but nowhere near as much as Sturrock. He is never going to be a fans' player – a scorer or creator of great goals, a flashy winger, a towering defender – and much of what he does is unappreciated by everyone except his manager and team-mates. He will nick a ball and deliver it to a team-mate to start an attack; he will close down players; he will hover omnipresently in the background, offering support; he will check opponents' runs before they have started. In the dressing-room, he is known as the Ghost – most people do not see him, but he puts the frights on those that do.

Saturday, January 14, 2002, Nationwide League

Plymouth Argyle 1
Stonebridge 20
Hull City 0

Plymouth Argyle (4-4-2): R Larrieu; D Worrell, P Wotton, G Coughlan, B McGlinchey; M Phillips (J Bent 87), S Adams, D Friio, L Hodges; M Keith (M Evans 67), I Stonebridge.
Substitutes (not used): C Adamson (gk), B Sturrock, J Beswetherick.
Hull City (5-3-2): P Musselwhite; B Petty, J Whittle, I Goodison, M Wicks, A Holt (D Beresford 74); T Whitmore, M Greaves (R Sneekes 61), J Johnsson (R Williams 74); G Alexander, L Dudfield. **Substitutes (not used):** M Glennon (gk), N Mohan.
Bookings: Whittle 27, Alexander 64.
Referee: C Wilkes (Gloucester). **Attendance:** 9,134. **League position:** 1st.

PAUL STURROCK: "This was a difficult game. Hull were still in the shake-up. We only won 1-0, which was scary. We had several games like this where we never looked out of sorts but we hung on. It would have been nice if we'd got a second but the system we were playing, with the two central midfielders sitting and Stoney playing just off the front, made us look much more solid but cut down on our opportunities. We had three convincing 1-0 wins against three big teams –

Rushden, Hull and Mansfield. This spell was the deciding factor on us being promoted.

"Stevie Adams was a big influence. They played a system I don't think they had ever played to hinder us, people wide to stop our full-backs. It caused them a lot of concern.

"Stevie has been a steadying influence all season. Our defence is always content when he's playing with them. They want him there because he reads the games so well. We don't have another one who can influence a game like him, who can steal things, who can be quick enough to close things down and make simple passes. He's the best player in the league without the ball. David Friio looked influential when we had the ball, but looked disappointing tactically when the other team had the ball in that position. He got to the stage when he didn't want to play. There's too many things go through his mind when he plays that position. Every time I said Adams was our best player, I got letter after letter saying I must have been watching a different game. If you'd ask any player defensively who they would like playing alongside them, they would say Adams, because he's such an influence to them."

KEVIN SUMMERFIELD: "Our nights out together were really important nights. At the LMA dinner, Matthew Lorenzo said obviously we had a really good team-spirit. I said, with the way we travel, we're away two or three days at a time, it's important we've got togetherness so it's important, else long coach journeys can become fractious. That all helps. Wottsie took the lead at a karaoke night at the Grecian Taverna. He's a hopeless singer, but he was first up. Neil Heaney was fantastic as Tom Jones. Maxie is a big Elvis fan and obviously does Elvis great; he got dressed up in all the gear. David Friio, in English, was superb. The wives were there, so it was a great night. I didn't get up – there weren't any songs in the songbook that were in Brummie. No Slade or anything like that.

"Hull, we dominated another 1-0. We were a little bit worried before the game We put a lot of thought into what they would come at us with, but they were very disappointing and, to me, they were more worried about us than what we were going to do, and they did nothing to us.

"We absolutely mullered them; quality midfield; forwards worked well together; the back four was very solid; the right-hand side – David and Buster -- absolutely killed them; great set-pieces. I put at the bottom of my notes that we wouldn't lose too many games playing like we did.

"We were aware that we needed to score more goals so we worked on crossing and finishing. That was our main route to scoring goals."

Not for the last time in the season, Sturrock ruled out any talk of promotion in the wake of the Hull victory. "We are in a position where we can only shoot ourselves in the foot," he admitted, "but, you know what it's like – tension, stress, worry can filter into teams very quickly. The only thing that will deter that is by winning games.

"At the end of February, we will have a clearer picture of what's going to happen to us."

In the home dressing-room, however, he chalked up a number, representing the points he thought Argyle would need to win promotion: that number was 83, meaning, by Sturrock's own reckoning, Argyle needed only 28 points from their last 20 matches to escape the Third Division.

Sturrock's message clearly got through to his troops, although there was no denying a confidence was spreading through the camp. "To be top of the league is where you want to be," said Paul Wotton. "I'm not going to kid anyone – we didn't expect to be there this season. But we are there, and we are there on merit.

"At the start of the season, I think we would have settled for a play-off position, but, as I say, we are rightly top of the table and I don't think anyone can argue with that. We have shown character, strength and determination, and we can play a bit."

Wotton's central defensive partner Coughlan said: "We have set ourselves some targets and the sooner we get them, the better, but we are not going to come out with any rash statements or start jumping ahead of ourselves. We have a long, long way to go. At the start of the season, finishing seventh would have been seen as a tremendous achievement and I don't see why those objectives should change. We have done well and seventh place is within our grasp because we have had a tremendous start."

Despite his ban on talking about promotion, Sturrock could not resist referring to it again on the eve of his side's visit to fourth-placed Shrewsbury. "It's in our hands to make sure we win all the games we need to be promoted," he said. "I'd much prefer to do it ourselves."

The visit to Gay Meadow was a thoroughly miserable affair all round for Sturrock and his players. Before the match, the players' kit had been sabotaged after being taken into the away dressing-room on the morning of the match. Water was poured into their boots.

During the game, Sturrock was laid low with a virus that had sprung up in the Argyle camp and was forced to spend most of the second half in the away dressing-room after complaining of feeling dizzy.

Argyle lost the match 3-1, and saw Shrewsbury become the only side to do the double over them during the campaign, despite taking a fifth-minute lead and seeing the home side reduced to ten men following the 16th-minute dismissal of Greg Rioch – Shrewsbury's tenth red card of the campaign. Perhaps the day's only good news was that Luton had failed to usurp Argyle at the top of the Third Division table after being unable to beat lowly Carlisle at home. Indeed, they had to come from behind to earn a 1-1 draw against the third-from-bottom placed side.

"Shrewsbury deserved it," said Argyle assistant-manager Summerfield, a former Shrewsbury player and coach. "We have been due one of those afternoons when things don't go right, and this was it. Somebody was going to give us a good turning-over and they have done it. We were second best – it's as simple as that.

"We had a great start but, for some reason, the sending-off really affected us big time. We just could not control the game when we should have been nicely set up to do so."

Sturrock, anxious not to spread his illness around the team coach, was driven home to Plymouth by chairman Paul Stapleton, who was eager to allay fears about his manager's health following the erroneous rumours when he was manager of St Johnstone that Sturrock had suffered heart problems.

Stapleton said: "I don't want anyone worrying about this being heart-related. It's not. It looks as though he's got a 'flu-type virus. He slept most of the way home and went straight to bed when he got in."

Saturday, January 19 2002, Nationwide League

Shrewsbury Town 3
Rodgers 45, Aiston 50, Lowe 83
Plymouth Argyle 1
Evans 5

Shrewsbury Town (4-4-2): I Dunbavin; D Moss, M Redmile, A Tretton, G Rioch; R Lowe, M Atkins, J Tolley, S Aiston (P Wilding 58); R Fallon (A Thompson 22), L Rodgers.
Substitutes (not used): T Malessa (gk), K Murray.
Sending-off: Rioch 16 (second bookable offence).
Bookings: Rioch 5, Lowe 25, Rodgers 59.
Plymouth Argyle (4-5-1): R Larrieu; D Worrell, P Wotton, G Coughlan, B McGlinchey; M Phillips (N Heaney 73), S Adams, D Friio, S Evers (M Keith 53), L Hodges; M Evans (I Stonebridge 53). **Substitutes (not used):** C Adamson (gk), J Beswetherick.
Bookings: Worrell 25, Evans 46, McGlinchey 88.
Referee: D Pugh (Merseyside). **Attendance:** 4,796. **League position:** 1st.

PAUL STURROCK: "All it was was a general virus that anyone could have had. After the game, I jumped in the car. I came home and went straight to my bed and lay there for five days. I could not get my head off the pillow."

KEVIN SUMMERFIELD: "I went to watch Shrewsbury play Bristol Rovers and spoke to lots of scouts who were very complimentary about us and what we were doing. Football people tended to be. When we played them, it was an absolutely terrible day. The dressing-room wasn't right. David Friio had a bad nosebleed before the game. It was one of those days when the lads couldn't do anything right, although it wasn't for the lack of trying. There were mistakes all over the field and there wasn't any pattern or shape. It was not our day. I put in the bottom of my book in capital letters 'WORST'. I had everybody in on the Sunday and stressed the importance of the team – if we were going to win games; we were going to have to win them altogether. We had got to the top of the league because we were a team."

Sturrock was still out of commission on the eve of Scunthorpe's visit to Home Park the following Tuesday, begging the question of whether the manager or the team would respond quickest to remedial treatment and be back to something like par.

Summerfield took training and afterwards said he felt Argyle were lucky to be playing so soon after their off-colour defeat at Shrewsbury, even if Scunthorpe were seeking to become the second side on the spin to complete a double over the Pilgrims.

"The way we're looking at it is that we're fortunate to have a game so soon after

Saturday's performance," he said. "The boys knew they were below par and have got the opportunity to put that right against one of the better teams in the division. If we'd sat in the dressing-room and dissected things, we'd probably still be there now – there was that much that went wrong.

"We haven't really spoken about what happened on Saturday – it's gone. It's roll-our-sleeves-up time."

Argyle duly limped and spluttered their way to an 11th home victory of the campaign without Sturrock and first-choice goalkeeper Larrieu, who succumbed to the same bug that had poleaxed his manager. Although, in the absence of anyone else, he was named substitute, the Frenchman spent the game isolated in physio Paul Maxwell's room so that he did not spread the virus. Sturrock's son Blair, unsurprisingly, was also affected by the Luggy lurgy.

The 2-1 victory might have been a tonic for Sturrock, but the general health of his players would have been subject to thorough examination after some wholly nasty alehouse football from their opponents, who would have been asked by the Football Association why six of their players were cautioned by referee Mick Fletcher.

The Pilgrims came from behind to register a character-filled victory, with Wotton's 44th-minute penalty cancelling out Martin Carruthers' 13th-minute opener, before the new Tynan proved to be the Pilgrims' match-winner for the second time in three home games. Marino Keith's 54th-minute decider was made by full-back David Worrell, who burst from his own half, caught Andy Dawson flat-footed by heading the ball past Dawson's right side while scooting around his left and collecting it behind the dizzy defender before centering.

"It was a brilliant goal," said Summerfield. "Dave read the play superbly and those are the ones that Dan scores – inside the six-yard box – and he's come good again today."

At the other end, Adamson made his one and only Argyle appearance and could not be faulted for Carruthers' opener, which was the first time Argyle had gone behind at Home Park since September the previous year. The same could not be said for the Pilgrims' defenders, who allowed Dawson and Steve Torpey too much time to tee up Carruthers.

Having lost the lead, Argyle then lost McGlinchey with a broken ankle that was to sideline him until the very end of the campaign. They rallied to go in on level terms when Hodges was slipped in by Ian Stonebridge and went down as he attempted to take the ball around goalkeeper Tom Evans. Evans, who looked harshly treated by Fletcher, was spared the red card, but not from Wotton exacting maximum revenge with a trademark thunderclap penalty.

McGlinchey's injury gave Jon Beswetherick the opportunity to regain his favourite left-back position and Summerfield said: "Bezzie had a great game. His attitude has been magnificent. He has had to be patient because Brian has played superbly for us." Beswetherick was also given a vote of confidence by Northern Ireland B international McGlinchey, his friend and rival. "Bezzie deserves his chance," said McGlinchey. "I hope he does well."

Tuesday, January 22 2002, Nationwide League

Plymouth Argyle 2
Wotton pen 44, Keith 54
Scunthorpe United 1
Carruthers 13

Plymouth Argyle (4-4-2): C Adamson; D Worrell, P Wotton, G Coughlan, B McGlinchey (J Beswetherick 16); M Phillips, S Adams, D Friio, L Hodges; M Keith (M Evans 88), I Stonebridge. **Substitutes (not used):** R Larrieu (gk), S Evers, N Heaney.
Scunthorpe United (4-4-2): T Evans; A Dawson, S Thom, M Jackson, N Stanton; M Sparrow, W Graves (J McCombe 90), A Calvo-Garcia (L Hodges 75), P Beagrie; M Carruthers (B Quailey 72), S Torpey. **Substitutes (not used):** C Bennion (gk), T Barwick.
Bookings: Evans 43, Stanton 59, Torpey 64, Graves 68, Beagrie 78, Thom 83.
Referee: M Fletcher (Warley). **Attendance:** 5,804. **League position:** 1st.

PAUL STURROCK: "Obviously, with Romain being out we had to bring in a goalie who had never played with our back four. We lost a goal very early on to a team that was a very good offensive side with a reasonable defence. When we dragged ourselves out of the mire, it showed character again. When you are sitting in the house, you daren't put the TV on. Barbara had gone to the game and I knew she was coming back. When I eventually turned the Teletext on, I was a relieved man because all the other results had gone our way as well. With Luke being a bag of washing, we would have had to put Romain on, but it would have been a real push.

"Losing Brian was a blow, but it gave Bezzie the opportunity and he never let us down from then until the end of the season. He played very, very well. The problem would have been if it had been the right-back, because Stevie was too influential in midfield, but that's football – sometimes you just have to hope that what you've got will see you through."

KEVIN SUMMERFIELD: "David went home ill on the Sunday; Wottsie and Blair were both ill on the Monday; Romain caught it on the Tuesday and couldn't play, so whether we were sickening for it on the Saturday, you don't know. Maxie was trying to get Romain fit but we had the Doc in and he was absolutely adamant he couldn't play, so he sat in Maxie's room. Chris proved more than capable. We went a goal down, but they got through it. Everything in the game was stacked against us. The character

was immense to come through and win that game against a good team. They played much better than they had up there."

Sturrock senior and Larrieu both returned for the visit of Oxford United for a game which marked the opening of the revamped Lyndhurst side of Home Park, completing the rebuilding of the three sides, other than the main grandstand, more or less on schedule. As a superstitious man, Sturrock would have loved the portent of the date on which the stand was opened – appropriately enough for a team built by a Scot and a ground rebuilt by a Scottish company, it was Burns' weekend.

Having already equalled the Pilgrims' points tally for the whole of the previous season – 58 – with 18 games in hand, Sturrock was keen to break the 60-point barrier before trips to nearest rivals Luton and Swansea and a home match against Mansfield. "We've got two naughty away games coming up and then a big game at home," he noted. "It would be nice to start this wee run of four games with a victory. The most important thing is to keep achieving, churning out points and slowly getting where we want to get to."

Cautious as he was, even Sturrock must have realised that mere promotion, welcome and overdue as it might be, would be a severe underachievement after his Pilgrims had marked the official raising of Home Park's capacity to more than 20,000 by whupping Oxford 4-2. With around 20 points needed from their last 17 matches, Argyle could have shown relegation form and still been promoted: the championship, and 100+ points, had to be their aim.

How could they be stopped? Oxford manager Ian Atkins thought he had the answer twice. The Oxford manager sent out a 5-3-2 formation designed to stifle, saw the Pilgrims sweep into a 2-0 lead, through Coughlan and Hodges, switched it to 4-4-2 and briefly got back on terms before a double from Stonebridge settled things in Argyle's favour.

Coughlan judged the flight of Wotton's floated free-kick better than Oxford goalkeeper Andy Woodman to convert at the far post for the opener, and then the underappreciated Hodges stooped low to nod home a cross from David Worrell, receiving a fearful whack on the hip for his bravery.

Argyle were cruising on their showboat again. Coughlan shot from the centre-circle and Oxford would not have got back in the game had Keith not leant back at the wrong moment when poised to convert a sweeping move that ended with Stonebridge's cheeky reverse back-heel into his striker partner's path.

Like the previous week, Argyle's ascendancy gave them the excuse to get sloppy, and Dave Morley and Paul Powell levelled the score. Morley profited from some

poor defending following a free kick needlessly conceded, and there was an element of Keystone Kops about Powell's goal, which came after the ball fell at his feet when Worrell allowed a floated cross to hit him on the back. Larrieu, having come to collect an anticipated backpass, was left stranded.

Argyle got back on track with Stonebridge's first in first-half stoppage-time, the 20-year-old finishing off a cute four-man free-kick routine in which the scorers of the first two goals played their part, and killed the game off 22 seconds after the interval. The attack was initiated by Beswetherick and ended by Stonebridge after Woodman had shovelled Keith's grass-cutting drive into his path.

"I'm very pleased with the result," said Sturrock, "but a wee bit disappointed that that's two games now when we've gone ahead and looked very sloppy for a spell after scoring. They were two Plymouth-made goals that brought them back into the game."

Stonebridge was not the only young striker with a significant double to his name: 19-year-old Mark Sheeran came off the bench to make only his fourth league appearance – all as substitute – and scored twice in the final nine minutes to give Darlington a 3-2 victory over Luton. He could now get drunk in Plymouth when he wanted for life without having to pay.

The two results put Argyle seven points ahead of the team which was rapidly becoming their only serious rivals for the Third Division title, who they were due to face next. Not that Sturrock was looking that far ahead after beating Oxford.

"What about your next game?" he was asked.

"We've got Bridgwater in a friendly on Wednesday," he replied. "I'm looking forward to it."

Saturday, January 26 2002, Nationwide League

Plymouth Argyle 4
Coughlan 21, Hodges 24, Stonebridge 45, 46
Oxford United 2
Morley 34, Powell 41

Plymouth Argyle (4-4-2): R Larrieu; D Worrell, P Wotton, G Coughlan, J Beswetherick; M Phillips, S Adams, D Friio, L Hodges; M Keith (M Evans 50), I Stonebridge.
Substitutes (not used): C Adamson (gk), C Taylor, S Evers, N Heaney.
Oxford United (5-3-2): A Woodman; S Ricketts, A Crosby, D Morley, M Bound, P Powell; D Savage, R Quinn, D Whitehead (M Omoyinmi 76); P Gray (P Moody 49), A Scott.
Substitutes (not used): S Guyett, S Stockley, M Thomas.
Bookings: Crosby 45, Quinn 69.
Referee: B Curson (Burbage). **Attendance:** 8,239. **League position:** 1st.

PAUL STURROCK: "Oxford was a great game. We defended a bit poorly and it could have been 8-4. We had a chance to go 3-0 up when Dan missed the sitter of the season, and they went back and scored two goals. After the two goals we coasted home. It kind of petered out. We never scored lots of goals in games because we weren't that kind of team I'll take 1-0s and 2-0s – a win's a win's a win."

KEVIN SUMMERFIELD: "It was great game and we ended up seven points clear of Luton. It was now us and them. We went to Barnet to watch Fulham play Arsenal in a reserve game and Joe Kinnear was at the game so Paul shouted down to him 'Alright Joe' and he's turned round and had laugh. 'See you Saturday."

CHAPTER 13

THE build-up to Argyle's visit to Kenilworth Road, which some were suggesting could decide the destination of the Third Division title, was quieter than the previous encounter between the two sides had been, but you could sense an intense undercurrent in the Argyle camp.

Central defender Graham Coughlan – 'Joe Soap'- claimed the match-up between the division's two top sides was "just another game." He said: "We don't care who we play. Saturday is just another game worth three points."

"Joe Kinnear is an experienced manager who has been around, so who am I to question him?" he asked. "I don't know where he was coming from, but it does not worry me. He's entitled to express his opinions. According to him, they are going to win the league by the end of February, so there is obviously only second place to play for."

Argyle's supporters were keen to put another one over on Luton's manager. "Are You Watching, Joe Kinnear?" had been their favourite chant of the season, closely followed by "We're Just An Average Side", and Argyle manager Paul Sturrock recognised their desire for a victory.

"Some things have been said that have upset our fans," said Sturrock, "but we need to be disciplined in our approach. We don't want any bad injuries or sendings-off. There's a bit of an edge to the game, especially after what was said before and after the previous match. People have put so much importance on this game, but it is just another Third Division game between two teams chasing three points." Yeah, right, and the Mona Lisa's a half-decent sketch.

The day before the match had seen intense activity at board-room level as the five-man consortium which had agreed to buy out previous chairman Dan McCauley on the eve of the season completed the deal. Having originally agreed to pay McCauley £2 million for his shares, and the money his company Rotolok had loaned the club, over two years, the consortium closed the deal earlier. McCauley, his financial commitment to Argyle over, duly resigned.

Ever since the announced board-rrom changeover at in August, negotiations had been going on about the finalisation of the share-sale. McCauley had declined to talk to anybody on the board about the sale except chairman Paul Stapleton, so everything was channelled through him. Eventually, after weeks of talks, the matter had been resolved.

"It was felt we should repay all the money now," explained Stapleton. "It became

evident that Dan, who had had sole control for so many years, found it difficult to work with a new set of directors and that was probably pertinent because he was owed such a large amount of money. Because we agreed to repay the money, Dan probably thought it was time for us to get on with things ourselves. He will be very welcome in the boardroom and the directors' box."

McCauley said: "I can't devote the time and attention needed so I think it's better to part amicably. My heart is still at the club. I just can't afford the time needed. It has been a long drawn-out process but it is done now. I don't know how they have done it, but they have, and congratulations to them."

PAUL STAPLETON: "There had been a lot of negotiations and paperwork and bits and pieces with Dan and Sean [Swales, McCauley's accountant]. There was a lot of toing and froing between Plymouth and Rotolok. The worst day of all was Christmas Eve. Dan was annoyed with a newspaper article that gave John McNulty a lot of credit for the new stadium and wanted him to resign. In my opinion, John deserved a lot of credit as he had spent 18 months on the project, and, anyway, the independently written article had not been prompted by John. I was trying to pin Dan down on certain things but all he wanted to do was talk about John McNulty.

"What we were trying to do was raise money from outside lenders, but, every time we tried to raise money, Dan said he didn't want to do it. He never had control, but he stopped us borrowing cash, so, in the end, we had to come up with a different way to buy him out.

"Paul knew about the ownership problem and was talking about resigning. Dan was for letting him go. He said there were plenty of good managers around. I was worried. I met Paul and Kevin Summerfield and then phoned Dan. He said: 'Tell Paul, if you get the money, I'll do the deal. I'll resign.' I don't think he thought we could get the cash, but I told him we'd got the cash and we'd do the deal. Paul was still unhappy and was talking about holding a Press conference on Boxing Day. He wanted something done on Christmas Eve, which was impossible, from a legal point of view. I gave Dan a letter of intent on Boxing Day, which Paul seemed to accept, although he wasn't happy.

"It was weird, being top at Christmas, having a full-house here, a lot of people in the boardroom, including the Eden Project, but still nothing had been finalised.

"Dan said he might think about keeping the club. I said: 'You've got no chance.' I asked him about signing the paperwork. He said he was going away on February 2 and if he didn't get the cash in...' I told him he was

hampering us. We then got to the stage where we had a deal sorted out – except he wanted three things in it that were non-negotiable. At the hotel on the eve of the Shrewsbury game, I told him we couldn't do a deal unless they were negotiable. He said they were negotiable – we could talk about anything.

"On the Monday, I rang Sean and told him what Dan had said and could we negotiate? He said they were non-negotiable. It was a nightmare. I said to him to tell Dan there'd be a Press conference the following day and we would be resigning, Paul would be resigning, and that we had the support of the council. We'd had enough.

"Dan sent me a fax, saying he thought we were out of order and had misjudged the situation, but we had put him in a position where he had to resign and leave. If we gave him his money, he would go. We spent the next ten days putting the money together. We managed to do it, although I don't think he thought we would because of the conditions he'd put on the sale. People still think he still has some sort of control – he has got none whatsoever – he's got 75 shares out for 60,000.

"It could have gone either way – it could have been six months and out. I don't think he realised the feeling for this board and what it had done. The fans would never have had him back if he had decided against signing. He'd gone so far, he'd have to do it.

"We went to Luton and lost, but that was secondary on the day."

PETER JONES: "We wanted to be able to run the club as a proper business and we didn't see any problem in having loan facilities – not an overdraft, but investment loan facilities – set up as a business to help us. We did arrange certain options for setting up working capital and they were never satisfactory as far as Dan was concerned.

"One of the reasons was that he never felt comfortable about borrowing money commercially in order to pay himself back. Bank guarantees were another issue. He was always uncomfortable about what he called Last Man Standing – the last director would remain responsible for the debts of the club.

"There were times when we got a bit worn down by it but, at the same time, we knew how important it was for the club that we should hang on and try and get it sorted."

PHILL GILL: "It became apparent that the goalposts were beginning to

shift towards the corner flag at an early stage. Promises were being broken in terms of timescales on certain things and it just became more and more difficult to get things resolved.

"It got to the stage where, in the run-up to Christmas, what should have been signed and sealed by October at the latest was becoming more and more unlikely to be done. The structure of the deal had changed dramatically. It put everybody under immense strain. Paul Stapleton was facing most of it; it was an unbelievable situation.

"I think Dan's position would have been untenable if he'd changed his mind. The fans hadn't been with him for a long time and it would have been far more difficult for him to carry on than he realised. Because he was physically removed from Plymouth, he hasn't seen as much of the bad stuff; by the same token, he wasn't on hand to see the feelgood factor that was happening at the club. Perhaps if he had done, he would have taken a whole different approach to things.

"We didn't win. We just got what we wanted. What had been agreed."

Argyle went into the Luton match without Brian McGlinchey, flu-victims Kevin Wills and Joe Broad, and influential midfielder Jason Bent, who had returned from a month-long stint on Gold Cup duty for Canada with a hamstring injury, and were comprehensively beaten 2-0, with both goals coming in the last ten minutes.

There remained 16 matches for the Pilgrims to seal their promotion but the games most concerning Paul Sturrock after the dissatisfying defeat were those being played in the mind. Sturrock blamed himself for the Pilgrims' apparently negative psyche that let a pumped-up Luton dictate the pace and direction of the game and slice Argyle's lead at the top of the Third Division to four points.

The 'what-we've-got-we-keep' attitude had served Argyle well but, although Sturrock wanted to jettison that cautious approach in favour of a more open style, he discovered his players were finding it more difficult to shake the habit. "That was a game where one team wanted to win and one team didn't want to lose," he said, after Kevin Nicholls' 80th-minute penalty and Steve Howard's header seven minutes later had secured victory for the cock-a-hoop Hatters. "The team that wanted to win won the game.

"Sometimes a manager does create a mentality like we have. Because our away form was so abysmal, something had to change. I made the change and I'm worrying now that we are just waiting not to lose a game, instead of going for the jugular. I think it's at this time of the season, with teams scrapping away as they

are for all sorts of things, that we went out and did the business – I'll be very pleased with three wins and a couple of draws from our last eight away games."

Sturrock's selection had indicated his eagerness to open out: 4-4-2, instead of 4-5-1, with Marino Keith and Ian Stonebridge leading the line; and an inverted midfield, with Buster Phillips and Lee Hodges swapping flanks, to counteract the threat of Jean-Louis Valois. Phillips, though, found it hard to support David Worrell in the containment of Luton right-back Emmerson Boyce and winger Adrian Forbes, who had the sort of game players like him enjoy roughly once every three seasons.

"I wanted to try something different," said Sturrock. "We could have come here, played our old away style, and really shut up shop, but I think it's important we pinch some points away from home."

Kinnear called the result "a 2-0 massacre" which is the sort of spin that goes down well in his own kingdom, but conveniently ignored the fact that his attractive but largely guileless side was 11 minutes away from being held to a goalless draw by a "massacred" team. To come so near to taking a point on a day which Kinnear admitted saw Luton at their season's best and Argyle pretty well at their season's worst should have been a source of comfort to the fed-up Green Army.

The match turned on two moments. After Romain Larrieu had turned a shot from Forbes on to a goalpost, substitute Michael Evans initiated a breakaway which ended with him crossing to Stonebridge at the near post. Stonebridge attempted a back-heel, but there was not enough pace on the ball and goalkeeper Carl Emberson flopped gratefully on the goalbound trickler.

Immediately, Worrell tripped Matt Taylor for a stone-cold penalty. Sturrock said: "I don't think we would have lost the game had the penalty not gone against us. I felt we were looking strong and starting to cause problems at the other end, but there's no excuses – Luton deserved to win the game."

Howard duly completed the "massacre", heading in Forbes' nod-on of Valois' corner, and both he, with a thunderous shot, and Coughlan, with a far-post header, hit the bar as Argyle opened up the game. Too little, too late.

Kinnear was predictably beside himself after the victory, and, equally predictably, laid down a title-challenge to the Pilgrims. "We probably saved our best performance for the team that's top of the table," said the Luton Lip. "It was a 2-0 massacre, really. They're a decent side, and the league table proves that, but they more than met their match.

"Even if they had gone ten points clear, I don't think it would have been all over

because they were nine points clear of us earlier on and then we had a run and clawed them all back, so it's been nip and tuck throughout the season.

"It's not for me to criticise them. We were the better side. We had more will to win and created the better opportunities. We slaughtered them down the sides. Taylor and Valois ripped the heart of them out wide.

"The title-race is as it has been. There's three of us there – Mansfield, ourselves and Plymouth. I don't think anyone else is in with a shout."

The defeat could not prevent the Pilgrims from notching up another significant milestone on their march to the championship. The following Monday saw them celebrate 100 successive days as the leaders of their division – a boast which no other club in the country could come close to making.

Saturday, February 2 2002, Nationwide League

Luton Town 2
Nicholls pen 80, Howard 87
Plymouth Argyle 0

Luton Town (4-4-2): C Emberson; E Boyce, D Bayliss, R Perrett, M Taylor; A Forbes, M Spring, K Nicholls, J-L Valois; D Crowe (A Brkovic 88), S Howard.
Substitutes (not used): M Ovendale (gk), P Hughes, A Skelton, I Hillier.
Booking: Nicholls 44.
Plymouth Argyle (4-4-2): R Larrieu; D Worrell, P Wotton, G Coughlan, J Beswetherick; L Hodges, D Friio, S Adams, M Phillips (S Evers 62); I Stonebridge (N Heaney 84), M Keith (M Evans 73). **Substitutes (not used):** C Adamson (gk), C Taylor.
Bookings: Friio 45, Heaney 89, Evans 90.
Referee: P Joslin (Newark). **Attendance:** 9,585. **League position:** 1st.

PAUL STURROCK: "I'll put my hands up. I tried to outfox Joe and it backfired totally. If we'd played our 4-5-1, we might have got something, but we played 4-4-2, put Buster on the left and Hodgy on the right and it never worked. I should have gone with Mickey that day, because his height would have been a big influence on the game – he was a big influence when he came on as substitute. When you say how indifferent we were, we were still 0-0 until the penalty with 10 minutes to go. Just before that, we had two really good opportunities – Stoney had one he should have done much better with and Sean Evers was blocked on the edge of the area.

"I'd played the game down too much, I think, because I didn't want the players getting too hyped up and risk a sending-off. Our two strikers never got started, never looked content, looked sluggish and slow. Marino looked a bag of washing. We let too many crosses come into our box and, had it not have been for Romain that day, we would have taken a drubbing.

"We just sat on the bench and said: 'If we're going to get a result here, it's going to be 0-0'. I think Joe got it right...but I think that was the first thing he said about us all season that was correct! It was a poor day, a poor result. The problem was that the fans were really up for it that it was a bitter pill for them to swallow, which I think the players appreciated because they knew they had let the fans down. We didn't play."

KEVIN SUMMERFIELD: "We could have lost 3-0 or 4-0 playing 4-5-1, so you will never know whether the changes were right or not. On the day, they were much better, even though they didn't score until the 80th minute. It was one to forget. We didn't come in on the Sunday, which was a change. We thought: 'Let's have day off and come in on Monday.' We had a long discussion. It was a bit doom and gloom although we were four points clear. I said: 'Why do we need to lose another game?' If we played anything like we could play, we didn't need to worry. There weren't that many big games to come and, if we got back to what we'd been doing, there was no reason why we should lose any games."

Sturrock and his players spent the following Monday deconstructing the Pilgrims' season to try and ensure that it did not destruct.

Sturrock called his squad into Home Park for a team brainstorming session following their fourth successive defeat away from base, which meant Argyle had not travelled home following a success since their 1-0 victory at Southend the previous November.

A rearranged Tuesday night fixture at Swansea offered them the chance to arrest that particular slide but, first, Sturrock was eager to make some points and to hear what his players thought of the situation. Sturrock emerged with food for thought after wide-ranging discussions that encompassed such diverse subjects as training methods, travel arrangements and eating habits.

"I've voiced my concerns and they've given me their opinions," said Sturrock. "It was a very fruitful meeting. Normally I talk and they listen, but it wasn't one of those. Seven or eight of the boys stood up and said things, which was needed. They have got to be happy in their minds."

The most important thing that Sturrock learned was that his players were so content playing the 4-5-1 system that had served them well on their travels, they were loath to give it up at such a late stage. "It is up to us to make sure that the gap between us and the chasing pack at the end of February is exactly the same as it is now," he concluded. "You do not win promotion without winning some games away from home."

In one way, Sturrock could not have wished for a better game for his Pilgrims to give themselves a fresh start – the Swansea game was originally scheduled to have been played on New Year's Day – and he rang in the new by handing his son Blair and winger Neil Heaney full debuts.

Sturrock repaid his father's faith by getting the only goal in a 1-0 win that re-established the Pilgrims' seven-point lead at the top of the table. Sturrock struck in the 39th minute after Swansea had failed to clear a cross by Heaney, and his dad could not hide his paternal joy.

"As a dad, I'm delighted," he said. "Your son is playing professional football and he has scored a goal. A lot of people in Scotland will take note of that.

"I should judge my laddie as a manager, and sometimes I don't do that. Maybe I have taken the easy option with him. It has been very easy not to rock the boat with others by not putting him in, but he got his chance and responded well. I'm pleased for him, because he works hard at his game.

"I thought we played very well in the first half, but it was the same old story – we went 1-0 up and decided we would hold on to what we had got. Swansea chucked everything into our box in the second half, which made it very difficult, but the players showed great character and I'm very pleased.

"I have taken on board some of the things the players raised in our meeting and I'm settled in my mind about what they want to do away from home. I don't think we have rolled our sleeves up and really battled away from home for a long time."

Tuesday, February 4 2002, Nationwide League

Swansea City 0
Plymouth Argyle 1
Sturrock 39

Swansea City (3-5-2): R Freestone; C Todd, A Mumford, N Sharp; T Evans, N Cusack (D Lacey 88), S Brodie, J Coates (L Jenkins 70), M Howard; S Watkin (J Williams 70), M Sidibe.
Substitutes (not used): J Jones (gk), K O'Leary.
Booking: Mumford 42.
Plymouth Argyle (4-1-4-1): R Larrieu; D Worrell, P Wotton, G Coughlan, J Beswetherick; S Adams; B Sturrock (I Stonebridge 74), D Friio, L Hodges, N Heaney (J Broad 74); M Evans.
Substitutes (not used): C Adamson (gk), M Phillips, M Keith.
Bookings: Beswetherick 79, Stonebridge 90.
Referee: S Tomlin (Lewes). **Attendance:** 4,060. **League position:** 1st.

PAUL STURROCK: "This was the most important game of the season. The players' message had been point blank – in no uncertain terms, they told

me they wanted to play 4-5-1 away from home which is something I'd been trying to wean them off. We weaned them straight back on to it again. Put fresh legs in in the shape of Heaney and Blair, although their fitness was not going to let them play a whole game. Mickey Evans had not played much so we went in with three fresh pairs of legs.

"I think it had to be said. We'd come off a real resounding defeat and I wanted to hear what they wanted to say. We sat them down and home truths came out – certain things were said by them; I had my say; Summers had his say. The thing it kept coming back to was that 70 to 80 per cent of the team wanted to play 4-5-1. I don't think they understood why we'd played 4-4-2 at Luton.

"For the first half, we played very, very well and got the goal, but, in the second half we started to have problems with their 3-5-2 and we got battered. When, we walked off the pitch at the end, I had in mind that that was the game that settled us. We had Mansfield to come, and if we'd lost at Swansea we would have gone into that one with two defeats in a row, they were flying, and if we'd lost that the season could have just petered out. This was a big key game.

"It wasn't until we got to the hotel that I decided Blair merited his first start. He got a goal but blew a gasket so early and after that we diced with death – they hit the post, the bar and we let people cross from all sorts of places. But the system we play is a very tiring system. By the last quarter of the season we were firing on fumes and the system doesn't allow you to dominate games for the entire 90 minutes. We had a lot of games late on when we were under the cosh.

"If we'd come out with a defeat, I don't think we'd have been the team we were from then until the end of the season, we'd have been hot and cold, up and down. It was the first time I'd seen relief in the team. They knew they hadn't played well, but they showed a determination and a will to win. They'd bit and scratched and got result. They dirtied their hands for a result and got it.

"Blair wasn't in the team when we left Plymouth. Barbara asked me before we'd left whether he'd be in the team and I said he wouldn't start. I toyed with the idea and I just felt he merited a start after what he had done as a substitute. To be fair, Neil crossed and he scored, so it wasn't a bad decision."

KEVIN SUMMERFIELD: "The team for Swansea took more deliberation than any other. We went into the pre-match and we didn't know the team. I

still had to do the team book and all the set-pieces. I'd never left it so late. They battered us in the second half and we just hung on. The bar saved us and Romain saved us. The last six minutes were basically played in their corner. [Swansea manager] Colin Addison wasn't happy. We had the ball in the corner and they just couldn't get it off us and he turned to me and Paul on the touchline and said: 'You'll get football done away with, playing like that.' The boys were more buoyant afterwards than any other game previous to that."

Blair Sturrock's reward for re-igniting Argyle's away form was to be dropped to the substitutes' bench for the visit of third-placed Mansfield to Home Park the following Saturday. "I'm pleased for Blair," said his dad, "but I picked the team for Saturday on the way to Swansea and was committed to it as long as things went well."

Sturrock also revealed he had forbidden himself and his players from looking at the Third Division table, believing that an unhealthy pre-occupation with the fixtures and results of Argyle's promotion rivals – like Luton and Mansfield – meant the Pilgrims were in danger of losing their focus.

He said: "I feel our fan-base, our management team, and our players have, for about the last month, looked at our fixtures, at matches other teams have got to play, and at league tables that dramatically change from week to week. I feel that this has put an apprehension into the team.

"We should ban ourselves from looking at the league table, take each game as it comes and, if we win, it's three points nearer our goal. We need to focus on our games to come, rather than what is happening behind us. I totally refuse to look at anything now. I'm not going to look at papers or Teletext in that respect, and I hope my players can turn off to that as well.

"I see so many teams playing mind-games with themselves, or they get worried because other teams are catching up. I don't want that to happen. I want us to focus on getting the points I feel we need to be mathematically safe of being promoted."

The week had been mentally and physically wearying for the Pilgrims. Defeat at title-rivals Luton drained the spirits, while the midweek victory at Swansea was uplifting, but muscle-sapping.

"I blame myself for the Luton performance and result," said Sturrock. "Sometimes managers have to put their hands up and say 'I contributed'. I did contribute to that defeat, but that's water under the bridge now – learned from

and forgotten about. Management is all about making mistakes and learning from them. I found that out early in my career and I've lived by that code ever since.

"To bounce back on Tuesday was important. If it had gone pear-shaped, we could have gone into the Mansfield game with our heads around our ankles."

When Argyle's players lifted the Third Division championship, their minds surely would have gone back to the first week of February as the moment when the title was won. A week after limping home from Luton, tails between their legs and severe doubts in their minds whether they could regain and retain the form that had taken them to the top of the Third Division, they added to their midweek victory over Swansea by knocking over Mansfield 1-0, while Luton were losing at Rochdale. Joe Kinnear now had the ten-point gap he believed his side could make up.

However much Sturrock downplayed the importance of Friio's 85th-minute winner against game opponents and true promotion contenders, you could tell he knew how precious the three points were. At the end of most games, he normally thrusts his hands in his jacket pockets and departs without a fuss: this time, he twice saluted the grandstand with clenched fist and gritted teeth.

The game's kick-off was delayed by 15 minutes to allow the then largest Third Division crowd of the season – 14,716 – in as memories of the past and a vision of the future merged: the Devon Expressway backed up to Marsh Mills; Lower Home Park car-park closed by 2.10pm; queues all around the ground. Those who said they would not return to Home Park until Dan McCauley had left the club, and no longer bound by that promise, contributed significantly to the huge turn-out.

The first half was, thought Sturrock, 'a non-event'. The only mark made by much-vaunted 24-goal striker Chris Greenacre was over Wotton's left eye, after catching the Argyle captain with an unseen elbow, and the nearest Argyle's opponents came to scoring was when a Gaelic-Gallic cock-up between Larrieu and Coughlan nearly resulted in the latter chalking up a Devonport end oggie.

Sturrock had what he called 'a wee chat' with his players at half-time, which is managerspeak for something infinitely more horrendous, and they responded by moving up through the gears. The Pilgrims, though frustrated by Mansfield's disciplined defence, always looked the more likely winners, and Larrieu had little difficulty maintaining his 18th clean-sheet – a target he had had in mind since discovering no team had failed to win promotion after achieving such a feat.

Some strong running by Beswetherick won a corner, from which Wotton supplied the cross that Friio converted at the near post for his 10th goal of the season. The

Frenchman later thanked the huge crowd for their help. "I can't believe the atmosphere," he said. "It is like we are in the Premiership. It is incredible. It was like having an extra player. The crowd pushed us on to the end to get a result."

Saturday, February 9 2002, Nationwide League

Plymouth Argyle 1
Friio 85
Mansfield Town 0

Plymouth Argyle (4-4-2): R Larrieu; D Worrell, P Wotton, G Coughlan, J Beswetherick; M Phillips (N Heaney 82), S Adams, D Friio, L Hodges; M Evans (M Keith 76), I Stonebridge (B Sturrock 82). **Substitutes (not used):** L McCormick (gk), J Broad.
Bookings: Adams 30, Friio 42.
Mansfield Town (4-4-2): K Pilkington; B Hassell, S Reddington, A Barrett, A Tankard; L Lawrence, L Williamson, M Pemberton, W Corden; C Greenacre, D Kelly. **Substitutes (not used):** A Asher, M Bingham (gk), A White, J Clarke, D Jervis.
Bookings: Barrett 25, Tankard 68.
Referee: D Crick (Worcester Park). **Attendance:** 14,716. **League position:** 1st.

PAUL STURROCK: "I'd made up my mind before the Swansea game what the side would be because we were a settled unit winning games with the formation and the personnel. People will find it very strange that I had two teams during the season – a home team and an away team – but it worked for us. I'm a great believer that there are certain people who play very well at home and not very well away, and vice versa.

"There were certain players who came and knocked on my door who were unhappy about it but they didn't have a debate because I just put the results down on the table and they couldn't argue. I understood their disappointment, but they appreciated the situation

"We couldn't play our away formation at home, although we did try a variation of it for a wee spell midseason when we lost quite a few goals.

"I felt we played very well. Our goalkeeper had his quietest game against one of the most free-flowing forward teams in the division. Apart from the last ten minutes, they weren't at the races and I'm disappointed we didn't come out more worthy winners on the day. It was a difficult week – three games, two away from home, two against two of your closest rivals. To come out of it with six points out of nine...if somebody told me at the start of the week we'd get that, I would have taken it.

"We dominated the first half and hadn't scored, so I gave them a wee kick up the arse at half-time. There was a period about that time of the season that I didn't think people were taking enough responsibility for scoring

goals. David Friio and Graham Coughlan had a lot of pressure on them, so I was hoping other people would grab the cudgel."

KEVIN SUMMERFIELD: "Mansfield was going to be a big game. We'd played second and now we were playing third. It was pretty tactical because they were such a good team, so we needed to be on our toes. Set-pieces proved decisive. The most important thing about set-pieces is delivery. You can have runs, you can get free, you can have all the brilliant moves, but, without the delivery, you won't get anything."

Argyle's next fixture looked a formality – the whole of the Third Division, and 42 points, separated the Pilgrims from Halifax, but that was a problem in itself, according to Sturrock. He believed, firstly, that the Yorkshire club's financial predicament and the surge of confidence given to the Pilgrims by their two victories since the disappointment at Luton could prove their downfall.

"The whole of the country will have this down as an away banker," he said. "Everybody's thoughts will be on an away win, but we went up there last season on the back of a reasonable run and when they were around the same place in the league, and we lost 2-0.

"Now they've got the added incentive that some of them are worried about their livelihoods because of the sale of the football club – teams usually get bolstered from that, and we've got two key players injured who will need fitness tests, which is worrying me and which reduces us to firing on fumes as far as the squad is concerned. So there's a lot to look out for.

"We have got to be very much up for this one. We have got to be focused, and we've got to go for it."

A swift double strike just before half-time ensured another valuable three points for the Pilgrims, who hit the 70-point mark for the season in their 33rd game and allowed the normally cautious Sturrock to drop his guard a little. "It's a negative factor for the other clubs, looking at us on that pointage," he said. "We've set a target we want to aim for and all we're doing is chipping away at that."

A massive pile-up on the M1 delayed some of the Green Army's footsoldiers, but they need not have worried. Argyle's players seemed sympathetic and spent much of the first half-hour churning out nothing much. A lob by Mark Richards, thwarted by Larrieu, proved to be the catalyst for the Pilgrims, and Hodges had an effort ruled out for offside before the same player finished off yet another set-piece, Coughlan's header from Beswetherick's free-kick setting him up at the far-post.

Coughlan also began the move that led to the Pilgrims' second with a defensive header. Steve Adams, Kevin Wills and Stonebridge kept the ball moving forwards and a special goal was on the cards until Halifax captain Paul Harsley intervened to send Wills sprawling in the penalty area. Wotton converted with his usual zeal.

The Pilgrims spent much of the second half displaying all the confidence and assurance – if not the surgical finishing – of a team so emphatically outpointing the rest of the division, much to the delight of their fans whose day was made complete by the news that Luton had dropped another three points at home, losing 3-2 to a 90th-minute goal by Scunthorpe's Matthew Sparrow. "Plymouth have been the most consistent side by a mile," said Luton manager Joe Kinnear afterwards. "I can't see us winning it now – it's their title." No-one at Home Park was taken in by the mind-games.

"I'm obviously pleased with the result," said Sturrock, "although our passing disappointed me. We had chances at 2-0 to kill the game off and we then could have stored up a lot of energy we had to expend." A little picky, perhaps? "That's my job. When you, as a manager, can handle a performance and say 'there's nothing I can change', I think you've got problems."

Sturrock also revealed that outcast striker Steve Guinan had left the club after settling up the remaining few months of his contract with the Pilgrims. Guinan, 26, had been out of favour all season. He had not been allocated a squad number and had been training apart from the first team.

Saturday, February 16 2002, Nationwide League

Halifax Town 0
Plymouth Argyle 2
Hodges 41, Wotton pen 43

Halifax Town (4-4-2): B Richardson; A Woodward, C Clarke, G Mitchell, M Clarke (P Wright 29, G Jones 66); S Houghton, P Harsley, S Bushell, I Fitzpatrick (C Middleton 83); M Richards, S Kerrigan. **Substitutes (not used):** R Herbert, P Crookes (gk).
Booking: Fitzpatrick 42.
Plymouth Argyle (4-5-1): R Larrieu; D Worrell, P Wotton, G Coughlan, J Beswetherick; B Sturrock (M Phillips 71), K Wills (J Broad 51), D Friio, S Adams, L Hodges; I Stonebridge. **Substitutes (not used):** L McCormick (gk), M Keith, N Heaney.
Referee: T Parkes (Birmingham). **Attendance:** 2,330. **League position:** 1st.

PAUL STURROCK: "The players were so professional, it was unbelievable. They were so up for the game. The first ten minutes were a bit ropy, but after that it was 2-0 and it could have been four or five. We just sat on it but we had a lot of chances. It was a naughty one – they were fighting for their lives and we were going for the title. Funnily enough, a couple of weeks

later, Kidderminster went up there and got tatted. I'd played it down but winning the title was in my mind. You didn't want to mention anything like that because of that dreaded complacency."

KEVIN SUMMERFIELD: "We were really concerned about this game because they had all these big lads, but I thought we played really well. They were two great goals – a great free-kick for the first goal and a really well-struck penalty. It was a real good day for us because Luton lost. We picked up a lot of injuries on the day, so we would have been struggling at Rochdale, although that was called off. Blair got a really nasty ear injury and had to have it stitched. The Doc had told him he had to protect it, so Maxie decided to tell him he had to have it bandaged. On the Monday, Maxie put a great big dressing on it and taped up his head. He came out for training and the lads were absolutely killing themselves. It just shows how gullible footballers can be."

Sturrock need not have worried about conserving energy as the Pilgrims' Tuesday night match at Rochdale was called off after heavy rain left their ground, which they shared with local rugby league outfit Rochdale Hornets, waterlogged and unplayable.

Neither should Sturrock have been surprised – it was the fifth time in two seasons that the fixture had fallen foul of the weather. Argyle travelled fruitlessly to Spotland in November and December the previous season, when the game was rained off, while a third attempt to play the game in the new year was thwarted by frost, as was the first attempt to play the 2001-02 match.

The full significance of the new date for the game – March 26 – would not become evident for a few weeks, but Sturrock was not unduly concerned about the postponement. "I wouldn't have wanted to play on a wet pitch that wouldn't have enabled us to put a rhythm to or passing," he said. "We would like to get the games over as quickly as possible and don't want a fixture pile-up at the end of the season, but maybe it was for the best." Luton used the rain-off to cut Argyle's lead over them and the rest of the division to ten points by beating Bristol Rovers 3-0.

Sturrock spent much of the rest of the week pursuing his long-term interest in Dundee's Scottish Under-21 international Lee Wilkie, who had spent several weeks on loan at Home Park the previous season. Dundee accepted a bid from Argyle for their player, who had fallen out of favour with manager Ivano Bonetti, but in the end, Wilkie could not agree personal terms with the Pilgrims and stayed at Dens Park, forced his way back into the first team, and, by the end of the season, became a full international under new Scotland manager Berti Vogts.

Argyle's next fixture was the visit of Kidderminster Harriers to Home Park, although Sturrock's concern was that too much attention was being paid to the Devon Expressway Derby at Home Park the following Tuesday. "My worry as a manager is that people are focusing on Exeter, rather than Saturday. I will be telling the players in no uncertain terms to forget about Exeter. If things don't go right against Kidderminster, I will be reassessing the team for Tuesday.

"We've come up against hurdles all the time this season and said that this or that is the important part of the season – well, this is the important part of the season again."

The latest Saturday afternoon goal in Home Park's history – at, appropriately enough for a football game, around 6.06pm – ensured Argyle remained on course for the Nationwide Third Division title, giving them a 2-1 win over Jan Molby's side.

The lateness of Wotton's penalty winner in the 81st minute of playing time was down to a power-failure half-an-hour before the scheduled kick-off, which was delayed for an hour and a half while necessary repairs were made. Hundreds of fans were stranded outside the computer-linked turnstiles and many of them went home after receiving a soaking made worse by the sound of Travis's 'Why Does It Always Rain On Me?' insensitively bellowing out from the club's PA.

Those who endured until the problem was fixed must have initially wondered why they had bothered. Standing in the rain is one thing: watching a complete shower is another. Argyle were so poor in the first half that, had the lights gone out again, no-one would have complained.

After the game, Sturrock was still in the dark. "Delighted with the result; disappointed with the performance," he summed up. "There was a lethargy about us, a disjointedness. Putting your finger on it is difficult. We've rested the players this week – now we've got to ask whether we rested them too much."

In keeping with the theme of the day, Argyle failed to spark for most of the opening 45 minutes, and then not until they were a goal behind, apart from when Kidderminster goalkeeper Stuart Brock excellently prevented Adams from converting the move of the match.

Adams was clearly the victim of a foul in the build-up to Drewe Broughton's 33rd-minute opener – even opposition manager Molby recognised it as "the only 50-50 decision that went our way all day". The ball broke to Ian Foster, who crossed for Broughton to head home, with Coughlan caught between tracking back and appealing for the free-kick that never was.

Argyle's second-half revival did not begin until Sturrock made a triple substitution in the 65th minute, replacing Phillips, Hodges and Stonebridge with Sturrock, Heaney and Keith. None was directly involved in the build-up to Coughlan's equaliser within two minutes, but the presence of three new attackers lining up for Beswetherick's corner maybe caused enough disruption to allow the Dubliner to power home a header and cancel out his previous error.

After that, there was only going to be one winner and Argyle might still have found it had they not been handed it on a plate by Scott Stamps, who raised both hands when challenging Sturrock junior for a header and was penalised when the ball hit one of them. Wotton dispatched the gift with his usual amount of restraint, i.e. none.

Molby blew the second fuse of the afternoon over both goals (no corner, no penalty) and the referee, but that was merely displaced frustration in seeing his injury-hit side shock the Third Division leaders, yet leave unrewarded for their efforts. Meanwhile, Luton also had to come from behind to beat York 2-1 at Kenilworth Road.

"It was okay," said Sturrock, of his side's performance, "but, if we keep playing for only 45 minutes, it's not going to be okay, so we have got to get to the bottom of this."

The win meant Argyle would qualify for the play-offs if they completely blew their season: if they completely blew their season, they would be in no shape to contest the play-offs."

Saturday, February 23 2002, Nationwide League

Plymouth Argyle 2
Coughlan 67, Wotton pen 81
Kidderminster Harriers 1
Broughton 33

Plymouth Argyle (4-4-2): R Larrieu; D Worrell, P Wotton, G Coughlan, J Beswetherick; M Phillips (B Sturrock 65), S Adams, D Friio, L Hodges (N Heaney 65); M Evans, I Stonebridge (M Keith 65). **Substitutes (not used):** L McCormick (gk), J Broad.
Kidderminster Harriers (4-5-1): S Brock; I Clarkson, A Sall, C Hinton, S Stamps; T Bird, D Bennett, A Smith, B Davies (C Larkin 63), I Foster; D Broughton.
Substitutes (not used): J Danby (gk), S Shilton, L Ayres, I Joy.
Booking: Stamps 79.
Referee: R Beeby (Northampton). **Attendance:** 8,758. **League position:** 1st.

PAUL STURROCK: "Rochdale was a nightmare. We went all the way up there. I was sitting in the bus reading a book and the boys were sleeping in

the hotel when we got the call saying the game was off. It hasn't been a happy camping ground for us. Until later on. We were starting to worry about all these rearranged games. I wanted to stick them at the end of the season, hoping we'd have enough points to make them insignificant, but it didn't work out that way.

"We brought Lee down, the chairman talked to him, I talked to him, and we seemed to be on the same wavelength. Lee had a couple of financial concerns at home and wanted to make sure the move would safeguard him, which would have meant he would be one of our highest wage-earners. I wasn't prepared to put him above certain players, but we made him an offer which we thought was reasonable and he declined it.

"I'm sure I'll lose a lot more players because of it, but I wasn't prepared to break the bank. He went back, and they had a couple of injuries and stuck him in; they've shaken hands and everything's rosy for him. Berti Vogts sees him in a couple of games, thinks he does very well, and the next minute he's playing for Scotland.

"No regrets. If I was to worry about bad players I'd signed and good players I'd lost, I'd be hanging in my garage by now."

"Kidderminster were the one team this year that I felt was a really good footballing team. I didn't feel that they were strong enough defensively and I'm thankful they had one or two injuries when they played against us. Sometimes they played a bit too much football. They gave us a hard time. We had to come from behind to win the game and they caused us real concerns. With a derby coming up, it was a worry people were thinking ahead. The substitutes worked again; we scored two minutes after the changes.

"The game was about three minutes from being called off. I was thankful we got through it because I didn't want another game put back, especially as they had the injuries. To be fair to Jan Molby, he wanted the game on as well because he already had a lot of catch-up to do anyway."

KEVIN SUMMERFIELD: "Everything's a routine. You eat at the right time, drink at the right time, you warm up, come back in, go out – you're ready, so, just by delaying it, everything's thrown out of kilter. They played well. They had a go at us. We were lethargic again. We'd been playing lots of games and doing a lot of travelling."

CHAPTER 14

THERE might be little love lost between supporters of Argyle and Exeter City but, on the eve of the 70th derby match between the two rivals, the managers of the two sides appeared to be members of a mutual admiration society.

Paul Sturrock had taken the Pilgrims to the very brink of promotion on the back of the Nationwide Third Division's best away record, and recognised the similar achievement of John Cornforth, who would be standing in the adjacent dug-out. "We've got a form away team coming to play us," said Sturrock. "He's worked hard at it; he's brought some organisation to the place; and he's got a very settled team. I think those ingredients are why he's got success."

Cornforth, who had taken over from Noel Blake following Argyle's 3-2 victory at St James' Park earlier in the season, was equally complimentary about the neighbours. "It will be our last chance to do well against Plymouth for a while because they will be promoted," he said. "I think they will win the league."

Sturrock was aware of the Returning Heroes Syndrome, with ex-Pilgrims Sean McCarthy, Martin Barlow and Chris Curran among those available to Cornforth. He said: "Sean and Chopsy [Barlow] were very influential in the last game, and I don't see it being any different this time. In fact, everyone will be well up for it and they will all be buoyed with confidence as far as what they have achieved away from home recently.

"They will want to upset the applecart, so it does put an edge on the game. We've been out of sorts in our last couple of games here, so it should be interesting."

McCarthy, who had an impressive record of seven goals in ten Devon derbies, was, unsurprisingly, relishing his first return to Home Park since being released by Sturrock the previous summer. "I enjoy derby games," he said. "They are always good games to play in and there is nothing bigger than Exeter-Plymouth, especially in the Third Division. They need a few more points to win the championship, but we are looking to get into the play-offs, so it has the makings of a good game."

Whether it was a good game depended entirely on your viewpoint. It certainly was not very good for McCarthy, who was red-carded only seven minutes after coming on as a 69th-minute substitute for a needless elbow on the already-wounded Graham Coughlan. It was a toss-up which was louder – the boos which had greeted his arrival or the cheers which saluted his dismissal.

It was, however, a great night for Argyle, who hosted the Third Division's

biggest crowd of the season – again – by some 1,500 people. They witnessed their heroes win 3-0 to maintain their ten-point advantage at the top of the table in most glorious style against their bitterest rivals.

It was not a bad night, either, for Marino Keith, who scored twice after Steve Adams' second goal of the season had given Argyle a fifth-minute lead. Keith's second was screamer to finish things off and make it clear that the Devon Expressway rivals would not be playing in the same league the following season. Indeed, it was possible to argue that they were not in the same league on the night.

For the first time since the three-quarters rebuilding of Home Park, the atmosphere generated by the crowd and the home side's play were in perfect synchronicity: the fans wanted to shout, and the team gave them plenty to shout about. Looking at the overflowing ground and flowing Argyle possession, it was entirely possible to forget you were watching Third Division football.

Apart from two long-range efforts from Exeter's clearly confident Andy Roscoe, the Pilgrims dominated a pulsating first 45 minutes to the extent it could have been any-score-you-like-nil by the break. As it was, two goals were their reward for a half of enterprise and endeavour.

Yet, for all their crisp, clean passing and movement, the two goals were about as scrappy as you could get. The first, after five minutes, was due almost entirely to the most wicked of left-wing crosses by Jon Beswetherick, whose delivery, hit with venomous pace, cajoled Exeter goalkeeper Stuart Fraser into coming for a ball which tantalisingly curled away from him at the last minute. He fumbled, and the ball dropped between Keith and Adams, who managed to shovel the ball towards the vacant net. The latter claimed, with some embarrassment, the final touch from a mere yard.

For the next half-an-hour, the Greens poured forward and the purple-shirted visitors showed great heart to keep them at arms' length. Ian Stonebridge, whose contribution to the Pilgrims' cause could not have been greater, pulled a fine save out of Fraser with a low shot, and Paul Wotton fired a 30-yard free-kick narrowly wide of the post with the young goalkeeper well beaten.

The damn burst in the 29th minute and, once again, Beswetherick played a vital part. His free-kick from midway inside the Exeter half found the head of Keith, whose flick-on was deflected past Fraser by Curran, the former Pilgrim making an unhappy return to the ground on which he starred during Argyle's 1995-96 promotion-winning campaign.

The good ship Pilgrim ploughed on with the wind in her sails and her crew in

excellent voice. Keith put the game beyond doubt in the 74th minute with a goal about which there was no doubt, the Scot lashing Curran's weak clearance past a helpless Fraser from 30 yards on the full. The home fans remained standing until the end and they kept singing – 'Stand Up For the Champions'. After 18 home games unbeaten, it was impossible to deny them their optimism.

"It was a good all-round performance," Sturrock said, "but the two strikers were the key to the first half. Stoney and Marino gelled together very well. The result was what we wanted – it's another three points towards our target."

Tuesday, February 26 2002, Nationwide League

Plymouth Argyle 3
Adams 5, Keith 29, 74
Exeter City 0

Plymouth Argyle (4-4-2): R Larrieu; D Worrell, P Wotton, G Coughlan, J Beswetherick; B Phillips (N Heaney 87), S Adams, D Friio, L Hodges (K Wills 87); M Keith, I Stonebridge (B Sturrock 82). **Substitutes (not used):** L McCormick (gk), J Broad.
Booking: Adams 7.
Exeter City (4-4-2): S Fraser; B McConnell, A Watson, C Curran, G Power; G Tomlinson (G Breslan half-time), G Cronin (P Buckle 80), K Ampadu, A Roscoe; C Roberts, S Flack (S McCarthy 69). **Substitutes (not used):** A van Heusden (gk), P Read.
Sending-off: McCarthy 76 (violent conduct).
Bookings: Flack 17, Tomlinson 22, Cronin 40, Watson 67.
Referee: G Cain (Bootle). **Attendance:** 16,369. **League position:** 1st.

PAUL STURROCK: "I honestly believe this was our best performance at home this season because we turned a lot of our play into goals. There's been lots of other great performances at home but we won 1-0 and never really convincingly beat a team. This was one game when we were totally up for it. I was worried about the game because of the Rochdale trip and the game against Kidderminster but I needn't have worried because they were wired and ran right over the top of them on the night.

"There was a great atmosphere. The crowd was magic. I think Marino Keith was outstanding. He had a difficult time – he missed pre-season, he'd been out the year before, he came down here and we thrust him straight into games and I think he hit a wall, but periodically he showed what he's capable of. After Luton, you wouldn't have given him a game ever again, yet a week and a half later, he played unbelievably.

"Sean would probably have liked to have done something in that game but it didn't work out the way he would have wanted. As I've said all along, he was a marked man by referees by then – he just had to look at a player and he'd get sent-off. Funnily enough, they started to play much better when

they went down to ten men. We never handled ten men all season. It was a strange scenario – every time we went down to ten men, it seemed to bolster us, but when other teams went down to ten men we never really got to grips with it and use the width and cause them concern.

"Cocko was a worry, because Wottsie at that time wasn't training a lot because of a back and hip injury.

KEVIN SUMMERFIELD: "You never knew what Exeter would do after the way they played against us at St James' Park but basically, we turned the tables on them. They'd won six from eight away; they were much more comfortable away from home. Everybody was up for the game – Exeter home and Exeter away are the games everyone wants to see, even if we're both bottom of the league. There's massive pressure and you just do not want to lose face. On the night, it was possibly one of our most complete performances in all aspects of the game.

"The players know the importance of these games. The game up there was really exciting. It was fierce and fast. We were helped because it rained and it was a quick pitch. We'd worked quite a bit on the forward movement, the two strikers working together, because of Exeter's lack of pace. We didn't say a lot before the game and I was watching the lads, and Friio and Dan just sat in the dressing-room, never moving, looking forward. That's the way the whole team started. The only worry you'd have if somebody was so hyped up and so focused is that they'd go over the top but we didn't. Good goals; good play; everything was good about the game."

The victory over Exeter helped Sturrock earn the February Nationwide Third Division manager of the month accolade from the Football League's sponsors, the announcement of his third monthly award of the season coming on the eve of the Pilgrims' visit to Macclesfield. Sturrock, though, immediately declared he did not want a repeat of his side's form the previous month.

The Pilgrims had won five of their six matches during February but had, however, begun the month with a defeat at Luton, and Sturrock was determined to avoid a similar fate at Moss Rose. "We don't want to start with a defeat again, because we want to distance ourselves from everybody else," he said. "The only way we can do that is by winning games. We don't want people chewing on our coat-tails."

Nationwide media manager Chris Hull said: "It is a magnificent effort by Plymouth Argyle, and, in particular, Paul Sturrock. The club accrued 15 points out of 18 in the month; the fan-base and the potential of the club are being realised, as we saw in midweek. This is a hat-trick of awards for Paul. He's a

delightful character and we are thoroughly looking forward to coming down next week to hand over his third award."

Sturrock had insisted that all his players be invited to the by now familiar surroundings of Chambers restaurant when the award was presented, and dedicated the honour to them and the fans. He said: "The last couple of times, I've emphasised how important the chairman and the board and everyone working for the club have been, but the players are the people who run over the white line and make the decisions which determine if you win or lose.

"The fans have been like an extra man. They gave us the edge in the Kidderminster game. Managers are the ones who get their name on the trophy, but I'd like to think that everybody involved with Plymouth Argyle are winners."

Sturrock got his wish at Moss Rose the following day. Argyle did not lose, but Chris Priest's 90th-minute goal earned the Silkmen a 1-1 draw and, with Torquay unable to help out their fellow Devonians by losing 1-0 to Luton at Plainmoor, the Pilgrims' lead at the top of the Third Division was cut to eight points.

If the Devon Expressway Derby had been a superb advert for Third Division football, the first 45 minutes at Macclesfield would have put the Plymouth and District Junior League to shame. The only point of interest came when Romain Larrieu superbly tipped over a free-kick from Richie Lambert.

Argyle raised their game after some choice words by Sturrock at the interval and took the lead midway through the half after Kevin Wills, who had earlier been seen a completely justifiable shout for a penalty turned down, was fouled on the edge of the penalty area. Beswetherick's free-kick was parried high by goalkeeper Steve Wilson and Coughlan headed the dropping ball into the roof of the net.

Priest, the former Everton player who had been the subject of a transfer bid by Sturrock the previous season, had displayed a tendency to play well against Argyle and the cynics on the away terrace were not the least bit surprised to see him sneak in at the far post to sweep home Jon Askey's right-wing cross at the death.

Despite the disappointment of seeing two points disappear so close to the final whistle, Sturrock was magnanimous. "I've no complaints with the draw," he said. "Macclesfield played well and really merited a point. We think we can hold the lead and just sit back, but they came back at us. We have not lost – that's the main thing to emphasise – and we have gained another point towards where we want to go."

Coughlan, still sporting a shiner after the previous Tuesday's collisions with Geoff Breslan's head and McCarthy's elbow, was similarly generous. "I would say our performance was very poor," he said, "but we live to fight another day. The easy part is getting to that line – crossing it is extremely hard. But we are still there."

Saturday, March 2 2002, Nationwide League

Macclesfield Town 1
Priest 90
Plymouth Argyle 1
Coughlan 71

Macclesfield Town (3-1-4-2): S Wilson; D Tinson, S MacAuley, D Adams; D Smith; D Whitaker, C Priest, C Byrne (S Hitchen 66), K Lightbourne (J Askey 73); L Glover, R Lambert.
Substitutes (not used): L Martin (gk), D Ridler, K Monroe.
Bookings: MacAuley 45, Adams 62, Askey 90.
Plymouth Argyle (4-5-1): R Larrieu; D Worrell, P Wotton, G Coughlan, J Beswetherick; B Sturrock, K Wills (J Broad 87), S Adams, D Friio, L Hodges; I Stonebridge (M Keith 90).
Substitutes (not used): L McCormick (gk), C Taylor, M Phillips.
Booking: Hodges 90.
Referee: P Dowd (Stoke-on-Trent). **Attendance:** 2,557. **League position:** 1st.

PAUL STURROCK: "We didn't merit anything apart from a draw. Our first half was so poor it was unbelievable. I had to change a couple of things in the second half to get their minds set on going forward, which we didn't seem to do. We just sat and waited and waited and waited for them to score. For once, we paid the price for it. We'd hung on and eventually they sneaked one, but I couldn't argue with the draw. I wouldn't have argued with a defeat that day. Football's like that – there were plenty of times we went to other paces and sneaked things we didn't deserve.

"I liked Priest – he had always been very influential when I'd seen him.

"Because we cut the season by two weeks, all these games were coming thick and fast. How we got through the season with the few injuries we had was an amazing feat."

KEVIN SUMMERFIELD: "Macclesfield had been playing well and they've got a lot of good players, so we knew it was going to be a tough game. Their pitch is tight. It was going to be interesting how we coped with going back to 4-5-1 after Exeter. First half, we were just awful. We could not get to grips with them. They had too much movement and we could not get near them. We never got the ball. We could have gone in 3-0 down at half-time. After half-time, when we reorganised the midfield three, we got on top of the game and pounded them for much of the rest of the game, deserved to

go in front; then a bad error cost us a goal. We should have cleared the ball on the left-hand side, didn't, they crossed and Joe Broad didn't track his runner. When we walked off the pitch, we were gutted. We'd lost two points in the 90th minute and that could have been crucial, the way it was getting so tight at the top.

"We'd been three, four, five six points clear, but you were still always looking over your shoulder. We'd always got a gap, so we could lose one and still have something in hand. But, when we lost a point or more here and there, the pressure really came on. Would it have been easier if we'd been coming up on the rails? That's even more credit to the boys, that they had been top of the division for so long. They were desperately keen to hold on. That may have made every game really tense.

"This was one of the few occasions when there was a bit of a slanging match in the dressing-room, and, again, that could relate to the pressure. Usually they were very placid; they'd show it without it being aimed at anybody. But, with it being a late goal, you come in – Luton had won – you're still seething about the goal. If it had been 20 minutes before, it wouldn't have happened; everybody would have calmed down and we'd have carried on. But we were that close to the final whistle. It was unusual. After everybody had had their say, everyone held their hands up and it didn't linger. It was forgotten."

Sturrock was unconcerned about the closer proximity of Luton, and Mansfield, to the top spot that his Pilgrims had occupied for 128 consecutive days on the eve of their home fixture against lowly York City. "I think that's going to happen periodically between now and the end of the season," he said. "We are going to have our wee troughs and they're going to have their troughs. We've just got to make sure we have fewer troughs than they do."

More on Sturrock's mind was claiming the three points against York which would put the Pilgrims within sight of the points total that he set his players at the beginning of the year – 83 – that he believed would be enough to take Argyle up.

"The important thing for us is the 80-point mark," he said. "It's the penultimate hurdle before promotion. It would be a great psychological boost to everybody to reach it. The opportunity's there – a home game and three points to play for."

Argyle's players duly complied with their manager's wishes after, as he would no doubt have put it, 'biting and scratching' their way to a 1-0 victory over the financially-troubled Minstermen in a match which saw another five-figure crowd

witness two firsts: the first legitimate sending-off of the league campaign, when David Worrell was red-carded for two bookable offences eight minutes after half-time, and the consequent first – and, as it turned out, only – appearance of the season of Craig Taylor.

Taylor, who had broken his ankle almost a year previously, was sent on as Sturrock reorganised his defence following the dismissal of Worrell, who was booked for barely evident encroachment at a 47th-minute free-kick and then sent off six minutes later for petulantly throwing the ball away after the award of a free-kick against the Pilgrims.

As a result of referee Phil Prosser's summary justice, Argyle were left hanging on to an own goal by Graham Potter in the final minute of a first half they dominated. Somehow, the determined manner of their eventual triumph made victory all the more sweet, though Sturrock was beside himself when it came to explaining Worrell's actions.

He said: "He had a yellow card. He realised he had a yellow card and knew he was on one more. He then mouths at the referee and petulantly chucks the ball away. It's just absolutely insane. In the position we are in the league...I was agog. I could not believe what I was actually seeing from that player, who is perhaps the most disciplined of them all.

"It near enough cost us dear at an important time. In home games, you have got to take your three points and it's difficult enough playing 11 against 11 without going down to ten men, which made us have to go on the back foot, made us have to play a bit more protective.

"I made my views very plain as he came off the pitch and he and I will have a little chat. You can rest assured he'll come under the disciplinary code of the club.

"Our first-half performance was reasonable and we always looked as though we'd nick a goal. It was an own goal but, to be fair, we had a few chances and we were looking forward to getting on top as the second half went on, and making it easier for ourselves. That was obviously taken away from us with the situation.

"I was very, very pleased with the result but bitterly disappointed with the way we have had to go about our business to get the result."

Potter's own goal was in the bizarre category. Wotton's free-kick was helped on by Hodges, but was going nowhere dangerous until the York full-back took a unilateral decision to clear the ball and succeeded in heading it past his aghast goalkeeper Alan Fettis.

After that, York's territorial dominance was so great that when Stonebridge engineered a breakaway in the final ten minutes, Friio's shot which was beaten out by Fettis was the Pilgrims' lone effort on their visitors' goal in the whole of the second half.

Sturrock said: "York pumped a lot of things into our box but we blocked and handled most of the crosses. They huffed and puffed. At the end, we've got to be pleased in difficult circumstances.

"It was a worry, but I knew the players knew how to play the shape. I was reasonably confident we would hold out and a draw wouldn't have been the worst scenario. I was appreciative the players knew what to do."

Tuesday, March 5 2002, Nationwide League

Plymouth Argyle 1
Potter og 45
York City 0

Plymouth Argyle (4-4-2): R Larrieu; D Worrell, P Wotton, G Coughlan, J Beswetherick; B Phillips (B Sturrock 64) S Adams, D Friio, L Hodges; I Stonebridge, M Keith (C Taylor 59). **Substitutes (not used):** L McCormick (gk), K Wills, N Heaney. **Sending-off:** Worrell 53 (two bookable offences). **Bookings:** Phillips 29, Worrell 47.
York City (5-3-2): A Fettis; G Potter, G Hobson (S Wise 73), M Basham, J Parkin, M Hocking; N Richardson, C Brass, L Bullock; A Mathie, L Nogan. **Substitutes (not used):** R Howarth (gk), C Smith, A O'Kane, L Wood.
Bookings: Parkin 50, Brass 55, Bullock 58, Hobson 61.
Referee: P Prosser (Albrighton). **Attendance:** 10,801. **League position:** 1st.

PAUL STURROCK: "I'd watched them a couple of times before this game and they actually looked not a bad side, but they just seemed to lose their way all the time. I was worried about this game. The previous season, they had battered us at times. We didn't play well on the day and they played well. At that stage, people had worked out there was a way to handle Plymouth Argyle and they came very much in that vein.

"When we went down to ten men, Craig Taylor had to come on and put in a really good 20 minutes defending the box. It was always going to be difficult for him, but he did well and I was very pleased with him. There were other permutations I could have done – I could have brought Stevie Adams back, but I didn't want to lose his influence in midfield. I think he played for about four minutes at right-back before we made the change.

"To be sent off for petulance is something I'll never understand in a footballer because you'll never change a referee's mind. I can see a point talking

to a referee at half-time or at the end of the game – but through a game...two bookings like that put us under severe pressure. All the games were important by then and to play 40 minutes with only 10 men and one goal up put us under severe pressure. It upset me because he showed a side of his game I'd never seen in the past. He's very level-headed and docile, but he got over excited and we could have paid the penalty.

"David got fined the maximum within the PFA guidelines and was told if it happened again, it would be much more. He was very, very apologetic. After the heat of the moment had gone, he appreciated his stupidity. That's the kind of lad he is."

KEVIN SUMMERFIELD: "We'd had them watched and everyone had said how cumbersome their back three was, so we'd done a lot of work, trying to make that work in our favour, but we just never got started in the game. We always have a nightmare when Phil Prosser's the referee. There's always something happening. In Paul's first game in charge, he sent Chris Leadbitter off at Chester. The goal was a massive injustice. That was the bit of luck we had.

"We always had discussions about the bench. Wottsie had been having a problem with his hip and back and had missed bits a pieces of training. I think that may have been one of the only occasions that Craig was on the bench for a home game, and that was because we were a little bit concerned about Wottsie. At the end of the day, he proved the perfect substitute when Dave went off. They had a big lad up front and pumped ball after ball after ball into the box and Craig is probably the best header of a ball at the club. He went straight in, Wottsie went to full-back, and we carried on what we'd been doing and defended the box really well.

"It was out of character for Dave. It looked like the frustration of the evening. It looked like it was hard work out there. To be fair, he was really low after the game. These things happen. If it never happens again to him, he will have learnt his lesson."

A sheepish Worrell was amongst the players who attended the following day's luncheon at Chambers, where Sturrock was formally presented with his Nationwide Third Division manager of the month award for February. He was handed a giant brandy goblet and joked: "After last night, I hope David Worrell will fill this up for me." Worrell duly did, with orange squash. Sturrock thanked him, but growled: "You're still fined."

Nationwide media manager Chris Hull said: "It's not usual the manager invites all his players but I think that's quite indicative of the chap: he invites all his

back-room team, the chairman's here, directors, all the players. He realizes it's not just one man's success – it's a collective pursuit."

Sturrock said: "We've brought the players along because they are the mainstay of the club and the reason we are in this position. It's a wee 'thank you' to them."

Adams and Hodges received further reward the following day when they signed deals to extend their contracts with the club until the summer of 2004. Adams was given a one-year extension to his existing deal, while Hodges, whose contract had been due to expire at the end of the season, earned himself a two-year deal. It left Beswetherick as the only player who would be out of contract in the summer, and Sturrock said negotiations had begun with the left-back.

Sturrock also said that he had revised upwards, by three points, the promotion points-target he had set his players. "The revision is for promotion," he said, ignoring thoughts of the Third Division championship. "We won't look further than that until we get it."

Argyle's lead over Luton was cut to five points the following Saturday, when the Pilgrims' match at Darlington fell foul of the weather. The game was called off only two hours before the scheduled kick-off, by which time most Plymouth-based Argyle supporters had nearly completed a six-hour trek from Devon, but referee Fraser Stretton was left with no choice after a heavy rainstorm and a subsequent snow shower left Feethams unplayable.

Meanwhile, Luton came from a goal down to defeat Rushden and Diamonds 2-1 at Nee Park. "While the players were twiddling their thumbs, everybody else caught us up," summarised Sturrock, who was eager to rearrange the postponed Darlington match for the Monday following their scheduled April 13 visit to Carlisle.

Before that switch of dates was confirmed, Luton caught up further on the Pilgrims in midweek, when they beat Exeter 3-0 at Kenilworth Road to move within two points of the leaders, having played two matches more. Their manager, Joe Kinnear, who had earlier conceded the Third Division title to Argyle, had now apparently changed his mind. "We can overhaul them," he said. "I want the title as much as I want promotion."

Hatters' striker Steve Howard, who scored two of the goals as Luton cruised past Argyle's Devon neighbours, was also bullish. "I was pretty sure we were going up," he said, "but now I think we can catch Plymouth. Let's put it this way: if we keep winning our games, they are going to have to do ever so well to stop us overtaking them."

Unlike most of his club's supporters, Sturrock welcomed Luton's run and con-

gratulated them on their efforts. "Any team that has seven wins in a row, including some very difficult away games, deserves every credit," he said. "I'm quite pleased Luton have made it a very competitive league. There should be an edge to us now that will hopefully take us through the rest of the season.

"We have really got to go for it now. The picture has been painted and it's up to us to make sure it doesn't get any different. The only way we can do that is by winning games."

Argyle's 20-week reign as Nationwide Third Division leaders would come to an end if they failed to beat Leyton Orient at Home Park and Luton – who boasted a superior goal-difference – won at home to Kidderminster the following Saturday.

Sturrock said: "Our record is comparable to Luton's and there is no reason we should in any way feel inferior or worry about it. We're in the driving seat. At the end, the proof will be in the pudding – if we fail, it will be because of our results." It was difficult to assume he was not talking about the title.

Argyle maintained their two-point lead over Kinnear's side – who beat Kidderminster 1-0 for their eighth straight win – with a thoroughly confusing 3-0 Westcountry victory over the men from the Orient.

Here were the Third Division leaders being outplayed by lowly Leyton – who included David Partridge in their line-up – for large chunks of the match, yet still managing to stretch their unbeaten home record to 20 games with an ultimately comfortable victory.

There was Dubliner Graham Coughlan, a centre-back with two career goals to his name before joining the Pilgrims in the summer, climbing to the top of Argyle's scoring charts with his ninth goal of the campaign – a prouder Paddy on St Patrick's weekend you could not hope to find.

And there was Paul Sturrock, eager for points to maintain his side's promotion push in the face of Luton's onslaught, yet sympathising with his counterpart.

"This was our worst home performance of the season," was Sturrock's unequivocal opening gambit afterwards." If I was the manager of Leyton Orient, I would be deeply upset," and there was no denying that Paul Brush was upset, not least of all because he thought Stonebridge was offside when he opened the Pilgrims' account after seven minutes.

Coughlan, who made the opener with a sublime length-of-the-field pass after winning back the ball on the edge of the area following Adams' mistake, said earlier in the season: "On a Saturday, eight or nine players might play well, two

may not play well. We get them through it: the following week, they get us through it." This was one of those Saturdays, except the figures were more or less reversed, with Coughlan one of the few who helped his team-mates claim their win bonus.

The other was Romain Larrieu, who enhanced his reputation for being tete et epaules the best goalkeeper in the division with a double save from Steve Watts that could best be described as being indescribable. Suffice to say that Watts was barely a yard from goal and had two bites at the cherry, but still Larrieu turned the ball away for a corner. He guarded his clean-sheets so zealously – and this was his 22nd of the season – that even his old mate Laurent Robert would have had trouble beating him. "Romain earned his corn," conceded Sturrock. "He made a couple of saves that changed the complexion of the game. We went straight down the other end and scored. That's football. Beggars can't be choosers."

Coughlan added the second at the far post 12 minutes from time, converting centre-back partner Wotton's corner, and substitute Evans drove home the third three minutes later.

The strange day concluded with Sturrock talking about promotion and the title, without actually mentioning either by name. "We are focused on our performances and results," he said. "We want to get to the finishing post as far as the top three is concerned, then we can battle our corner for the icing on the cake.

"At the end of the day, we have got to take each game as it comes" – and, with two managerial cliches in one sentence, normality returned to Home Park.

Saturday, March 16 2002, Nationwide League

Plymouth Argyle 3
Stonebridge 7, Coughlan 78, Evans 81
Leyton Orient 0

Plymouth Argyle (4-4-2): R Larrieu; D Worrell, P Wotton, G Coughlan, J Beswetherick; M Phillips (J Bent 76), S Adams, D Friio (B Sturrock 82), L Hodges; M Keith (M Evans 55), I Stonebridge. **Substitutes (not used):** L McCormick (gk), N Heaney.
Booking: Worrell 64.
Leyton Orient (4-4-2): A Bayes; A Harris, D Smith, D Partridge, M Lockwood; A Newton, C Hutchings, S Canham (D Barnard 86), J Martin; S Watts (A McLean 86), I Christie. **Substitutes (not used):** G Fletcher, B Jones, G Morris (gk).
Bookings: Watts 82, Partridge 90.
Referee: M Fletcher (Warley). **Attendance:** 9,438. **League position:** 1st.

PAUL STURROCK: "Darlington was a frustration because they had body-count missing big time and I knew they would be stronger later in the sea-

son. The referee phoned me when I was about 20 miles away and told me the pitch wasn't fit for a game. In the end, he had my vote because I wanted to have a pitch where we could play our football.

"It's a nightmare. You're peaking for 3pm and it doesn't happen, there's a lot of frustration and pent-up energy.

"Joe Kinnear's team had gone on a fantastic run. I'd have fancied my chances. It was going to be real torrid end to the season. Nobody would have predicted that one team would finish with 102 points and another with 97. If somebody had said that at the start of the season, no-one would have believed them. We would have been expecting to run away with the league but there they were just two points behind.

"David Partridge played in this game and I thought he did well. Their two centre-halves were the key to how well they did that day. By the end of the season, most teams who came down here played quite well. One, they knew how to stop us and two, we're a type of team who at home are a bit more open and will let teams play in front of us, which means they get a lot of the ball. It was never 3-0 – it was an absolute travesty they didn't get a draw out of that game. The boy up front had three gilt-edged chances before we scored. Romain made two tremendous saves and we cleared shots off the line.

"I think Mickey Evans' substitution was very influential. We had never upset them with height. Mickey came on and all of sudden things aren't coming straight back to us and they are on the back foot. A change of tactics influenced the game."

KEVIN SUMMERFIELD: "They gave us a real tough game – pressed us, pushed everybody on – and we just couldn't come to terms with it. We like our full-backs on the ball so much, and they wouldn't let us. We lost our composure, hit too many long balls. The game turned when Evo came on. We scored two set-pieces and we defended set-pieces and crosses well."

At the end of the week, the next game to come was at Lincoln, where victory would see the Pilgrims achieve the upwardly-revised, terribly conservative, points target of 86 that Sturrock had set his side to be sure of winning promotion. However, as far as he was concerned, only Plymouth Argyle could prevent Plymouth Argyle from stumbling over the finishing line now.

"We've got four games in ten days coming up," he said, "which is tough. It's important how we mentally approach these games, because we might

get knocked off our perch...or we might do the business as far as pointage is concerned. These are big games."

Certainly the next one was much bigger than the Lincolnshire Senior Cup semi-final, the Red Imps' previous match in which their first team went down 2-1 to Grantham, which is about as embarrassing as it gets. Sturrock, though, was in a mood to see menace in Sticker Under-11s, and rallied his troops accordingly.

He said: "They're in a bit of a slump at the moment [three successive defeats, the last two at home; no goals scored] but they might be geed up for the top-of-the-table team coming – it will give a bit of an edge to them. I'm not taking anything for granted and I anticipate a difficult 90 minutes."

Sturrock's caution was at least partially caused by the fact that he would have to rearrange his defence for only the third time during the season, thanks to David Worrell's one-match suspension for his sending-off against York. Steve Adams returned to the right-back slot in which he had begun the season due to Worrell's injury, with Jason Bent restored to the midfield.

It took a terrific 71st-mniute goal from substitute Stonebridge to separate the two teams and punish hosts who enjoyed plenty of possession but did not seem to know what to do with the ball once they reached Argyle's penalty area.

On the subject of enjoyment, Argyle players celebrated after the 1-0 victory in a manner that suggested they would be playing Second Division football the following season.

On the final whistle, they sprinted across to the jubilant travelling support. Wotton and Friio swung on the crossbar, Hodges joined in the fans' chants, and Larrieu celebrated with a giant inflatable champagne bottle. Chairman Paul Stapleton and his deputy Peter Jones joined the players in greeting the fans, and there was an amusing moment when they found themselves being congratulated by co-directors Phill Gill and Nic Warren, who had been standing on the away terrace.

There was, however, technically still some work to be done. Argyle remained one point away from arithmetical confirmation of their promotion. One dull, scrappy point from their midweek visit to Rochdale – weather permitting – would put the issue beyond any doubt.

Sturrock was as pragmatic as ever. "I'm disappointed with the way we played," he said. "I can't believe we didn't show the urgency that I would expect from a team in the position we're in. We could have made it much easier for ourselves. We just seemed to be sluggish again."

Luton? Oh yes, they destroyed Halifax 5-0 at Kenilworth Road to extend their unbeaten run into double-figures. The frustration of Hatters' manager Joe Kinnear was so tangible it was felt 150 miles away in Lincoln, where the slimmest of victories kept the Greens two points clear of the Luton Lip and his men.

Saturday, March 23 2002, Nationwide League

Lincoln City 0
Plymouth Argyle 1
Stonebridge 71

Lincoln City (4-4-2): A Marriott; J Barnett, G Brown, P Morgan, S Bimson (P Gain 76); K Black (P Smith 76), I Hamilton (T Battersby 83), J Walker, A Buckley; L Thorpe, D Cameron. **Substitutes (not used):** D Horrigan (gk), M Bloomer.
Plymouth Argyle (4-5-1): R Larrieu; S Adams, P Wotton, G Coughlan, J Beswetherick; M Phillips (B Sturrock 61), J Bent, D Friio, K Wills (I Stonebridge 61), L Hodges; M Evans. **Substitutes (not used):** L McCormick (gk), J Broad, C Taylor.
Referee: T Parkes (Birmingham). **Attendance:** 4,019. **League position:** 1st.

PAUL STURROCK: "Eighty-three points was the initial target. I had looked at the stats and 83 had never not got promoted. We got to eighty-three and we were still not quite sure of being promoted. It was quite scary. We revised it to 86, which we got at Lincoln. It was a poor performance and we looked out of sorts. The pitch didn't help. It was very bumpy; hard and really difficult to get a rhythm going. We had one or two half-chances, which we didn't take.

"Stoney got us the win with a great finish. We had a right go because I brought Blair on at the same time and we changed to 4-4-2 and all of a sudden the momentum went to us. We had four or five chances, as they couldn't handle us. Everybody was happy because we got to eighty-six points. I told them if they'd won that day it was a certainty, no way anybody would catch us. When they won, although statistically we still needed one point, I felt in my mind no-one would catch us.

"A lot of people talk about the relationship between the players and the fans and you saw it that day. The fans were a wee bit taken aback by the players' response to the win, knowing that it still wasn't statistically certain. I think it was just the relief of it all."

KEVIN SUMMERFIELD: "We knew if we got a result here, things were likely to happen. Points went out of the window apart from the points we won and the points Luton won. Nobody else was going to catch us at this time. The day was a comedy of errors. The hotel was two minutes from the

ground but half an hour after we left, we had to phone the ground to ask for directions. Malc, the driver, went the wrong way. We were in the middle of nowhere. The ground was in Lincoln, the hotel was in Lincoln, you could have walked from the hotel to the ground in five minutes. Dave Tall phoned the club from the coach and they had to talk us in. I had to get off the coach and walk straight in and hand the team-sheet to the referee.

"The pitch was awful. It was warmish day and what is usually a good football game, because they like to get the ball down and play, never really got going. We had an off day; we didn't get numbers into the box; we didn't get enough quality balls into the box; the balance of the midfield wasn't right. Steve Adams played right-back and that may have had an effect. Steve was a massive factor in away games and, although Jason came in and played really well, we still missed something balancewise. Then Ian scored a wonder goal and that was the difference. The lads knew that Luton had won 5-0 and they knew their own win was a really big win."

PHILL GILL: "I don't feel that being on the board should come between me and supporting the club the way I feel. Under duress, I wear a suit and go in the boardroom on home games, but at away games, the craic is much better with the fans.

"It also enables me to share the experience with my son, Terry. The whole season was an incredible time for both of us, especially a teenager like Terry – he went from watching the players from the terraces to being on first-name terms with them. One minute, they were his heroes; the next, he was chatting to them like he'd known them forever. It must have been amazing for him.

"Watching from the terraces had its funny moments, too. When Wottsie scored at Halifax, I caught his eye as he was celebrating. He was shocked. He didn't know until then that I didn't always go in the directors' box. He told all the lads afterwards 'You'll never guess who I saw on the terraces – Gilly'."

CHAPTER 15

PAUL Sturrock was in no mood to pursue the point his Pilgrims needed to make sure of promotion to the Nationwide Second Division at a mercifully dry and sunny Spotland on March 26, 2002. "I think the important thing is to win the game," he said. "If we start focusing on a point, on not losing...I don't think you can approach games like that."

Rochdale were one of several teams chasing the third automatic promotion spot behind championship rivals Argyle and Luton, and Sturrock said: "This is a big game for Rochdale as well – they will be right up for it – so we are going to have to focus on the win. Our players appreciate we could go five points clear at the top. It's a game that could create a bit of space for us.

"I think the championship is the thing they are talking about more than anything else now. They've been on top so long, they are all geared to that – getting the icing on the cake. The worry is maintaining the momentum. The only way you keep the momentum going is by winning games. We want to get over this hurdle and keep the second hurdle in sight – the only way we can do that is by getting three points, instead of one."

Sturrock was committed to bringing back David Worrell after the right-back's one-match ban, but was not about to make other changes. He said: "I won't change my philosophy. It's stood me in good stead most of the season. A couple of times, I've meandered off to escapism and cavalierness and it's cost me dear, so I think we should be disciplined as we have been in the past.

"David will go straight back in, though. You want the back four you have decided on and David's one of those."

Despite his natural caution, Sturrock insisted every member of the first-team squad travelled to Spotland...just in case there was something for them to celebrate afterwards.

Argyle suddenly being in a position to be the first side in England to claim promotion had caught many people unawares. The reason they had failed to realise that Argyle could finish the job off with a draw at Spotland was because the Third Division table appeared to show that three teams – Luton, Mansfield and Cheltenham – would still be able to overtake them unless the Pilgrims won. However, with Mansfield and Cheltenham still to play each other, it was now impossible for the fourth-placed team to finish the season with more than 86 points – Argyle's total going into the Rochdale game.

The scene was set. Rochdale's small, but welcoming, ground became the focus of Argyle's most important game since the 1997-98 relegation decider a few miles down the road at Burnley. Around 1,000 Argyle supporters took a day off or threw a sickie to be there and they did not go home disappointed.

Four years after being relegated amid tears at Turf Moor, and just 17 months after Paul Sturrock's appointment as manager, the Pilgrims shook the Third Division dust from their feet.

A 3-1 victory which for the first hour of their encounter with Rochdale at Spotland looked thoroughly unlikely, but which underlined the Pilgrims' resilience and resolve that typified their season, proved more than enough to ensure Argyle could finish no lower third place in the table.

A goal down to Paul Simpson's 55th-minute bolt from the blue and against the ropes with less than half an hour to go, Argyle gutsed their way back into the game – and into the Second Division – with strikes from substitute Marino Keith, centre-back Graham Coughlan and midfielder Lee Hodges to complete their season's first objective with still six matches to go.

Their supporters had been singing it with increasing conviction as the season had progressed, but that Tuesday night the Green Army received unequivocal arithmetically confirmation of their boast: the Greens were going up.

Dale had been quicker out of the blocks, Kevin Townson catching Paul Wotton in possession before Romain Larrieu proved why he was rated the division's top stopper with two superb saves. The first, a flying one-handed parry to his right after Clive Platt's head connected powerfully with David Flitcroft's cross from the right wing, was nothing short of world class: the second, an acrobatic tip over of Townson's long-range effort, was not far behind. The 27 scouts representing Premiership and First Division clubs would have taken note.

A pattern developed, with Argyle attempting to stay faithful to their patient passing as much as the uneven surface would allow, and their hosts trying to release their width players was quickly as possible. Alan McLoughlin, their former Irish international, was the lynchpin.

Argyle's reliable defence planted itself like a green wall across the edge of the 18-yard box. When it was breached, Larrieu was there to break hearts, swatting Lee Duffy's rasper over the crossbar. The Pilgrims continued to keep Dale, defeated once in their previous nine matches and unbeaten at home since the previous December, at distance – trouble was, Dale were beginning to find their range and narrow in on the target.

Not so Argyle. Hodges and lone forward Evans worked an opening for Friio which represented the Pilgrims' best chance, but the French midfielder was caught between power and placement and the resultant beggar's muddle was predictably easy for opposition goalkeeper Matt Gilks to deal with.

The half ended as it had begun, with Rochdale forcing the pace and getting nearer breaking the deadlock. From a corner unnecessarily conceded by Worrell, Simpson's kick squirmed through to Platt, whose tame shot fooled Larrieu – who had been used to dealing with more high-octane stuff – and trickled through to hit a post. Seconds later, Richard Jobson headed Flitcroft's cross over the crossbar. Argyle, though, managed to reach the interval on level terms and with the least of their pre-game objectives intact. Just.

The Blue waves continued after the break. Coughlan made a rare error, fly-hacking the ball to let Platt in on goal, but Adams covered superbly and muscled the tall forward off the ball. Wotton was booked for a clumsy challenge on the slippery Simpson as Argyle continued to find Spotland as difficult venue as had Luton, Shrewsbury and Hartlepool, who had all returned from Greater Manchester well beaten.

The form Larrieu was in, it was going to take genius or a fluke to beat him, as it proved, though only Simpson will know which category his outrageous lob from wide on the left belonged in. It was impossible to say that Rochdale did not deserve their break, though.

Coughlan went close to levelling from a corner on the right, but the momentum was well and truly with the home side and Flitcroft fired in a low shot which Larrieu scrambled wide of his post.

Then, the genius of Sturrock. Or was it luck? Argyle threw on three substitutes around the hour mark, presumably on the basis that they could not do worse than what was already out there, and were immediately back in the match thanks to one of them.

Wotton fired in a free-kick from 30 yards which Gilks could not hold and Keith, left out altogether from the squad at Lincoln the previous Saturday, pounced from a yard to crack the ball into the roof of the net. The goal understandably appeared to suck some life out of Dale who, having been on top for so long, could be forgiven for wondering how they had not shaken off the Pilgrims.

Argyle, now playing 4-4-2, with Adams having given way to Neil Heaney and Evans substituted by Ian Stonebridge, managed to play further up the field, gaining ground as the old legs of McLoughlin, Simpson and Jobson tired. They forced a corner on the left and Wotton swung it in. Gilks fluffed again and

Coughlan shovelled the ball in from less than the yard that his former Livingston team-mate had opened the Greens' account.

Two minutes later, Hodges set the seal on a memorable final 25 minutes, snaffling up a loose ball after a break down the left from Friio and curling the ball around Gilks from 10 yards. Lost in the welter of emotion that followed was the fact that the defeat was only Rochdale's second at home all season, and that alone spoke volumes for the result.

The job, though, was only three-quarters done. To fail to win the Third Division title after spending nearly 22 consecutive weeks staring down with disdain from the summit on their 23 rivals would be deflating, and Sturrock immediately targeted the divisional championship after his side had celebrated in traditional style by spraying their hoarse and still delirious supporters with champagne from the Rochdale directors' box.

"That's great, promotion's magic, but obviously the championship's the thing we've got to aim for now," said Sturrock, who had burst through the doors leading to the directors box into the glare of the television lights clutching a bottle of bubbly at the end of each outstretched arm and looking for all the world like the messiah the Argyle supporters greeted him as.

"We enjoy these two or three days but we get back to work on Thursday afternoon for the challenges ahead – six games. We can have one slip up. We've still got three difficult away games to come. Obviously we want to make sure we keep pegging away and the only way we can do that is by beating Bristol on Saturday.

"The boys have worked hard. It's been a squad that has got us promoted. Any manager carries a bit of luck and, to be fair, we have had players who have gelled much quicker than we ever expected. We've worked hard as a squad, but Lady Luck smiles on you and certain players have gelled well with the rest.

"The team spirit's been fantastic. I think that's been a big bonus because I think there's been games this year we would have lost last season. That game tonight would have gone away from us. The boys have realised that every point's a prisoner and we go for it."

Sturrock revealed promotion had been on his mind since much earlier in the season. He said: "When I did think about it was when we drew 0-0 at Kidderminster. I thought things were shaping up the right way. You wouldn't have thought it after the first two or three results, although I wasn't worried about the performances."

Sturrock, who took over at Home Park on Hallowe'en 2000 with the good ship Pilgrim holed below the water-line and becalmed in the middle of the Third Division, followed in the footsteps of only six other men to have steered the club into more bountiful waters: Bob Jack (1930), Jimmy Rae (1952), Jack Rowley (1959), Tony Waiters (1975), Dave Smith (1986), and Neil Warnock (1996).

Like Warnock only, his success came at the first real attempt; unlike the mad as chips Yorkshireman, he saved his club's followers the ecstatic agony of promotion through the play-offs by the simple expediency of making sure Argyle had not been headed in the table by another club since October 28, some 21 weeks previously.

When the euphoria surrounding the result subsided, Sturrock's next trick would be to attempt bring the first championship to Home Park for nearly half a century, equalling Rowley's feat in the first season after the regional Divisions Three were abandoned. Argyle supporters had dreamed of players to succeed Jimmy Gauld and Wilf Carter, Johnny Williams and Neil Dougall: suddenly they had them.

Each and every one could stand proudly shoulder to shoulder with the heroes of previous promotions. To the list including Sammy Black and Ray Bowden, Jumbo Chisholm and Maurice Tadman, Alex Govan and Reg Wyatt, Billy Rafferty and Paul Mariner, Tommy Tynan and Kevin Hodges, Ronnie Mauge and Mick Heathcote were now added: Romain Larrieu, David Worrell, Jon Beswetherick, David Friio, Graham Coughlan, Craig Taylor, Brian McGlinchey, Sean Evers, Michael Evans, Ian Stonebridge, Buster Phillips, Steve Adams, Lee Hodges, Paul Wotton, Martin Gritton, Kevin Wills, Marino Keith, Jason Bent, Blair Sturrock, Joe Broad, Neil Heaney and Luke McCormick – the men who won Plymouth Argyle promotion in 2002.

One of Paul Sturrock's Manager of the Month awards

Nuff said

The end of the season; the beginning of some serious partying

Paul Sturrock salutes Home Park after receiving his title-winners' medal from Nationwide

Argyle captain Paul Wotton with the spoils of a long, hard, season

Argyle players enjoying a traditional open-top bus ride around Plymouth prior to their Civic Reception

**Argyle chairman
Paul Stapleton**

The kings of the Third Division in Plymouth's Royal Parade

Left to right: Peter Jones (vice-chairman), Paul Stapleton (chairman) and director Phill Gill

On the balcony at the Civic Centre reception

244

PLYMOUTH ARGYLE: NATIONWIDE DIVISION THREE CHAMPIONS 2001/2002

PLYMOUTH ARGYLE 2001/2002

STEVE ADAMS
BORN: 25.9.80, PLYMOUTH
SIGNED: 1.8.98
PREVIOUS CLUBS: TRAINEE
LEAGUE APPEARANCES 2001-02: 40(6)
LEAGUE GOALS 2001-02: 2
CUP APPEARANCES 2001-02: 4(2)
CUP GOALS 2001-02: 0

CHRIS ADAMSON
BORN: 4.11.78, ASHINGTON
SIGNED: 10.1.02-07.2.02 (LOAN)
PREVIOUS CLUBS: WBA, IK BRAGE(L), MANSFIELD(L), HALIFAX (L)
LEAGUE APPEARANCES 2001-02: 1
LEAGUE GOALS 2001-02: 0
CUP APPEARANCES 2001-02: 0
CUP GOALS 2001-02: 0

JASON BENT
BORN: 8.3.77, TORONTO
SIGNED: 21.9.01
PREVIOUS CLUBS: FSV ZWICKAU, COLORADO RAPIDS, TORONTO LYNX
LEAGUE APPEARANCES 2001-02: 16(5)
LEAGUE GOALS 2001-02: 4
CUP APPEARANCES 2001-02: 3(1)
CUP GOALS 2001-02: 1

NICKY BANGER
BORN: 25.4.71, SOUTHAMPTON
SIGNED: 24.8.01-26.11.01
PREVIOUS CLUBS: SOUTHAMPTON, OLDHAM, OXFORD, DUNDEE, SCUNTHORPE(L)
LEAGUE APPEARANCES 2001-02: 3(7)
LEAGUE GOALS 2001-02: 2
CUP APPEARANCES 2001-02: 1
CUP GOALS 2001-02: 0

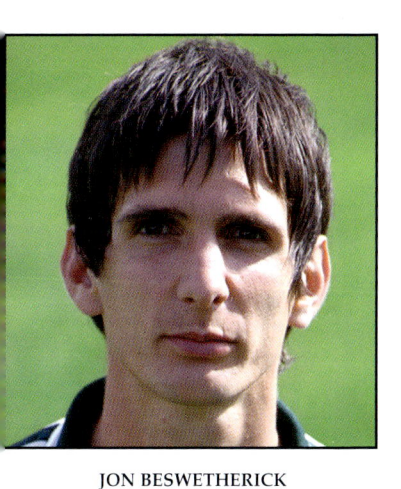

JON BESWETHERICK
BORN: 15.1.78, LIVERPOOL
SIGNED: 01.8.95
PREVIOUS CLUBS: TRAINEE. MOVED TO SHEFFIELD WEDNESDAY AT END OF 2001-02 SEASON
LEAGUE APPEARANCES 2001-02: 27(5)
LEAGUE GOALS 2001-02: 0
CUP APPEARANCES 2001-02: 2(2)
CUP GOALS 2001-02: 0

JOE BROAD
BORN: 24.8.82, BRISTOL
SIGNED: 01.8.00
PREVIOUS CLUBS: TRAINEE, YEOVIL(L)
LEAGUE APPEARANCES 2001-02: 1(6)
LEAGUE GOALS 2001-02: 0
CUP APPEARANCES 2001-02: 0(1)
CUP GOALS 2001-02: 0

PAUL CONNOLLY
BORN: 29.9.83, LIVERPOOL
SIGNED: 01.8.00
PREVIOUS CLUBS: TRAINEE, BIDEFORD(L)
LEAGUE APPEARANCES 2001-02: 0
LEAGUE GOALS 2001-02: 0
CUP APPEARANCES 2001-02: 0
CUP GOALS 2001-02: 0
(PAUL CONNOLLY WAS AN UNUSED SUBSTITUTE IN 3 LEAGUE AND 1 CUP MATCHES IN 2001-02)

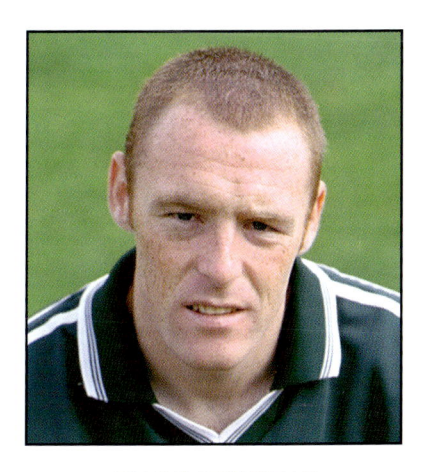

GRAHAM COUGHLAN
BORN: 18.11.74, DUBLIN
SIGNED: 27.5.01, FREE
PREVIOUS CLUBS: BRAY WANDERERS, BLACKBURN, SWINDON(L), LIVINGSTON
LEAGUE APPEARANCES 2001-02: 46
LEAGUE GOALS 2001-02: 11
CUP APPEARANCES 2001-02: 6
CUP GOALS 2001-02: 0

DEAN CROWE
BORN: 06.6.69, STOCKPORT
SIGNED: 10.8.01-5.11.01 (LOAN)
PREVIOUS CLUBS: STOKE, NORTHAMPTON(L), BURY(L). MOVED TO LUTON ON 29.8.01
LEAGUE APPEARANCES 2001-02: 0 (1)
LEAGUE GOALS 2001-02: 0
CUP APPEARANCES 2001-02: 0
CUP GOALS 2001-02: 0

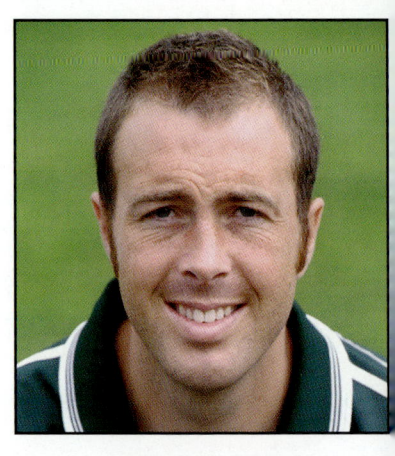

MICHAEL EVANS
BORN: 01.1.73, PLYMOUTH
SIGNED: 23.3.01, £30,000
PREVIOUS CLUBS: BLACKBURN(L), SOUTHAMPTON, WBA, BRISTOL ROVERS
LEAGUE APPEARANCES 2001-02: 30(8)
LEAGUE GOALS 2001-02: 7
CUP APPEARANCES 2001-02: 4(1)
CUP GOALS 2001-02: 0

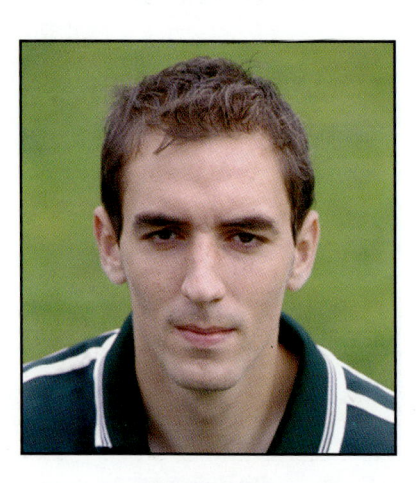

SEAN EVERS
BORN: 10.10.77, HITCHIN
SIGNED: 08.3.01
PREVIOUS CLUBS: LUTON, READING, ST JOHNSTONE(L), STEVENAGE BOROUGH(L)
LEAGUE APPEARANCES 2001-02: 3(4)
LEAGUE GOALS 2001-02: 0
CUP APPEARANCES 2001-02: 1(1)
CUP GOALS 2001-02: 0

DAVID FRIIO
BORN: 17.7.73, THIONVILL
SIGNED: 1.12.00, FREE
PREVIOUS CLUBS: NIMES OLYMPIQUE, EPINAL, ASOA VALENCE
LEAGUE APPEARANCES 2001-02: 41
LEAGUE GOALS 2001-02: 8
CUP APPEARANCES 2001-02: 6
CUP GOALS 2001-02: 3

MARTIN GRITTON
BORN: 1.6.78, GLASGOW
SIGNED: 1.8.98
PREVIOUS CLUBS: PORTHLEVEN, YEOVIL(L), SHELBOURNE (L)
LEAGUE APPEARANCES 2001-02: 0(2)
LEAGUE GOALS 2001-02: 0
CUP APPEARANCES 2001-02: 0(1)
CUP GOALS 2001-02: 0

NEIL HEANEY
BORN: 3.11.71, MIDDLESBROUGH
SIGNED: 4.12.01, FREE
PREVIOUS CLUBS: ARSENAL, HARTLEPOOL(L), CAMBRIDGE UNITED(L), SOUTHAMPTON, MANCHESTER CITY, CHARLTON ATHLETIC(L), BRISTOL CITY(L), DARLINGTON, DUNDEE UNITED
LEAGUE APPEARANCES 2001-02: 1(7)
LEAGUE GOALS 2001-02: 0
CUP APPEARANCES 2001-02: 0
CUP GOALS 2001-02: 0

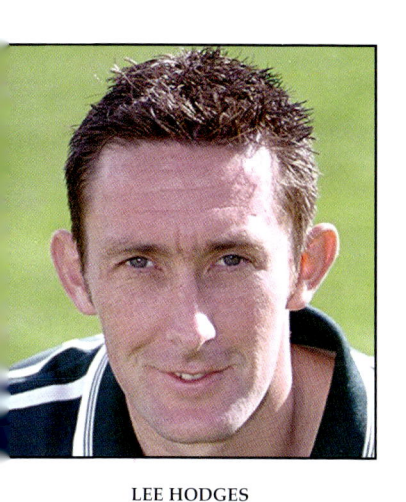

LEE HODGES
BORN: 4.9.73, EPPING
SIGNED: 17.8.01, FREE
PREVIOUS CLUBS: TOTTENHAM HOTSPUR, WYCOMBE WANDERERS(L), BARNET, READING
LEAGUE APPEARANCES 2001-02: 42(3)
LEAGUE GOALS 2001-02: 6
CUP APPEARANCES 2001-02: 6
CUP GOALS 2001-02: 0

MARINO KEITH
BORN: 16.12.74, PETERHEAD
SIGNED: 06.11.01, FREE
PREVIOUS CLUBS: FRASERBURGH, DUNDEE UUNITED, FALKIRK, LIVINGSTON
LEAGUE APPEARANCES 2001-02: 13(10)
LEAGUE GOALS 2001-02: 9
CUP APPEARANCES 2001-02: 0(2)
CUP GOALS 2001-02: 0

ROMIAN LARRIEU
BORN: 31.8.76, MONT DE MARSAN
SIGNED: 4.12.00, FREE
PREVIOUS CLUBS: MONTPELLIER,
ASOA VALENCE
LEAGUE APPEARANCES 2001-02: 45
LEAGUE GOALS 2001-02: 0
CUP APPEARANCES 2001-02: 6
CUP GOALS 2001-02: 0

LUKE McCORMICK
BORN: 13.12 15.8.83, COVENTRY
SIGNED: 8.11.99
PREVIOUS CLUBS: TRAINEE
LEAGUE APPEARANCES 2001-02: 0
LEAGUE GOALS 2001-02: 0
CUP APPEARANCES 2001-02: 0
CUP GOALS 2001-02: 0
(LUKE MCCORMICK WAS AN UNUSED SUBSTITUTE IN 40 LEAGUE AND 6 CUP MATCHES IN 2001-02)

BRIAN McGLINCHEY
BORN: 26.10.77, DERRY
SIGNED: 1.12.00, FREE
PREVIOUS CLUBS: MANCHESTER CITY,
PORT VALE, GILLINGHAM
LEAGUE APPEARANCES 2001-02: 26(3)
LEAGUE GOALS 2001-02: 1
CUP APPEARANCES 2001-02: 4(1)
CUP GOALS 2001-02: 0

MARTIN PHILLIPS
BORN: 13.3.76, EXETER
SIGNED: 08.8.00, £25,000
PREVIOUS CLUBS: EXETER,
MANCHETSER CITY, SCUNTHORPE(L),
EXETER(L), PORTSMOUTH,
BRISTOL ROVERS(L)
LEAGUE APPEARANCES 2001-02: 37(2)
LEAGUE GOALS 2001-02: 6
CUP APPEARANCES 2001-02: 5
CUP GOALS 2001-02: 2

IAN STONEBRIDGE
BORN: 30.8.81, LEWISHAM
SIGNED: 1.7.99, FREE
PREVIOUS CLUBS: TOTTENHAM HOTSPUR
LEAGUE APPEARANCES 2001-02: 29(13)
LEAGUE GOALS 2001-02: 8
CUP APPEARANCES 2001-02: 5(1)
CUP GOALS 2001-02: 1

BLAIR STURROCK
BORN: 25.8.81, DUNDEE
SIGNED: 12.10.01, FREE
PREVIOUS CLUBS: DUNDEE UNITED, BRECHIN CITY(L)
LEAGUE APPEARANCES 2001-02: 4 (15)
LEAGUE GOALS 2001-02: 1
CUP APPEARANCES 2001-02: 0(2)
CUP GOALS 2001-02: 0

CRAIG TAYLOR
BORN: 24.1.74, PLYMOUTH
SIGNED: 20.8.99, £30,000
PREVIOUS CLUBS: DORCHESTER, SWINDON
LEAGUE APPEARANCES 2001-02: 0(1)
LEAGUE GOALS 2001-02: 0
CUP APPEARANCES 2001-02: 0
CUP GOALS 2001-02: 0

KEVIN WILLS
BORN: 15.10.80, TORBAY
SIGNED: 1.8.98
PREVIOUS CLUBS: TRAINEE
LEAGUE APPEARANCES 2001-02: 13(5)
LEAGUE GOALS 2001-02: 0
CUP APPEARANCES 2001-02: 2(2)
CUP GOALS 2001-02: 0

DAVID WORRELL
BORN: 12.1.78, DUBLIN
SIGNED: 23.1.01, £25,000
PREVIOUS CLUBS: BLACKBURN, DUNDEE UNITED
LEAGUE APPEARANCES 2001-02: 43
LEAGUE GOALS 2001-02: 0
CUP APPEARANCES 2001-02: 5
CUP GOALS 2001-02: 0

PAUL WOTTON
BORN: 17.8.77, PLYMOUTH
SIGNED: 10.7.95
PREVIOUS CLUBS: TRAINEE
LEAGUE APPEARANCES 2001-02: 46
LEAGUE GOALS 2001-02: 5
CUP APPEARANCES 2001-02: 6
CUP GOALS 2001-02: 1

MARLEY MALONGA WAS ALSO NAMED IN A FIRST-TEAM SQUAD DURING THE 2001-02 SEASON. HE WAS AN UNUSED SUBSTITUTE IN THE LDV VANS TROPHY MATCH AT CHELTENHAM BUT FAILED TO COME ON.

Paul Wotton with another important squad member, physio Paul Maxwell

Tuesday, March 26 2002, Nationwide League

Rochdale 1
Simpson 55
Plymouth Argyle 3
Keith 65, Coughlan 80, Hodges 82

Rochdale (4-4-2): M Gilks; L Duffy, R Jobson, G Griffiths, M Doughty; D Flitcroft (K Durkan 80), A McLoughlin, M Oliver, P Simpson; K Townson (S Jones 75), C Platt.
Substitutes (not used): N Edwards (gk), S Coleman, G Atkinson.
Plymouth Argyle (4-1-4-1): R Larrieu; D Worrell, P Wotton, G Coughlan, J Beswetherick; S Adams (N Heaney 63); B Sturrock (M Keith 62), J Bent, D Friio, L Hodges; M Evans (I Stonebridge 62). **Substitutes (not used):** C Taylor, L McCormick (gk).
Bookings: Wotton 51, Hodges 66.
Referee: M Pike (Barrow-in-Furness). **Attendance:** 4,457. **League position:** 1st (promoted).

PAUL STURROCK: "We were battered for the first 20 minutes. Rochdale were right up for it because it was an important game for them, too. At half-time it was 0-0 and I told them 'We don't deserve to be 0-0, you've not played to the standards you can, let's have a go. Let's go 4-4-2 – they're not expecting it.' We started the half very well and then conceded a goal. I was worried about that but then we played another for ten minutes before I thought fresh legs were needed and I put the subs on. Mickey had run his race, Blair had run his race and it was important we had a go. Stevie Adams was taken off because we didn't need what he gave us; Jason and David played central midfield. Rochdale never handled the changeover and we scored three goals very rapidly.

"The one thing I've found is that a change of system and a change of personnel is very influential. It's not the same in Scotland, where everybody knows everybody else, but down here, because we only play each other once a season, it's more difficult to keep track of styles of players and systems. We definitely won a lot of games through our substitutions.

"Wottsie fell over and that set the tone. Romain made two great saves in the first half – and at 1-0 he had a fantastic save that kept us in it. I think Simpson meant the goal. That's the type of lad he is. He has that in his armoury. We had never handled the width players – they had put crosses in for fun. We were defending in our box.

"The players were disappointed how badly they'd played in such a big game. After the wee chat we had at half-time, we decided we'd have a right go.

"Winning promotion was a relief. I'm not a great celebrator, I never have

been. It was a mild relief. I was pleased for everybody and it was time to party. It was a coming together of all the hard work on the training-ground, looking after the diet, all the travelling all over the place; it all came to one thing and we gained the promotion that I think we merited over the season.

"I remember a few times when things have happened in cup finals and the like, when I have been kicked in the teeth. You can have huge disappointments with success as well as with failure. You have to stay on an even keel, but it isn't easy – you have to work at it. Saturday nights are terrible. I've kind of got over it, but it's still a stumbling block. I can't really have a life on a Saturday night if we've lost. It's all consuming, although I'm working a lot harder on it. I'm thinking: 'I should have done this, should have done that.' An example of that is Luton.

"There's very little you can do when they run out over that white line. Maybe a substitution here and change of system there sometimes benefits the team. We've been very lucky. There's been certain things we've done which has probably won us the game. But it's the players that win you or lose you games. When I'm going home, I'm weighing up the whole training process, and thinking about whether I should have had a word with someone, what should I do now, what should I change? By the end of the night, I'm ready and buzzing for Monday.

"I always have this problem with adrenaline. On a Sunday, I'm like a bag of washing and I just have to lie about the house, which is very irksome for my wife because it's the only day she can get me moving with the kids. I think that's her biggest disappointment.

"I didn't go back to Plymouth. I went to Scotland, which was a bit disappointing, because I missed out on the jollies.

"The support was magnificent and the relief of it all for the players was second to none. You could see the enjoyment and excitement in the changing-room and celebrating in the stand. Everybody was delighted. Gaining promotion was what we had set out to do, the icing would be the championship, but even if we'd got nipped by Luton for the title, it wouldn't have bothered me – the essence of the season was to get promoted.

"It was a very, very good night. Our away support had never had such a night. In the end, I think I'm pleased that the two big games were away from home, because our support away from home was fantastic all season. They had rocky years when three wins in a season was success and, all of a sudden, they've gained promotion and won a championship away from home. These people deserve it."

KEVIN SUMMERFIELD: "It was a funny game. We were so close but, like Luton, only one team started positive enough to win the game. They absolutely battered us. Romain was absolutely unbelievable, first half – save after save after save. Our 4-5-1 just couldn't cope. We just couldn't get the ball. It was like we'd never been together. I was nervous in the game; I think everyone was anxious, anticipating the end result before we'd earnt it. We were so lucky to in 0-0. We got to half-time and spent 10 minutes talking through what we should be doing and going through various things. At the end, the gaffer just said 'Right, shall we go 4-4-2' and the lads said 'Yeah, let's do it.' We'd just spent 10 minutes talking about 4-5-1! The game was still open, but we were now doing bits and pieces in their half which were causing them problems.

"The moment of the match was Stevie Adams' tackle on [Clive] Platt. The big lad went clean through with them 1-0 up. If that goes in, the game's lost, but he managed to come in and knock Platt off the ball. It was an unbelievable tackle. It was game-winning. From that, we made a couple of changes, went really positive and, once we'd scored our first goal, that was it, the lads knew we were going to win the game.

"The similarities for me were really odd. When I was at Shrewsbury, the year we were champions, we won promotion 2-1 on a Tuesday night at Rochdale. The celebrations with Plymouth were loads better. The fans were unbelievable, even when we were down.

"Everyone's got their own memories of that night and one of mine is weird. While we were celebrating, I put my thumb straight into the chairman's head and he couldn't stop bleeding. It was just a little nick, but it reminded me of the promotion with Argyle in 95-96. We were coming back from Darlington, last game of the season and, on the coach, Russell Coughlin bit Dave Smith's nose. All the way home, blood kept dripping down his nose.

"It was a big, big night and it was a massive relief for everybody. It was a great coach journey home. Jason was asleep most of the way home. He sits on his own; gets his headphones on and keeps his own bit of space. Second half, I thought we played fantastic football."

PHILL GILL: "Rochdale was an immense night. It was probably the night of the season. I came up with Peter Jones and he was quite nervous, but I was confident we'd win. As soon as we kicked off, I was more nervous than I'd ever been in my life. I watched the whole game through my fingers. As soon as we went 1-0 down I was confident again, What happened afterwards was great. I was so excited, I messed

up my video recording. Every time I thought I was turning the camcorder on, I was turning it off, and vice versa, so I've got half an hour of my feet and stairs and things."

No-one on the Argyle staff woke the following morning more proud than the Pilgrims' young captain Paul Wotton. A photograph of the 24-year-old Plymothian ecstatically grabbing his home-town club's crest on the front of his shirt and thrusting it towards supporters epitomised what Spotland meant to him, and them.

Four years earlier, another photograph of Wotton had captured a different moment in his life and of the history of the club: his tears at Turf Moor following relegation at the hands of Burnley on the final day of the 1997-98 season encapsulated the gloom of that day.

"I feel tremendous pride," said Wotton, who, like only his centre-back partner Coughlan, did not miss a single minute of Argyle's 2001-02 campaign after taking over the captaincy from the injured Craig Taylor the previous summer. "It is a great achievement. At the beginning of the season, this was beyond our wildest dreams.

"What happened at Burnley just makes you more determined to succeed. I said to Jon Beswetherick that what we had done made up for all the crap times – this is what you work for and you have to enjoy it. We had a few beers, but it's back to work tomorrow. We don't want to let it slip. There's one more thing to go for."

The player of the most famous goal in Plymouth Argyle's history led the chorus of congratulations to the Pilgrims. Ronnie Maugé, who headed the goal that beat Darlington to win the Third Division Wembley play-off final the previous time Argyle won promotion in 1996, said: "I'm delighted, I'm jealous and I'm happy for the fans – they've been through a lot."

Maugé, transfer-listed by Bristol Rovers and who did not play against his previous club as the Gas visited Home Park the following Saturday, also praised Paul Sturrock. He said: "I didn't know much about him when he came from Scotland but he is the man. His team has the best shape and is the best organised in the division."

Maugé's manager in 1996, Neil Warnock, shared his former midfielder's sentiments. "I'm absolutely delighted for everybody – the supporters in particular," he said. "Paul Sturrock, with his shrewd building and astute signings, has turned an average side into a very good side."

Tommy Tynan, who scored twice against Bristol City at Home Park in the pro-

motion-winning match of the 1986-86 season, also paid his compliments to the 2001-02 squad. He said: "They have proved themselves worthy as they have been up there all year."

The manager who bought Tynan back to Home Park for that promotion push, Dave Smith, believed the affect of Argyle's success would reverberate around the Westcountry. He said: "When I coach the kids on Saturday and Sunday, there are more youngsters in green shirts, which is always a tell-tale sign. I think the chairman and the board, and Paul Sturrock, with his experience, have been fantastic.

"I know Paul Sturrock always plays it cool, but I don't think he will be celebrating yet – we got promotion in 1986 and I said, 'no – we want the championship'. Let's hope that they are just two seasons away from the Premiership."

Sturrock's predecessor Kevin Hodges, who was sacked in October 2000 after two seasons in the Third Division, hailed Argyle's promotion as "wonderful news for the city". He said: "I'm delighted for the supporters and players – especially those players who have been there and sampled leaner times – but I'm particularly pleased for [chairman] Paul Stapleton, who has shown a vision and forward-thinking.

"The manager has done a tremendous job, and the club deserves this success. Everything is going in the right direction – things have fallen into place so quickly. Everything is positive for the club."

With the declared aim of the Third Division leaders to turn promotion into the championship, manager Paul Sturrock knew there could be no room for complacency against Bristol Rovers in what was sure to be an emotional homecoming for the players.

With Luton, who were five points behind Argyle – having played a game more – also still live contenders for the title, Sturrock said: "We have got to keep that space between us and Luton and the only way we can do that is by getting three points on Saturday.

"I'm really worried about the reaction. It's important we come down to earth again. I would hate to think the players think it is all over and that the fans just expect us to turn up and claim the three points. That type of thinking could cost us dear.

"We have come a long way down the road now, so it's important we achieve what we want to achieve. It's like stretching up for an apple on a tree. We are on our tip-toes now and can get a finger on it."

Sturrock, not exactly averse to having a good time, did not mind being cast in the role of party-pooper, as long as it helped Argyle take another step towards title. He said: "The fans are very important for two reasons: one is to back the team as the game's being played; two is to appreciate that the party spirit should be before the game, at half-time, and at the end.

"Then they can focus totally on the game as well. The backing of the crowd is very important to rekindle the players' focus because we could beat ourselves, in a way, and I want to take that out of the scenario."

Sturrock admitted getting the players' minds back on track had not been easy, but believed that failing to win the Third Division title after having spent the previous 22 weeks on top of the table would be a major disappointment that could affect their preparations for the Second Division the following season.

"It has been hard," he said. "There's a lot of back-slapping going on – a lot of joviality as far as the players are concerned. It is a worry. I would hate to think that we limply stumbled on to the end of the season, having shot ourselves in the foot regarding the championship. We would then carry a bitter taste into the summer.

"I think the championship's a must for everybody. I think we've tasted a celebration we will remember for a long time, but it's not very often you can have two of them. I think everybody at the club would like to have that second celebration."

Sturrock's trump cards were his own experiences in winning championships as a player (Dundee United) and a manager (St Johnstone), as well as those of his assistant Kevin Summerfield, who was a player-coach at Shrewsbury when they won the Third Division title eight years previously, and centre-back Graham Coughlan, who had a hat-trick of promotions under his belt after successes in 1999 and 2001 with Livingston.

That experience told him he might need to get nasty if any of his players took their foot off the gas against the Gas.

"I think those players' influence, my influence, Summers' influence – we've all tasted this kind of thing – is quite important," he said. "If the Hyde, instead of the Jekyll, is needed tomorrow, it will come out. They will know if I'm not happy. If my approach is right, I will expect my players' attitude to be right.

"If we lose or draw this game through the euphoria of a special day, it will leave a disappointment. Let's have a special day, but also a win."

After the emotions and exertions of Spotland, the Pilgrims produced a not unexpected hangover performance, but still managed to beat Rovers 1-0 for their 21st successive game unbeaten at Home Park. Keith's goal after 29 seconds provided an instant hair of the dog but the giddy expectations it raised gradually dissolved in the spring sunshine, and there were no more pleasant memories to add to a glorious, but exhausting, week.

The game was decided before the celebratory confetti thrown by fans among a crowd of 15,732 had been blown from the pitch. Rovers fluffed their kick-off, Argyle stole the ball, Stonebridge's run was blocked, the ball fell to Adams, who crashed it against the post, and there was Keith, sniffing like a Tynan of yore, to sweep it home.

After a couple of mulish free-kicks from Wotton, which were well saved by goalkeeper Scott Howie, Argyle decided they had done enough and invited the Pirates to plunder. Drew Shore was denied an equaliser when his shot hit teammate Ciaran Toner, before James Quinn rattled Larrieu's crossbar with a header from Mark McKeever's corner.

The pressure was relieved when Rovers' midfielder Wayne Carlisle was sent off after earning a second yellow card from referee Paul Danson for throwing the ball away following the award of a free-kick. Argyle were grateful of the extra time and space.

"A great day, a great crowd, and a great result, but poor fare as far as our performance was concerned," summarised Sturrock, after he and the players had completed a lap of honour to receive the fans' plaudits following the final whistle. "One of the nightmares of football is when you score early – what transpires is what you saw today: people drop a couple of gears, thinking it's going to happen, and don't make it happen.

"It would have been nicer if we'd got the second goal, but we'll take the result. The crowd have gone home happy and celebrated the day."

There was no time for Argyle to rest on their laurels, however. The following day, they were back on their travels for a Bank Holiday Monday fixture at, of all places, Hartlepool. With Luton, who were also confirmed of promotion following a 3-0 win at Swansea, hot on their heels, Sturrock set his team one, final points target. The arithmetic was simple. Luton, Sturrock reasoned, would reach 99 points if they won their remaining four games, therefore Argyle must aim for 100 – eight points more required from their final five matches at Hartlepool, Carlisle and Darlington, and at home to Southend and Cheltenham.

"I've said all along that I think Luton will win their last four games," said

Sturrock. "It's been a big season for them, as well as us. They are going to push us all the way to the end – it's up to us to make sure we don't slip up. The players appreciate the situation.

"Luton are a very good side. I knew they were going to push us all the way. The important thing for us is to reach the point where, statistically, they can't catch us. They have put an edge to us. Theirs is the first result the players think about when they come off and it's got the fans hyped up as well. Long may it last."

Saturday, March 30 2002, Nationwide League

Plymouth Argyle 1
Keith 1
Bristol Rovers 0

Plymouth Argyle (4-4-2): R Larrieu: D Worrell, P Wotton, G Coughlan, J Beswetherick; B Phillips (J Bent 81), S Adams, D Friio, L Hodges; I Stonebridge (B Sturrock 81), M Keith (M Evans 53). **Substitutes (not used):** L McCormick (gk), N Heaney.
Bookings: Keith 35, Beswetherick 40, Friio 58.
Bristol Rovers (4-4-2): S Howie; C Wilson, M Foran, S Foster, T Challis; W Carlisle, C Toner, D Shore, M McKeever (V Astafjevs 67); J Thomas, J Quinn. **Substitutes (not used):** R Clarke (gk), S Ommel, M Walters.
Sending-off: Carlisle 62 (second bookable offence).
Bookings: Carlisle 22.
Referee: P Danson (Leicester). **Attendance:** 15,732. **League position:** 1st.

PAUL STURROCK: "We had a training session which was in the frightening category. I started to worry but they were very professional in their approach to the Saturday. We set the tone of the game too quickly. Bristol never really caused us concern and we had a lot of half-chances which we never really took. It was a fans' occasion, they merited their day with the players. With six games to go, we let Luton back into the fray, but I think they needed to be brought back into the fray because they put an edge to us."

KEVIN SUMMERFIELD: "I wrote before the game 'How would we react?' We scored and then we could have all gone home. That was how memorable the game was. It was hard to write anything good about it afterwards. Even then, we created the best chances in the game. However we played, we knew we would work hard enough to make sure the other team doesn't get anything."

The weary Pilgrims ran out of legs and luck at Hartlepool, their fourth game inside ten days, three of which had involved 400-mile plus round trips. Midfielder Darrell Clarke made April fools of Argyle by scoring Pools' goal in their 1-0 Bank Holiday Monday victory at the Victoria Ground after Sturrock lost

a rare substitution gamble.

Sturrock's determination to chase a victory saw him switch from 4-5-1 to 4-4-2 in the final ten minutes, and he confessed afterwards that the move had probably cost the Pilgrims a point. He said: "I probably could have held on for 0-0 but the substitutions have worked for us recently. The fact it didn't was that one of our midfield players let their boy run for goal. Maybe I should have had a wee go ten minutes earlier than I did, but you can put that one down to the manager losing a point by trying to get all three."

With Luton having cut the deficit in the title race to two points with a 5-3 drubbing of promotion-hopefuls Mansfield – their 11th successive victory – and enjoying a far superior goal-difference to the Pilgrims, Sturrock was concerned fatigue might be the factor that cost the Pilgrims the title.

"The team looked weary-legged and that extra yard was just too much for them. In the second half, we looked as though we had definitely run our race. Boys were plodding out there. A lot has happened at this football club over the last week and a half."

Sturrock decided to give his players a rest and told them not to report for training until the following Thursday afternoon. "Maybe this is the kick up the backside our players needed," he said. "It's up to the management team to rest them and get a freshness back into their game. I think people see training as a chore."

It did not help that the game was played in fifth gear from start to finish, four minutes before which Clarke had latched on to Kevin Henderson's headed pass to fire the ball into Larrieu's net off a post. To put the result in some sort of perspective, it was only Argyle's sixth defeat in 42 league games.

Sturrock also appealed to the club's fans to help raise their weary heroes when they returned to Home Park to face Southend the following Saturday. "Come out and get behind the team on Saturday," he urged. "Let's try and win the title together – team, club and fans."

Monday, April 1 2002, Nationwide League

Hartlepool United 1
Clarke 86
Plymouth Argyle 0

Hartlepool United (4-4-2): A Williams; M Barron, G Lee, C Westwood, M Robinson; J Coppinger (A Boyd 79), D Clarke, R Humphreys, P Smith; G Watson (K Henderson 84), E Williams. **Substitutes (not used):** M Hollund (gk), P Arnison, J Easter.
Booking: Barron 75.
Plymouth Argyle (4-5-1): R Larrieu; D Worrell, P Wotton, G Coughlan, J Beswetherick; J Bent, K Wills (B Sturrock 63), S Adams (I Stonebridge 81), D Friio, L Hodges; M Evans (M Keith 81). **Substitutes (not used):** L McCormick (gk), N Heaney.
Bookings: Wills 14, Friio 75.
Referee: M Jones (Cheshire). **Attendance:** 3,725. **League position:** 1st.

PAUL STURROCK: "We were a spent force. We had run our race. We needed a few days to regroup, which we didn't get. We travelled on the Sunday and tried to rest, but there was never an edge to us. We had a lot more half-chances than they did in the first half but we ran out of steam in the second half and, after that, they battered us. I did a Rochdale and sent on the subs with about 20 minutes to go to try and chase the game and then Hodgy didn't puck up for a cross, they scored and we lost 1-0. It was about the only game we lost 1-0 in the season. There were more than a few times when we sneaked a 0-0 or even a 1-0 when we didn't deserve it so, at the end of the day, it evens itself out. I wasn't complaining. We had obviously won promotion which had put a bit of complacency into the players but we were tired, we had asked an awful lot of the players all season and I thought it had caught up with us."

KEVIN SUMMERFIELD: "We trained on the Sunday and went up. It was a real quality game – two different ways of playing and both worked when the team had the ball. We were causing mayhem going forward. Wottsie was getting the ball, transferring it to Bezzie, and Bezzie was rampaging forward, but we didn't have enough people to get on the end of his crosses. They were very clever, very good coming forward when they had the ball. Second half, our legs had gone. Darlington, Rochdale, Lincoln – this was our fourth long journey in two weeks. Luton kicked off early and we knew they'd won 5-3. We were constantly looking at Luton's fixtures and thinking 'Where are they going to get nipped?' We had this one as a possible where they might drop a point, and Hull, where they won 4-0, but not Macclesfield at home."

The Nationwide League season might have been slated to finish on April 20, but the signs during Argyle's disappointing 0-0 Home Park draw with Southend

were that the Pilgrims' campaign ended somewhere between Rochdale and Plymouth in the wee small hours of Wednesday, March 27.

The result allowed Luton, who racked up another impressive win in beating Hull 4-0 at Boothferry Park for their 12th successive three-pointer, to take over at the top of the Third Division on goal-difference after Argyle's 160-day stint as king pins. Both sides had 93 points, with Argyle's game in hand at Darlington apparently their only saving grace.

"It's a small squad that's played a long season," said Sturrock, after a third successive game in which Argyle were second best. "There's been hype about getting promotion and it's affected the players now that they've jumped that hurdle. It's very difficult to get them psyched up for games. Other than Mickey Evans, who worked his socks off, it was like watching a lot of ghosts out there.

"Southend were quicker, sharper, worked harder. It's not like us to be bossed and that just shows you what's happened to this team in their own minds. It's a mental tiredness, rather than a physical tiredness: too few have been asked to do too much."

There was not an ounce of criticism in his comments, and neither should there have been. In any other year, Argyle would already have been champions, and it was testimony to their achievements that Luton had to break an all-time club-record winning streak to draw level on points with them.

"It's still in our own hands," said Sturrock. "We've got the extra game, but the key to it is that we have got to win at Carlisle next weekend." He would have to do so without French midfielder David Friio, who was banned for the north of England double-header after passing the ten-bookings mark for the season.

As Sturrock had noted, Evans was the jewel in the muck of an encounter that would have been wholly unmemorable had it not have been for the Penalty That Never Was.

Referee Ray Olivier, who was as poor at his job as the Argyle players were at theirs, awarded a spot-kick to Plymouth after a handball in the penalty area, oblivious to the fact that the hand which struck the ball belonged to Evans.

After vigorous Southend protests, he checked with one linesman and declined to change his mind, then withdrew the award, to howls of protest from the Devonport end, after further consultation with his other linesman and the fourth official. Evans later held his hands up, again. "It wasn't the right decision for the championship," he said, "but, technically, it probably was. It was brave of the referee to change his decision.

"The lads are disappointed because we shouldn't be relying on penalties – we should have got something out of the game."

Saturday, April 6 2002, Nationwide League

Plymouth Argyle 0
Southend United 0

Plymouth Argyle (4-4-2): R Larrieu; D Worrell, P Wotton, G Coughlan, J Beswetherick; M Phillips, J Bent (B Sturrock 79), D Friio, L Hodges (S Adams 60); M Evans, I Stonebridge (M Keith 65). **Substitutes (not used):** L McCormick (gk), K Wills.
Bookings: Coughlan 55, Phillips 62.
Southend United (4-4-2): D Flahavan; S Broad, L Cort, D McSweeney, D Kerrigan; M Beard, S Thurgood, K Maher, D Searle; B Belgrave (A Wallace 65), P Whelan.
Substitutes (not used): L Johnson, A Clark, R Alderton, D Gay (gk).
Bookings: McSweeney 26, Maher 37, Wallace 75, Flahavan 90.
Referee: R Olivier (West Midlands). **Attendance:** 10,021. **League position:** 2nd.

PAUL STURROCK: "This was our poorest game as far as the performance was concerned – 0-0 was written all over it. They played very well and ours didn't reach the heights. It was disappointing. We gave them a bit of a torrid time in the last 15 minutes – Marino missed a sitter and their goalie made one or two good saves – but we never deserved anything. The penalty decision was justice – we didn't deserve it anyway. Luton nipped us, which was probably the best thing about that afternoon."

KEVIN SUMMERFIELD: "This was like a meaningless last game of the season; it was as if we couldn't wait to get all the pressure off, one way or another. Without doubt, it was taking its toll. Southend played a little bit similar to York – they pressed us – and there was nothing happening in the game. I wrote: 'We looked a tired team.' Luton had beaten Hull, we'd lost top spot, and the dressing-room was really low afterwards."

CHAPTER 16

IN hindsight, a somewhat unconventional build-up to Argyle's visit to Carlisle, though largely undesigned, was probably a huge factor in what was to follow.

Firstly, manager Paul Sturrock missed the first couple of days' training with a stomach upset, leaving assistant Kevin Summerfield in charge.

Barbara Sturrock got the blame for her husband's gippy stomach, which was a little harsh since she wasn't even there. "With my wife being away," said her old man, "I think I raided the fridge for something past its sell-by date. Blair was not feeling too well either, but we're fine now."

Then the Pilgrims' new away strip was unveiled. The predominantly tangerine outfit, which would be worn for the first time at Carlisle, demonstrated the esteem in which the Argyle directors held Sturrock. The colours were homage to their manager's lifelong connections with Dundee United and were likely to see more use than the white with green pinstripes, the 2001-02 away kit which had been used only twice.

The diversion caused by the new strip, and the change in the training routine brought about by Sturrock's illness, proved to be a breath of fresh air. Both Summerfield and Sturrock used the week to underline that, whoever won the Third Division title, Argyle had already achieved more than they had dared hope for.

Summerfield, who won promotion with Argyle as a mellifluous midfielder in Dave Smith's 1985-86 side, said: "You can measure our success whichever way you want to and it has been an incredible season – for supporters, players, staff, everybody involved in the club. It's all been a big buzz and it's been great.

"To me, this has been the hardest season I have ever been involved in – and that's without playing. Our success has heaped the pressure on us because everybody's been expecting us to do something: first promotion, then to be champions. If we'd come up on the blind side and sneaked into the promotion places, it would have been a completely different mind-set."
Later, a fully recovered Sturrock reiterated the message. "As I told the players, if we aren't going to win the championship, it won't be for lack of effort. That's all we can ask. We have had a fantastic season. Whatever happens now, I don't want people walking away from the season disappointed.

"If we don't win the title, the important thing is that we celebrate our achievement, rather than go away with our tail between our legs because we haven't won the championship."

Whether or not Sturrock's sentiments were a cunning ploy to take the pressure off his players, they certainly played as if they did not have a care in the world at Brunton Park, where their wonderful, crazy, beautiful, amazing, emotional, zany season scaled new heights.

While a significant number of Carlisle's disgruntled supporters spent the entire match parading around the perimeter of their ground, Argyle's fans were boosted by kilt-wearing Dundee United followers who had forsaken their own team to pay homage to the Pilgrims' manager and living Tannadice legend: their T-shirts bore the legend "Paul Sturrock's Tartan Army".

The terrace mix of Dundee tangerine and Argyle green received echo on the pitch, where Argyle previewed the following season's proposed away strip. Or more accurately, because the shorts were long on material, two-thirds of it: Day-Glo tangerine socks and slightly less luminescent shirts sandwiching conventional green. Some will not like it, but, as they used to say in an era when such acidic colours were last popular, "whatever turns you on" and most Argyle followers would cheer a team wearing sky-blue pink polka-dots if they won while wearing it.

The Scottish contingent helped add to the surreal nature of the afternoon. With the Tangergreens 2-0 up, thanks to a peach from Marino Keith and a jaffa of a free-kick by Paul Wotton, and so in control of the game that they had silenced what remained of the home support, a cheer appertaining to nothing on the pitch went up from the Argyle fans. From the following chants, it became apparent they believed Luton were being beaten 2-0 at home to Macclesfield, but the cheering had in fact emanated from their Celtic brethren to salute a Dundee United goal relayed over the border by radio.

The score at Kenilworth Road was, and remained, 0-0, which meant the Pilgrims were back on top of the table by two points and had two chances to rack up the two points they needed to win their first championship since 1959 - at Darlington on the Monday and the following Saturday against Cheltenham at Home Park. Neither were easy matches, but the force was with the Pilgrims.

Sturrock said: "Macclesfield have the fourth-best away record in the league, but I didn't expect that result, as I think Luton wouldn't have expected us to slip up last week. That's football. It's evened itself out again and the players are on a high because they know Darlington's a big, big game for them.

'I wouldn't want the championship to go to the last day and put an edge to the game. I would like to finish it at Darlington and the only way we can finish it is by a three-point win. A draw's no good for us because we can still get nipped on

goal-difference, so the important thing is to make sure we are professional. I think the players are up for it now."

They were certainly up for it against Carlisle. Sturrock kept an earlier promise to be adventurous by selecting a three-man midfield – Jason Bent, Steve Adams and Lee Hodges – and Ian Stonebridge playing link-up between it and strikers Marino Keith and Michael Evans. On a crumbling surface that made passing football impossible, and merely controlling the ball difficult, Stonebridge played the role to perfection, and his team-mates followed the letter of Sturrock's instruction.

The opener, after 20 minutes, had been honed on the training-ground, and came after Wotton's dead-ball deliveries had already caused mini-mayhem in the opposition box. Graham Coughlan, a shoo-in for Pilgrim of the season, delivered long to Evans, who flicked on for Keith to dispatch the sweetest of left-foot volleys – a tangerine dream, indeed.

Argyle never again looked like leaving without the maximum return and Wotton put the issue beyond doubt after Stonebridge had been fouled by Lee Andrews, thumping home the subsequent free-kick from 30-yards with a tracer-bullet that never rose more than three feet from the turf.

Sturrock said: "We had prior knowledge how the pitch was going to play and had to adapt and change our game completely. The players adapted very well. You couldn't run with the ball – you just had to make sure it went forward. For us to try and pass the ball on that surface would have been a total lottery. he second goal got a slight deflection but Marino's was a wee bit special. We had few half-chances before he scored but it was the icing on the cake as far as exactly the move we'd been working on in training worked, him and Mickey linking up."

Saturday, April 13 2002, Nationwide League

Carlisle United 0
Plymouth Argyle 2
Keith 20, Wotton 53

Carlisle United (4-4-2): P Keen; M Birch, L Andrews, M Winstanley, D Rogers; J Allan (S Bell 66), T Hopper (W McDonagh 69), M Jack, B McGill; R Foran, I Stevens (S Halliday 59). **Substitutes (not used):** A Thwaites, M Nixon.
Bookings: Hopper 40, Rogers 50, Halliday 64.
Plymouth Argyle (4-3-1-2): R Larrieu; D Worrell, P Wotton, G Coughlan, J Beswetherick; J Bent, S Adams, L Hodges; I Stonebridge; M Keith, M Evans. **Substitutes (not used):** L McCormick (gk), B McGlinchey, M Phillips, B Sturrock, J Broad.
Referee: M Cowburn (Blackpool). **Attendance:** 3,080. **League position:** 1st.

PAUL STURROCK: "Summers and I sat down after Southend, had a beer

in the coaches' room, and decided we hadn't scored many goals recently. Summers seemed to feel, and I agreed, that a lot of players had run their race as far as scoring goals was concerned. Summers felt we had to put more goalscoring type players on the park – 4-4-2 wasn't working at home, 4-5-1 wasn't working away, so we had to come up with something else. We tried two up with one off in training. While I was off, Summers worked on that with the players.

"The worry for me was that we were filling their heads with too much too quickly. I went up to Carlisle, still worried and still committed to 4-5-1. Then we had a few beers at the hotel.

"We had decided that we would use the new strip at Carlisle before the Darlington game was rearranged. We thought it was going to be the last away game of the season. I felt a freshness was needed all the way through. The nightmare was when we stripped, the shorts were enormous. Gigantor would not have got in any of them. It wasn't too bad for some of the boys who are a bit fat-arsed, but on people like Buster, they were falling off them. They would have been more worried about keeping their shorts up, than on the game.

"We said we'd go back to the green but the players wanted to try the new strip with green shorts so we tried it on and it looked absolutely magnificent. Much better than the tangerine shorts. The players liked it. We had information that the pitches at Carlisle and Darlington were in a bit of a state and we wouldn't be able to pass the ball the way we liked to away from home, so a change of style of play was developed as well - we were going to play a lot of diagonal balls, a lot of back-to-front balls because if we weren't going to gain anything by our passing, we were going to have to be a lot more positive.

"All these changes freshened everyone up. Again. There was an edge to them again, plus their will to win was unbelievable. If I'd been able to get to the bookies after seeing my lads 10-15 minutes before the Carlisle and Darlington games, I would have won myself a fortune. There was no way we were going to lose either of those games.

"The fans' expectations of the championship had been so high because of the Luton scenario, which I think also affected the players. Their nervousness and twitchiness was evident. We thought we had to get three points to keep the championship alive – who would have thought that Macclesfield would hold Luton 0-0 at Luton? Had we both won that Saturday, everything still would have been alive for the final game of the season.
"I looked at the pitch and thought what we are going to see is what we will

get. There was no way you could even judge a player on that day, it was all about winning the game. We scored two excellent goals. Marino's was the best of the season, I would say, but it was a wee worry until we got Wottsie's because we had four or five chances we could have done better with. It was never really in doubt, though; everyone who was at the game will appreciate what a professional performance it was. When we went 2-0 up, we shut up shop. We gave then a couple of chances, which was quite unusual because David Worrell was involved in a couple of them and Cocko and Wottsie allowed boys through. It was an important win.

"The cheers from our fans had me running up and down the line trying to find out what had happened at Luton. I was told it was still 0-0, so we were all kind of flummoxed."

KEVIN SUMMERFIELD: "I watched a video of the previous four or five games and it looked a struggle. Apart from Rochdale, we weren't looking bright and lively. How did we change it? We could not go with the same things we had been doing. We needed to do something, just to make the players have a fresh thought, rather than just doing the same things. We had two or three different permutations that we tried. We needed to score goals, so we needed as many people on the pitch who could score a goal. The pitches at that time weren't particularly conducive to our passing game; they were getting bobbly and dry. That was the way we looked at it.

"Dan, Stoney and Mickey had to play; David was suspended, so we lost a goal-threat that way. With having three forwards, you needed legs in the middle of the park. Hodgy would always stodge away and you knew what you were getting with him. He looked happier in there, a change from doing the miles down the left wing without reward. He got a new lease of life; it was like he was playing his third game of the season, not his third from last. Bent and Adams gave you pure legs and all three could defend.

"We weren't going out in the old kit. It was like the first day of the season – we had a new kit on. They went out fresher for the game. If only you'd seen the shorts on Buster – you could have made the whole kit out of Buster's. Wotton and Evans were the only two that wanted to keep them on because they were the only two who looked slim in them.

"Dan's first goal was frightening. That's the sort of thing he can do. He can score the shitty ones; he can score the spectacular ones – that's the type of player we haven't had. It was a fantastic goal. Considering they had only been playing the system for two or three days, it was a right good result. They played it really, really well and looked comfortable doing it.

"Luton was the bonus. Monday night we could go for it. It was a great dressing-room afterwards."

Sturrock's final team-talk of the record-breaking Pilgrims' 2001-02 travels included the stern reminder to his players that failure was not an option, not that anyone in the camp was contemplating anything else.

Argyle would win the Nationwide Third Division championship – and create club history – if they beat Darlington at Feethams, whereas a draw or defeat would have left them needing to take something from the following Saturday's visit of Cheltenham to Home Park. That was not a position Sturrock wanted to be in, especially as Cheltenham could have required a point, or points, to win promotion themselves.

After the team had relocated to their Darlington hotel on the Sunday following their victory at Carlisle, he said: "I think it's important that we go for it tomorrow. Even a draw would mean that, if we lost on Saturday, we could miss out on the title on goal-difference."

Victory would see the Pilgrims lift their first championship for 43 seasons and reach 99 points for the season, a total that would see them take over from Bob Jack's 1930 Third Division champions as the most successful Argyle side ever. Sturrock, speaking after taking a training session at Middlesbrough's sumptuous training headquarters ten minutes drive from the team hotel, said: "The players are well up for it. The worrying aspect is, if we go one-down they might think 'it doesn't matter, there's next week'. That's something I'm not looking forward to, but I think the players want to do it tomorrow. We've got the tangerine strip washed, so we're raring to go."

French midfielder David Friio's two-match suspension allowed him to attend the PFA Awards dinner in London that night at which he, Paul Wotton, Graham Coughlan and goalkeeper Larrieu were named in the Third Division team of the year. However, he pledged to link up with his team-mates at Feethams. "It's a real honour to be chosen for the PFA team, because it's voted for by the players," said Friio, who had spent much of the season getting up his fellow professionals' noses. "It's unfortunate more of the players have not been chosen because they have all done really well. If you are in the PFA team, it's because of the team."

Darlington proved fine hosts, waiving a previously imposed all-ticket restriction on away fans after pleas from the Pilgrims' board and mindful of supporters making last-minute decisions to attend the game. The move allowed as many Argyle supporters as possible who could swing time off work to witness the possibility of history being made.

The moment those fans, and tens of thousands of their kind all round Planet Earth, had waited a lifetime for arrived at precisely 9.08pm on Monday, April 15, when referee Fraser Stretton signalled the end of the Pilgrims' final away match of the season to confirm Sturrock's side as Nationwide Third Division champions for 2001-02.

Not since Sturrock was a three-year-old had Argyle won a championship, when Jack Rowley's men claimed the inaugural Third Division title of 1958-59, the season immediately following the abandonment of the North-South divide. They won the championship with a champions' display, too. No 1-0 to the Argyle, but a thorough and systematic 4-1 dismantling of opponents by goals of quality and distinction.

Evans began the party in the tenth minute, Keith doubled the lead in the 17th minute and trebled it 11 minutes later, with the impeccable Bent icing the championship cake in the 59th minute after wretched Darlo had got into the game through Ian Clark's 33rd-minute penalty.

It was somehow appropriate that the Pilgrims' achievement should have come at 380 miles away from Home Park at Darlington, for their success had been built on slugging out results after slogging up the motorways to England's far-flung football outposts. Those fans who threw an impulsive sickie to be at Feethams will know exactly how tiring travelling can be.

Supporters and players had been on something of an emotional switchback ride during the Pilgrims' end-of-season run-in but the Pilgrims' destiny always remained in their own feet and the victory at Darlington brought about ecstatic scenes not associated with Argyle since...well, since March 26, actually – but it does not appear to be a bad habit to get into.

Once again, Paul Sturrock's men were invited to invade an opposition directors' box to allow them to be greeted by ecstatic supporters that had invaded foreign soil; once again, the bubbly was sprayed hither and thither, making the players one big tangerine cocktail of sweat and champagne; once again, the chants went up 'Are You Watching, Joe Kinnear?' – except, this time, the players joined in. With gusto. They joined in, too, when the fans hailed the manager who had led them on this amazing odyssey – 'There's Only One Paul Sturrock'.

Sturrock had declared immediately after Saturday's victory at Carlisle that he would change both personnel and system to keep things fresh, but it sounded like a bluff then and so it proved.

So delighted was he with the easy way his players adapted to the new 4-3-3 formation that had been introduced to the training-ground only the previous week,

in which Ian Stonebridge played off the front pairing of Keith and Evans, that the only way he was going to leave it on the tactics board was if injury so dictated.

Same team, same colours. To call Sturrock superstitious is akin to describing David Beckham as underexposed, and once Argyle's new away strip of tangerine shirts and green shorts had debuted so successfully at Carlisle, he was always going to plump for it at Feethams, Football League regulations and finding a suitable laundry facilities permitting.

The ranks of Argyle's Green Army, many of who had overcome the sickness that prevented them from attending work earlier in the day, were swelled by a healthy contingent from Home Park: director of youth Stuart Gibson and goal-keeping coach Geoff Crudgington drove up, and the suspended Friio and chief executive David Tall arrived fresh...alright, they arrived from the previous night's PFA Awards.

Suddenly, after two days of waiting, hanging around hotels and travelling across country, it was here. The entry of the gladiators, the huddle, the whistle, the moment of destiny? The Green Army affected not to care – 'Que sera, sera, what-ever will be, will be, we're leaving Division Three' – but they cared all right – 'Are you watching, Joe Kinnear?'

Darlo were clearly rattled, a state of affairs not helped by the wall of noise from the Westcountry choir at their back. Paul Heckingbotton cracked first, allowing Bent to make ground on the right. Keith and goalkeeper Chris Porter challenged for his cross mid-goal and each caused the other to miss, but the ball reached Evans, whose trigger-finger was working better than it had the previous Saturday and he drew first blood from four yards. Chairman Paul Stapleton stood up to cheer from the directors' box and was immediately asked by a Darlington steward to sit down.

Argyle were in dreamland but received a wake-up call when a pass back to Larrieu hit a loose bit of turf and caused the French goalkeeper to slam the ball straight against the on-rushing Richard Hodgson. The ball trickled only just wide of the post.

The Pilgrims doubled their early lead with Keith's second goal in consecutive matches, and this was every bit as good as the first. Coughlan headed Porter's drop-kick back with percentage and Keith reacted first, outpacing the back-four to the ball and firing first time past the now ill-positioned Porter from outside the penalty box. For vision and application, there was not a better goal all season.

Argyle were cruising. Every attack contained menace, every pass was a threat, every cross caused palpitations and every corner was a potential goalscoring

opportunity. No surprise, then, when Keith rose at the far post to apply the merest touch needed to Beswetherick's vicious inswinging corner from the right for the third goal.

Argyle were put out of their happy stride five minutes later when Larrieu brought down former Torquay midfielder Mark Ford for a penalty that Ian Clark converted, although Le Keeper can be grateful he and his team incurred no further punishment apart from Evans' yellow card for delaying Clark's kick to tell Larrieu which way the ball would go. He was right, too.

Half-time. What did Sturrock say to his Tangergreens? 'You're 45 minutes away from achieving what you play this game for in the first place, gentlemen. Don't muck it up now', perhaps?

Darlington manager Tommy Taylor used all three of his substitutes at half-time, injecting a triple dose of youth to go in pursuit of the early goal his side needed to make a game of it. They looked brighter in the opening stages of the second period, forcing three corners in succession, one of which caused Larrieu to flip Clark's delivery over his crossbar.

Argyle swatted away this puppyish insolence and removed any doubt about the destination of the Third Division championship just before the hour when Keith won a free-kick on the left. Wotton floated up a gentle sand-wedge, Coughlan challenged, and Bent picked up the loose and converted by nutmegging Porter from 10 yards.

Evans was fortunate to stay on the field, referee Stretton erring on the side of compassion when he settled on a tongue-lashing, rather than a second yellow card, after the Argyle goalscorer clattered into Porter. Keith took a fearful whack to the head after colliding with an advertising hoarding but stayed on in hope of a hat-trick, although Darlo were reduced to ten men when Atkinson limped out of the action.

It was too much for him, too much for his colleagues. Argyle were rampant, unbelievable, a class above Darlington, who were also beaten by the Pilgrims in the 1996 Third Division play-off final and, it seems, destined forever to be Argyle's fall guys.

After the champagne celebrations, Sturrock admitted: "You only taste these things once or twice in your career. As I said to the players afterwards, there's some that will never taste this again. The important thing is that we make sure we enjoy it.

"We've done it now. I think we'll party for a few days and look forward to a full-

house when we play Cheltenham on Saturday. The boys were up for it. We did the business. We went at them straight from the kick-off. Great goals as well. The front three were magnificent.

"It's strange. It's been a bit of an anti-climax for me. I did all my partying after Rochdale because the essence of this football club was to go up. Then, all of a sudden, we're starting to worry about championships.

"But we went the whole way. I'm very pleased for everyone involved at the football club. The fans have had a great time and the players have been magnificent. The attitude they showed to run over the top of Carlisle and Darlington in a row was superb.

"I knew there was no way we were going to lose this game tonight when I looked at the lads in the dressing-room ten minutes before kick-off. They were up for it all right."

Sturrock's Pilgrims had become the greatest Plymouth Argyle championship-winning side in the club's 116-year history. His achievement in leading his record-breaking side to 99 points, with a century unprecedented in modern history still a possibility from their last game against Cheltenham at Home Park the following Saturday, was unsurpassed by any other Argyle manager.

Argyle's 30 victories and nine draws from their 45 games was demonstrably superior to the record of the club on the only previous occasion they won the Third Division, under former Manchester United and England forward Jack Rowley in 1959 and it dwarfed the impressive showing by Jimmy Rae's 1952 Jumbo Chisholm-led Third Division (South) champions.

Most remarkably, the first Pilgrims of the 21st century put into the shadow the benchmark previously thought unreachable set by the Robert Jack-managed legends of pre-first world war Plymouth who, with Sammy Black and Jack Cock to the fore, swept all before them in the Third Division (South) in 1930.

Sturrock will have enjoyed the fact that he had completed a hat-trick of Scottish-inspired titles, in the wake of his countrymen Jack and Rae, but would have been embarrassed at the perfectly correct suggestion that he had already become a figure of greater importance than either in Argyle's history.

Monday, April 15 2002, Nationwide League

Darlington 1
Clark pen 33
Plymouth Argyle 4
Evans 10, Keith 17, 28, Bent 59

Darlington (4-4-2): C Porter; P Brumwell (P Campbell half-time), C Liddle, D McGurk, P Heckingbotton; M Convery (A Rundle half-time), M Ford, B Atkinson, R Hodgson (M Sheeran half-time); I Clark, N Wainwight. **Substitutes (not used):** S Betts, S Harper.

Plymouth Argyle (4-3-1-2): Plymouth Argyle (4-3-1-2): R Larrieu; D Worrell, P Wotton, G Coughlan, J Beswetherick; J Bent, S Adams, L Hodges (B Sturrock 87); I Stonebridge (B Phillips 87); M Keith, M Evans (B McGlinchey 87). **Substitutes (not used):** L McCormick (gk), C Taylor.

Booking: Evans 33.

Referee: F Stretton (Nottingham). **Attendance:** 4,089. **League position:** 1st (champions).

PAUL STURROCK: "I thought fresh legs might be needed but when I looked at how relaxed they were in Darlington, I though 'I'm just putting myself under pressure here and the pressure should be on the players' so we went with the same squad and same team. It was tense. Obviously we knew it was an important game. We didn't want to come back and face Cheltenham with anything hanging on the game. This was our get out of jail card, this was the extra game, this was the opportunity to put it out of sight. We went out there and ran over the top of them. They changed the formation three or four times because they just couldn't handle Stoney off the front. We'd worked hard on some new set-pieces and they couldn't cope with those.

"I said: 'This one's your extra one game, the one to enjoy, the one to work hard and get your result. Just go out there and give everything you've got. I would hate to think you came back in frustrated with your individual performances. Very few people win things in their career. What you will remember when you finish your career is that something sitting there on your mantelpiece.' I'm not a winder-upper. I'll discuss the game; Summers will go through the set-pieces. I'll maybe sit them down and have a quiet word with them.

"We went 3-0 up and then lost a goal, and then you worry about it again – a second goal would have put them back into it. They looked up for it when they came out for the second half and had a wee go, but in truth Romain never had that much to concern him. The penalty was a wee bit soft. I don't think it was a penalty; I think Romain took his hands away and the boy went down. It kept it interesting and maybe it was a good thing to happen – we could have got very complacent, the situation we were in. I overemphasised it that if we sat on it, we could be opening ourselves up for trouble.

"I would never have said anything. Football's got a habit of doing funny things, but their attitude over the two games was so professional. The way they were concentrating in the dressing-room, knowing what they had to do.

"Job done. That was it. I didn't taste the trip home this time either. I had three Guinnesses and three bottles of champagne before we'd left, a few beers on the bus and I fell asleep by Birmingham and woke up just as the bus was coming through the Home Park gates.

"It was just a bit of relief. We fulfilled all the supporters' expectations, which you don't do very often. We'd done everything they had wanted us to do and it was just like, job done, let's have a wee party."

KEVIN SUMMERFIELD: "We talked about it and the conclusion was that, the way we played Saturday, we had to play the same team. Whether they watched us on the Saturday, I don't know. The PFA people missed out on a highlight in their career. Hopefully, they will have the chance to go again. It was a massive honour for them. Everything had built up to this 90 minutes. We didn't say a lot to them – we didn't need to, you just looked at the changing room and, to a man, they were ready. We didn't have to say a thing. It was the same team. It was like they'd walked off at Carlisle, had a sit down and were ready to go and finish it off.

"We'd have beaten anybody that night. The system worked an absolute treat. They couldn't cope with it. Everyone was immense that night.

"Whatever anybody says now, no-one can say we weren't the best team – the league table shows that.

"We were there ages after the game and Gilly and Peter Jones were planning on going back to London. We said there was no way they should go back to London – if they did, they would regret it for the rest of their lives. So they got rid of the hire car and ended up coming back with us. Phill did a video of the trip coming back and it is so funny. We watched it with the kids and they were crying. That started five, six, seven days of celebration."

CHAPTER 17

ARGYLE could now enter their final home game of the season against Cheltenham at what was sure to be a near 20,000 capacity full-house Home Park the following Saturday with nothing to play for apart from pride...and the small matter of bettering the club and divisional points records.

Captain Paul Wotton said: "We wanted to get promotion, and we have done that; we wanted to win the title; and we have done that; now we have got one last step to take and hopefully we can break the 100-point barrier.

"Luton have pushed us all the way, but the league table doesn't lie and we are the best team in Division Three. We have proved so many people wrong and it's a great feeling to know they are quiet now." Are you listening, Joe Kinnear?

Paul Sturrock's reason for wanting to win was because the third promotion spot behind Argyle and Luton remained open between Cheltenham, Mansfield and Rochdale. "We have to do the right thing for everybody on the day," he said. "It would have been nice to have a real party, with both teams promoted, but that's not going to happen.

"I can assure all Rochdale and Mansfield supporters and officials we will give it 100 per cent. We will be as professional as possible. People have tried so hard to this season to gain promotion. I would hate to be involved in the scenario they are in and I promise everybody we will be going out to win. We shall be totally committed for the full 90 minutes."

After addressing the concerns of his opponents, Sturrock used his eve-of-game Press conference to send a final message to home supporters. That message, in essence, was 'Don't Expect Too Much'. He said: "A lot of fans will have me signing seven or eight players through the close-season — that's not going to happen. This is a long-term job. We have not got loads of money all of a sudden. I have got to be really certain about the types of players I bring to the club."

Sturrock's decision reflected the faith he had in his squad, and also his determination to set the club back along the lines of the five-year plan which, he reminded everyone, should see the Pilgrims established as a strong Second Division club inside the four remaining years.

"I've deliberated long and hard and I believe this squad of players, which was brought together to compete in a higher division, should taste it first," he said. "I've also got to taste the league to see what players to bring in. There's no point

in bringing players in untried and untested. If someone slaps me in the face as being of a real standard, then we'll take him.

"The five-year plan has kicked back in again. We're very hopeful we will be very competitive in the next league, but we just don't know. We will test the Second Division before we make a decision on it. I know fans will not want to hear these things; they'll want me to have three fantastic signings before the start of next season, but it's not going to happen because I can't take chances."

It was doubtful whether, for all the pints, tots and wee drams drunk by Plymouth Argyle supporters to celebrate the end of their extraordinary season following what was more a party than a match, a single one was raised to toast Joe Kinnear.

That is a pity, because the Luton Town manager had done more than any individual apart from Paul Sturrock to inspire the Pilgrims to what history will recognise as their greatest ever season.

A 19th home victory on the final day by a comfortable 2-0 margin, not only condemned Cheltenham to the play-offs – sweet revenge for the nastiness at Whaddon Road earlier in the season – but also ensured Argyle finished the campaign with 102 points, equalling the best ever by a side outside the First Division and only three points adrift of Sunderland's all-time 1999 best. All but one of those points came after the first three games of the season, too.

Argyle, though, would not have reached such heights had it not been for Kinnear. Certainly, the Hatters manager is, publicly at least, everything Sturrock is not: he has tickets on himself, as they say in Sturrock's motherland.

He has become such a figure of mockery among the Green Army, that this season's most popular terrace refrain has been 'Are You Watching, Joe Kinnear?' (to, loosely, 'Bread Of Heaven'). For the Cheltenham match, a group of lads came in T-shirts which spelled out the same question when they stood side by side, and the homemade banners included one which read: 'No Joke In Here – Argyle Are Champions.'

Not worthy champions, according to the most recent of Kinnear's anti-Plymouth ravings, which, aside from showing a lack of respect, was also wanting in historical accuracy: most ten-year-olds know that Sir Francis Drake, and not Lord Nelson, is associated with the city.

Earlier, he had suggested Plymouth was where people 'came to die', perhaps confusing 'people' with his own side's championship hopes, which received a fatal knockback at Home Park. On that occasion, Kinnear, the Luton players and

the club's official website came to the Westcountry so bumptiously confident of their own abilities, Sturrock was able to forego his team-talk: he merely pinned a copy of the offending remarks on the team notice-board and let Plymouth pride do the rest.

So it continued through the season. Whatever Luton did, Argyle simply had to go one better, and what Luton did was magnificent. For Argyle to remain unheaded on points by a side which set a club-record 12 consecutive victories and which ended their season on 97 points is phenomenal, and Kinnear should have respected that.

Thanks to the Luton Lip and his crazy assertions, Argyle broke club record after club record. They would not have reached anywhere near 100 points if Luton had not pushed them so hard, and Sturrock would not have learnt the depths to which his squad could dig, had they not been under so much pressure. Kinnear's assertion of Argyle's unworthiness was merely another prod for the Argyle players carry on ramming his words back down his throat, as they had been all season.

Chairman Paul Stapleton thanked fans for their support before the game, and urged everyone 'Let's party' but the Third Division champions were far from ready for that. They came out snapping and buzzing with such energy that you would not have thought that (a) it was Cheltenham that needed a point for promotion and (b) they have been doing considerably more drinking than training since the previous Monday.

After four minutes, Graham Coughlan, predictably and deservedly named player of the season before the game, sent Ian Stonebridge away down the left and the young forward's flat low pass to Jason Bent was expertly dispatched by the Canadian international. Twenty minutes later, Coughlan made sure of the points, a club record, and that he finished Argyle's leading goalscorer with his 11th of the season, which was the result of a complete cock-up by the Cheltenham defence.

Russell Milton and Michael Duff sound like a comic duo and they certainly produced a moment of complete comedy to send the ball spinning back towards goalkeeper Steve Book. Book dithered fatally and allowed Coughlan – insultingly called 'Joe Soap' by Kinnear earlier in the year – to nip in and poke the ball home. It is unlikely his 11 goals had come from a combined distance of 20 yards.

Coughlan had earlier done Plymouth Argyle fans a huge favour, relieving them of any agonising over whether to cast their player-of-the-season votes for one of the Third Division championship-winning club's leading goalscorers or top defenders by finding that the 27-year-old Dubliner sat easily in both categories.

Consequently, Coughlan was a shoo-in to win the award in what history will view as one of the greatest seasons in the Pilgrims' history. An honour, indeed, and even more so when you consider the sparkling form and consistency of his fellow defenders: David Worrell, Paul Wotton, Brian McGlinchey and Jon Beswetherick. Not to mention the Flying Frenchman Romain Larrieu, behind them, and his compatriot David Friio, just in front.

Any one of them might have pushed Coughlan – 6ft 2in and eyes of piercing blue – close if it had not have been for the unexpected extra he had, as his manager would say, brought to the party.

Eleven goals, many of them set up by his dead-eye dead-ball specialist centre-back partner Wotton, made him the Pilgrims' leading league scorer and that, to borrow another Sturrockism, is a wee bit scary. Not bad, either, for someone who, after netting once on the club's pre-season tour of Scotland, claimed he had used up his quota for the next two seasons.

He said: "As a centre-half, you just want to keep a clean-sheet and do well each week, first and foremost. Goalscoring is a bonus, but I've enjoyed it. It's been tremendous, considering I only scored two goals last year. Not only that, but I've got on the end of a one or two bits and pieces and set goals up, so my assist-rate is high as well.

"I'm going into games and I do believe, that if I'm not going to score, I'm going to create something. I think that's down to the boys who put the ball into the box. Their delivery has been tremendous all season and I've just been lucky enough to get on the end."

Luck, you suspect, had precious little to do with it. Coughlan came to Plymouth in the summer with two championship winning seasons with Livingston behind him, but still willing to learn under Sturrock.

He said: "I've totally changed my style of play, as the lack of yellow and red cards would suggest. I've only picked up three all season. I used to get involved in the game a little bit more, passing and things like that, but it's been a big turn-around for me, personally."

Coughlan's wholehearted commitment and heart-on-sleeve endeavour made him a big hit north of the border, but the Livi Legend was not immediately embraced on his arrival at Home Park, a fact not unconnected to the fact that he effectively – in both senses of the word – replaced club captain Mick Heathcote.

He said: "I used to get a few shouts like 'There's a train going back to Scotland in a minute; here's your fare.' Obviously it was hard, because I was replacing one of

the fans' favourites, but, in fairness to Mickey, he got around me in Scotland and helped me out. The boys and the gaffer have been tremendous to me. The rest is history, as they say."

History, indeed. Another clean-sheet for Coughlan and Company against Cheltenham established a new club-record of 27 shut-outs in one season.

Goalkeeper Romain Larrieu, runner-up to Coughlan as the fans' choice as player of the year, produced a few routine outstanding saves to preserve the victory, and then the party did begin.

The Argyle players disappeared into the tunnel only to reappear two-by-two – each pair hailed to uproarious applause from around the stadium. The Third Division best-of-the-season crowd of 18,00-plus was the biggest for a league game at Home Park since 21,000 saw a clash with Portsmouth on Boxing Day, 1986.

The players applauded back as they trotted to the centre circle, where a podium had been hastily erected by Nationwide. Around the circle, snappers snapped, TV crews tugged at leads and cameramen focused on the huge grins.

As Martin Hesp noted in the *Western Morning News*: "The podium was too small and the players clung to each other like sailors on a raft. It was a good metaphor though: having saved themselves from the stormy, battle-savaged seas of the bottom division, here they were – not only surviving, but victorious – setting sail in a green ocean to the fresh wind of acclaim.

"Each player lifted the trophy and was cheered, until we heard the loudest roar of the lot. It came last. It was, of course, for manager Paul Sturrock. Gulls heard that roar out on the Eddystone Light.

"The inevitable 'We Are The Champions' was cranked up on the public address system as the great posse of players, photographers, day-glow wrapped ground-staff, camera and soundmen, reporters and other sundry folk made their way around the ground.

"The rapturous fans at the Devonport end – who'd been partying, conga-dancing and goodness knows what throughout the second half – went crazy. And who could blame them? Moments like these don't come often – if ever.

"Outside it was carnival time. You could have been in Rome, Barcelona or Milan. Nine out of ten cars beeped their horns – every other vehicle carried a green banner or flag.

And on the main road out of town some jubilant fans had draped the biggest banner in Plymouth across a footbridge. The thousands who drove under it saluted – it carried one word that said it all: 'Champions'."

Cheers, Joe

Saturday, April 20 2002, Nationwide League

Plymouth Argyle 2
Bent 4, Coughlan 24
Cheltenham Town 0

Plymouth Argyle (4-4-2): R Larrieu; D Worrell, P Wotton, G Coughlan, J Beswetherick; J Bent, S Adams, D Friio, L Hodges; M Keith (M Evans 34), I Stonebridge (B Sturrock 79).
Substitutes (not used): L McCormick (gk), B McGlinchey, M Phillips.
Cheltenham Town (4-4-2): S Book; A Griffin, J Brough (N Howarth half-time), M Duff, J Victory; L Williams (N Tyson half-time), M Yates, J Finningan, R Milton; J Alsop (N Grayson 86), T Naylor.
Substitutes (not used): C Muggleton (gk), M Lee.
Booking: Brough 21.
Referee: S Tomlin (Lewes). **Attendance:** 18,517. **League position:** 1st.

PAUL STURROCK: "The Thursday of that week – if I'd breathalysed some of my players... They had three days partying. The worrying thing was that Cheltenham had drawn at Carlisle – we had been praying that there would be a nothingness to the game but, all of a sudden, we had to be professional in our approach because we knew Rochdale and Mansfield were still involved in the shake-up. We actually got a phone call from Rochdale. To be fair we told them we would be professional and I had a chat with the boys after training on Thursday, because it was so bad. I said 'How would you like to be the fellas at Mansfield or Rochdale?' We still had 100 points to aim for. The boys trained well on Friday – there was a bit of a buzz about them and then Saturday came along and, although we ran out of stream in the final hour, we had done very well – very professional, very organised.

"I think Plymouth was swinging that night."

"I love the running of a football club. I like the day to day stuff, sorting out transfers, man-management. I took a back seat for all that. I never can really get myself hyped up, I don't know why. As long as I've got a beer and some people to chat with about football, I'm a happy camper. A bit of banter and a laugh, I'm not really interested in that side of things. I'm sure there's some managers who would have put themselves right out in front. It was the players' night. I was very up tight going on the balcony of the civic centre. It's something I've never enjoyed.

"Three defeats in a row next season and I'm the worst manager they've ever had. You take the good with the bad and the bad with the good."

KEVIN SUMMERFIELD: "I think it would have been a different game if we'd played anybody else. Other than Luton, you could have picked any other team in the division and we would have struggled. Because of the history of what went on there, and the fact that they had to come to us and get something, we didn't need any winding up. Since we'd played up there, the lads had been waiting to get them back at our place. Cheltenham were a good team, but the boys in the dressing-room were keen to get into it. That game summed up the players more than anything – they were professional to go out after Monday, and everything else, and perform like that.

"It put the seal on an unbelievable, but exhausting, season."

PAUL STAPLETON: "To be physically part of this success and to have contributed to it is something you will never ever take away. No matter what happens at this football club, we have been part of it and it's been fantastic for the city, the fans, for everybody. We felt it as well – we're fans."

FINAL CHAPTER

THERE was almost a sombre postscript to Argyle's season. Two weeks after the final match of the season, Paul Sturrock and Phill Gill were travelling on the motorway to Bristol Airport to begin a holiday in Canada. Sturrock was driving Gill's BMW; Gill was a front-seat passenger. Suddenly, another car swerved across three lanes into the path of the BMW. A high-speed collision between the front end of Sturrock's car and the driver's side of the other car was inevitable. Sturrock managed to skew the front end of his car around just enough to avoid a total T-boning and the BMW's airbags did the rest. Police later told the Argyle manager and director that they might not have survived the impact had they been driving a less robust car.

> **PAUL STURROCK:** "That was a sobering moment. It brings a lot of things home about family and the importance of life, when your own life flashes in front of you. I'm highly delighted we're still here. You have to appreciate there was an instance, had we been in a different car, that we would not be here. That's a big, big thing. For people to die that way, when it's not their fault is...it's a sin. It really brings it home how crazy those motorways are, that accidents like that happen all the time."

Thankfully, as it was, Sturrock was able to spend the flight across the Atlantic reflecting on happier times. The final question he was asked in the compilation of this book was: what, for him, had been the defining moment of Argyle's season?"

> **PAUL STURROCK:** "This is a hell of a choice. There's always an apprehension about every game; there's always a worry about results, a worry about whether you've picked the right players, whether you're playing the right system. If you want to be a manager of a football club and you want to pay golf in the afternoon, party at night – you've got no chance.

"I think the defining moment was sitting at Rushden in the 44th minute after the start we'd had and all of a sudden scoring a goal to make it 2-1 and then having an absolute flippie with three or four players at half-time. We went out with the youngest, most inexperienced midfield we had all season and got a result, That for me was the cornerstone of the rest of the season because they had seen what hard work and attitude, and work-rate. They showed real character on the day. They fed off that. Exeter came pretty quick after that and we had to dig deep again. I don't know what would have happened if we hadn't scored that goal before half-time."

APPENDIX 1

FINAL 2001-02 NATIONWIDE LEAGUE
THIRD DIVISION TABLE

				HOME					AWAY					
		Pld	W	D	L	F	A	W	D	L	F	A	GD	Pts
1	Plymouth Argyle	46	19	2	2	41	11	12	7	4	30	17	43	102
2	Luton Town	46	15	5	3	50	18	15	2	6	46	30	48	97
3	Mansfield Town	46	17	3	3	49	24	7	4	12	23	36	12	79
4	Cheltenham Town	46	11	11	1	40	20	10	4	9	26	29	17	78
5	Rochdale	46	13	8	2	41	22	8	7	8	24	30	13	78
6	Rushden & Diamonds	46	14	5	4	40	20	6	8	9	29	33	16	73
7	Hartlepool United	46	12	6	5	53	23	8	5	10	21	25	26	71
8	Scunthorpe United	46	14	5	4	43	22	5	9	9	31	34	18	71
9	Shrewsbury Town	46	13	4	6	36	19	7	6	10	28	34	11	70
10	Kidderminster Harriers	46	13	6	4	35	17	6	3	14	21	30	9	66
11	Hull City	46	12	6	5	38	18	4	7	12	19	33	6	61
12	Southend United	46	12	5	6	36	22	3	8	12	15	32	-3	58
13	Macclesfield Town	46	7	7	9	23	25	8	6	9	18	27	-11	58
14	York City	46	11	5	7	26	20	5	4	14	28	47	-13	57
15	Darlington	46	11	6	6	37	25	4	5	14	23	46	-11	56
16	Exeter City	46	7	9	7	25	32	7	4	12	23	41	-25	55
17	Carlisle United	46	11	5	7	31	21	1	11	11	18	35	-7	52
18	Leyton Orient	46	10	7	6	37	25	3	6	14	18	46	-16	52
19	Torquay United	46	8	6	9	27	31	4	9	10	19	32	-17	51
20	Swansea City	46	7	8	8	26	26	6	4	13	27	51	-24	51
21	Oxford United	46	8	7	8	34	28	3	7	13	19	34	-9	47
22	Lincoln City	46	8	4	11	25	27	2	12	9	19	35	-18	46
23	Bristol Rovers	46	8	7	8	28	28	3	5	15	12	32	-20	45
24	Halifax Town	46	5	9	9	24	28	3	3	17	15	56	-45	36

APPENDIX 2

2001-02 NATIONWIDE LEAGUE THIRD DIVISION STATISTICS

Most wins (home): Plymouth Argyle 19
Most wins (away): Luton Town 15
Most wins (total): Plymouth Argyle 31
Highest points per game (home): Plymouth Argyle 2.56

Fewest draws (home): Plymouth Argyle 2
Fewest draws (away): Luton Town 2
Fewest draws (total): Luton Town, Mansfield Town 7

Fewest defeats (home): Cheltenham Town 1
Fewest defeats (away): Plymouth Argyle 4
Fewest defeats (total): Plymouth Argyle 6

Most points (home): Plymouth Argyle 59
Highest points per game average: Plymouth Argyle 2.56
Most points (away): Luton Town 47
Highest points per game average: Luton Town 2.04
Most points (total): Plymouth Argyle 102
Highest Points per game average: Plymouth Argyle 2.21

Best winning run: Luton Town 12
Best winning run (home): Plymouth Argyle 10
Best winning run (away): Cheltenham Town 7

Best unbeaten run: Plymouth Argyle 19
Best undefeated run (home): Cheltenham Town, Plymouth Argyle 21
Best undefeated run (away): Plymouth Argyle 12

Longest drawing run: Scunthorpe United 4
Longest drawing run (home): Cheltenham Town 4
Longest drawing run (away): Torquay United 5

Most goals scored (home): Hartlepool United 53

Highest goals scored average: Hartlepool United 2.30
Most goals scored (away): Luton Town 46
Highest goals scored average: Luton Town 2.00
Most goals scored (total): Luton Town 96
Highest goals scored average: Luton Town 2.08

Fewest goals conceded (home): Plymouth Argyle 11
Fewest goals conceded average: Plymouth Argyle 0.47
Fewest goals conceded (away): Plymouth Argyle 17
Fewest goals conceded average: Plymouth Argyle 0.73
Fewest goals conceded (total): Plymouth Argyle 28
Lowest goals conceded average: Plymouth Argyle 0.60

Best goal-difference (home): Luton Town +32
Best goal-difference (away): Luton Town +16
Best goal-difference (total): Luton Town +48

Most clean-sheets: Plymouth Argyle 27
Most consecutive clean-sheets: Plymouth Argyle 6
Fewest consecutive games conceding a goal: Plymouth Argyle 4

Fewest games without scoring: Luton Town 4
Fewest consecutive games without scoring: Luton Town 1
Scoring in most consecutive games: Scunthorpe United 19

Least time without scoring: Luton Town 141 minutes
Most time without conceding: Torquay United 622 minutes

Most penalties scored: Darlington 8
Most penalties scored against: Darlington 10
Fewest penalties scored against: Luton Town, Carlisle United 1
Most own goals for: Rushden & Diamonds 4
Most own goals against: Shrewsbury Town, Luton Town 3

Most goals: Steve Howard (Luton Town) 24
Best striker rate: Onandi Lowe (Rushden & Diamonds) 19 goals – 113 minutes per goal

Best average home attendance: Hull City 9,506
Highest home attendance: Plymouth Argyle (v Cheltenham Town) 18,517
Best average away attendance: Luton Town 5,170

Most yellow cards for (team): Luton Town 97
Fewest yellow cards for (team): Cheltenham Town, Lincoln City, Plymouth Argyle 42
Most red cards for (team): Shrewsbury Town 11
Fewest red cards for (team): Plymouth Argyle, Scunthorpe United 1

Most yellow cards against (team): Luton Town 90
Fewest yellow cards against (team): Lincoln City 40
Most red cards against (team): Scunthorpe United 11
Fewest red cards against (team): Carlisle United, Hull City 1

Most yellow cards (individual): Kevin Nicholls (Luton Town) 14
Most red cards (individual): Paul Stoneman (Halifax Town), Kris O'Leary (Swansea City) 3

THIRD DIVISION TEAMS, MATCHES SCORING FIRST

	M	W	D	L	F	A	GD	Pts
1 Plymouth Argyle (1)	30	26	2	2	57	15	42	80
2 Luton Town (2)	26	22	2	2	62	16	46	68
3 Mansfield Town (3)	26	21	2	3	58	25	33	65
4 Hartlepool United (7)	23	8	3	2	58	17	41	57
5 Cheltenham Town (4)	24	18	5	1	44	15	29	59
6 Rushden & Diamonds (6)	22	17	2	3	48	20	28	53
7 Hull City (11)	21	15	5	1	46	16	30	50
8 Rochdale (5)	21	15	4	2	34	13	21	49
9 Macclesfield Town (13)	16	11	4	1	25	11	14	37
10 Torquay United (19)	14	10	2	2	28	16	12	32
11 Shrewsbury Town (9)	27	18	7	2	51	23	28	61
12 Leyton Orient (18)	19	13	3	3	39	18	21	42
13 Lincoln City (22)	16	10	5	1	27	13	14	35
14 Scunthorpe United (8)	27	18	5	4	59	29	30	59
15 Kidderminster Harriers (10)	27	18	4	5	49	22	27	58
16 Oxford United (21)	15	9	4	2	27	12	15	31
17 York City (14)	22	14	3	5	37	21	16	45
18 Carlisle United (17)	19	11	5	3	35	19	16	38
19 Swansea City (20)	16	9	5	2	32	19	13	32
20 Southend United (12)	16	10	2	4	24	12	12	32
21 Darlington (15) 19	11	4	4	3	9	24	15	37
22 Bristol Rovers (23)	17	10	2	5	30	21	9	32
23 Exeter City (16)	17	9	5	3 2	6	22	4	32
24 Halifax Town (24)	15	6	4	5	23	20	3	22

THIRD DIVISION TEAMS, MATCHES SCORING MORE THAN ONE GOAL

	Pld	M	W	D	L	F	A	GD	PpG
1 Plymouth Argyle (1)	46	21	20	1	0	55	15	40	2.90
2 Kidderminster Harriers (10)	46	13	12	1	0	37	9	28	2.84
3 Bristol Rovers (23)	46	8	7	1	0	22	11	11	2.75
4 Macclesfield Town (13)	46	11	10	0	1	26	13	13	2.72
5 Mansfield Town (3)	46	21	19	0	2	58	25	33	2.71
6 Hartlepool United (7)	46	19	16	2	1	59	17	42	2.63
7 Luton Town (2)	46	30	25	2	3	84	31	53	2.56
8 Rochdale (5)	46	20	16	3	1	47	23	24	2.55
9 Rushden & Diamonds (6)	46	21	17	1	3	57	26	31	2.47
10 Hull City (11)	46	15	12	1	2	43	17	26	2.46
11 Shrewsbury Town (9)	46	18	13	5	0	48	20	28	2.44
12 Southend United (12)	46	12	9	2	1	33	16	17	2.41
13 Cheltenham Town (4)	46	21	15	5	1	50	22	28	2.38
14 Lincoln City (22)	46	10	7	2	1	23	13	10	2.30
15 Exeter City (16)	46	14	10	2	2	34	25	9	2.28
16 Torquay United (19)	46	15	10	4	1	33	20	13	2.26
17 Leyton Orient (18)	46	15	11	1	3	39	21	18	2.26
18 Carlisle United (17)	46	13	8	4	1	34	17	17	2.15
19 York City (14)	46	15	10	2	3	36	21	15	2.13
20 Swansea City (20)	46	19	11	7	1	44	27	17	2.10
21 Darlington (15)	46	19	12	4	3	48	31	17	2.10
22 Oxford United (21)	46	13	8	3	2	34	21	13	2.07
23 Halifax Town (24)	46	10	6	2	2	25	16	9	2.00
24 Scunthorpe United (8)	46	21	12	5	4	58	34	24	1.95

THIRD DIVISION TEAMS, MATCHES CONCEDING MORE THAN ONE GOAL

	Pld	M	W	D	L	F	A	GD	PpG
1 Plymouth Argyle (1)	46	8	3	1	4	15	17	-2	1.25
2 Luton Town (2)	46	11	3	2	6	27	30	-3	1.00
3 Mansfield Town (3)	46	15	4	0	11	24	43	-19	0.80
4 Rochdale (5)	46	12	2	3	7	21	34	-13	0.75
5 Shrewsbury Town (9)	46	16	2	5	9	24	38	-14	10.68
6 Exeter City (16)	46	23	4	2	17	27	61	-34	0.60
7 Southend United (12)	46	20	3	2	15	25	44	-19	0.55
8 Swansea City (20)	46	24	2	7	15	31	67	-36	0.54
9 Rushden & Diamonds (6)	46	13	2	1	10	21	36	-15	0.53
10 Oxford United (21)	46	19	2	3	14	25	44	-19	0.47
11 Scunthorpe United (8)	46	18	1	5	12	29	44	-15	0.44
12 Hartlepool United (7)	46	12	1	2	9	13	27	-14	0.41
13 Darlington (15)	46	18	1	4	13	24	54	-30	0.38
14 Cheltenham Town (4)	46	13	0	5	8	18	34	-16	0.38
15 Carlisle United (17)	46	19	1	4	14	20	44	-24	0.36
16 Bristol Rovers (23)	46	20	2	1	17	20	46	-26	0.35
17 Kidderminster Harriers (10)	46	13	1	1	11	12	30	-18	0.30
18 Lincoln City (22)	46	17	1	2	14	17	43	-26	0.29
19 Macclesfield Town (13)	46	11	1	0	10	9	30	-21	0.27
20 Torquay United (19)	46	16	0	4	12	16	43	-27	0.25
21 Leyton Orient (18)	46	20	1	1	18	22	59	-37	0.20
22 Halifax Town (24)	46	26	1	2	23	20	75	-55	0.19
23 York City (14)	46	19	0	2	17	20	53	-33	0.10
24 Hull City (11)	46	11	0	1	10	11	31	-20	0.09

THIRD DIVISION TEAMS, MATCHES SCORING FEWER THAN TWO GOALS

	Pld	M	W	D	L	F	A	GD	PpG
1 Plymouth Argyle (1)	46	25	11	8	6	16	13	3	1.64
2 Luton Town (2)	46	16	5	5	6	12	17	-5	1.25
3 Scunthorpe United (8)	46	25	7	9	9	16	22	-6	1.20
4 Cheltenham Town (4)	46	25	6	10	9	16	27	-11	1.12
5 Rochdale (5)	46	26	5	12	9	18	29	-11	1.03
6 Shrewsbury Town (9)	46	28	7	5	16	16	33	-17	0.92
7 Mansfield Town (3)	46	25	5	7	13	14	35	-21	0.88
8 Kidderminster Harriers (10)	46	33	7	8	18	19	38	-19	0.87
9 Southend United (12)	46	34	6	11	17	18	38	-20	0.85
10 Rushden & Diamonds (6)	46	25	3	12	10	12	27	-15	0.84
11 York City (14)	46	31	6	7	18	18	46	-28	0.80
12 Macclesfield Town (13)	46	35	5	13	17	15	39	-24	0.80
13 Hartlepool United (7)	46	27	4	9	14	15	31	-16	0.77
14 Hull City (11)	46	31	4	12	15	14	34	-20	0.77
15 Carlisle United (17)	46	33	4	12	17	15	39	-24	0.72
16 Exeter City (16)	46	32	4	11	17	14	48	-34	0.71
17 Lincoln City (22)	46	36	3	14	19	21	49	-28	0.63
18 Oxford United (21)	46	33	3	11	19	19	41	-22	0.60
19 Bristol Rovers (23)	46	38	4	11	23	18	49	-31	0.60
20 Darlington (15)	46	27	3	7	17	12	40	-28	0.59
21 Leyton Orient (18)	46	31	2	12	17	16	50	-34	0.58
22 Torquay United (19)	46	31	2	11	18	13	43	-30	0.54
23 Halifax Town (24)	46	36	2	10	24	14	68	-54	0.44
24 Swansea City (20)	46	27	2	5	20	9	50	-41	0.40

THIRD DIVISION TABLE, GOALS CONCEDED

	Pld	W	D	L	F	A
1 Plymouth Argyle (1)	46	31	9	6	71	28
2 Kidderminster Harriers (10)	46	19	9	18	56	47
3 Luton Town (2)	46	30	7	9	96	48
4 Hartlepool United (7)	46	20	11	15	74	48
5 Cheltenham Town (4)	46	21	15	10	66	49
6 Hull City (11)	46	16	13	17	57	51
7 Rochdale (5)	46	21	15	10	65	52
8 Macclesfield Town (13)	46	15	13	18	41	52
9 Rushden & Diamonds (6)	46	20	13	13	69	53
10 Shrewsbury Town (9)	46	20	10	16	64	53
11 Southend United (12)	46	15	13	18	51	54
12 Scunthorpe United (8)	46	19	14	13	74	56
13 Carlisle United (17)	46	12	16	18	49	56
14 Mansfield Town (3)	46	24	7	15	72	60
15 Bristol Rovers (23)	46	11	12	23	40	60
16 Oxford United (21)	46	11	14	21	53	62
17 Lincoln City (22)	46	10	16	20	44	62
18 Torquay United (19)	46	12	15	19	46	63
19 York City (14)	46	16	9	21	54	67
20 Darlington (15)	46	15	11	20	60	71
21 Leyton Orient (18)	46	13	13	20	55	71
22 Exeter City (16)	46	14	13	19	48	73
23 Swansea City (20)	46	13	12	21	53	77
24 Halifax Town (24)	46	8	12	26	39	84

THIRD DIVISION TABLE, CLEAN SHEETS

	Pld	CS	%CS
1 Plymouth Argyle	46	27	58.6%
2 Cheltenham Town	46	18	39.1%
3 Luton Town	46	17	36.9%
4 Kidderminster Harriers	46	16	34.7%
5 Rochdale	46	16	34.7%
6 Rushden & Diamonds	46	16	34.7%
7 Scunthorpe United	46	16	34.7%
8 Southend United	46	16	34.7%
9 Carlisle United	46	15	32.6%
10 Hull City	46	15	32.6%
11 Shrewsbury Town	46	15	32.6%
12 Leyton Orient	46	14	30.4%
13 Mansfield Town	46	14	30.4%
14 Hartlepool United	46	13	28.2%
15 Macclesfield Town	46	13	28.2%
16 York City	46	13	28.2%
17 Bristol Rovers	46	12	26.0%
18 Swansea City	46	12	26.0%
19 Darlington	46	11	23.9%
20 Exeter City	46	11	23.9%
21 Halifax Town	46	11	23.9%
22 Lincoln City	46	10	21.7%
23 Torquay United	46	10	21.7%
24 Oxford United	46	9	19.5%

APPENDIX 3
CLUB FACTS AND FIGURES
PLYMOUTH ARGYLE 2001-02

HOME PARK, PLYMOUTH, DEVON PL2 3DQ
Tel: 01752 562561 **Fax:** 01752 606167
Pilgrim Shop: 01752 558292, **email:** argyle@pafc.co.uk

DIRECTORS: PAUL STAPLETON (chairman), PETER JONES (vice-chairman), MICHAEL FOOT, PHILLIP GILL, DAN McCAULEY (until February 1, 2002), NICHOLAS WARREN

ASSOCIATE DIRECTORS: KEN JONES, JOHN McNULTY

CHIEF EXECUTIVE: DAVID TALL OBE

MANAGER: PAUL STURROCK

ASSISTANT MANAGER: KEVIN SUMMERFIELD

DIRECTOR OF YOUTH: STUART GIBSON

PHYSIOTHERAPIST: PAUL MAXWELL

COMMUNITY OFFICER: GEOFF CRUDGINGTON

CLUB CAPTAIN: CRAIG TAYLOR

TEAM CAPTAIN: PAUL WOTTON

VICE-CAPTAIN: GRAHAM COUGHLAN

CHIEF SCOUT: JOHN JAMES

CLUB DOCTOR: PAUL GILES

MEDICAL CONSULTANT: IAN STEWART

STADIUM MANAGER: COLIN WHEATCROFT

GROUNDSMAN: RICHARD WHITE

COMMERCIAL MANAGER: ANDY BUDGE

OFFICE MANAGER: CAROLE ROWNTREE

PILGRIM SHOP MANAGER: RACHEL FRY

CLUB ASSISTANT: PETER HALL

CLUB PHOTOGRAPHER: DAVE ROWNTREE

WEBMASTER: STEVE HILL

FORMED: 1886 (as Argyle Athletic Club)

TURNED PROFESSIONAL: 1903 (as Plymouth Argyle FC)

NICKNAME: THE PILGRIMS

RECORD LEAGUE VICTORY: 8-1 v MILLWALL, January 16, 1932 (Division 2); v HARTLEPOOL, May 7, 1994 (Division 2)

RECORD CUP VICTORY: 6-0 v CORBY TOWN, January 22, 1966 (FA Cup third round)

RECORD DEFEAT: 0-9 v STOKE CITY, December 17, 1960 (Division 2)

MOST LEAGUE POINTS (2 for a win): 68, 1929-1930 (Division 3 South)

MOST LEAGUE POINTS (3 for a win): 102, 2001-2002 (Division 3)

MOST LEAGUE GOALS: 107, 1925-1926 (Division 3 South) and 1951-1952 (Division 3 South)

HIGHEST LEAGUE SCORER IN A SEASON: JACK COCK, 32, 1925-1926 (Div 3 South)

MOST LEAGUE GOALS IN TOTAL: SAMMY BLACK, 180, 1924-1938

MOST LEAGUE APPEARANCES: KEVIN HODGES, 530, 1978-1992

RECORD TRANSFER FEE RECEIVED: £750,000, MICHAEL EVANS, FROM SOUTHAMPTON, March 1997

RECORD TRANSFER FEE PAID: £350,000 PETER SWAN TO PORT VALE, July 1994

SOUTHERN LEAGUE: Champions 1912-1913; runners-up 1907-1908 and 1911-1912

WESTERN LEAGUE: DIVISION 1 – champions 1904-1905; **DIVISION 1B** – runners-up 1906-1907.

FOOTBALL LEAGUE: DIVISION 3 – champions 1958-1959, 2001-2002; runners-up 1974-1975, 1985-1986; also promoted (play-offs) 1995-1996; **DIVISION 3 (South)** – champions 1929-1930, 1951-1952; runners-up 1921-1922, 1922-1923, 1923-1924, 1924-1925, 1925-1926, 1926-1927; **DIVISION 2** (best) – 4th 1931-1932, 1952-1953

SOUTH WEST REGIONAL LEAGUE: Champions 1939-1940

FA CUP: Semi-final 1984

FOOTBALL LEAGUE CUP: Semi-final 1965, 1974

APPENDIX 4

This letter, from a Dundee United supporter, was received by Paul Sturrock at the end of the season. Apart from explaining to uninitiated Sassenachs that an Arab is a follower of Dundee United, I will let it speak for itself.

"FIRST of all, may I apologise for never having written to you to wish you all the best at Plymouth. I was absolutely gutted when you left Tannadice. I personally thought it was too early for you to go, but I understand your reasons completely – and they've been vindicated at Home Park.

"I took the chance of going to Brunton Park for the Carlisle game with my dad (also an Arab). It was great to see so many Arabs down there and some old faces from the past. We were obviously there to see how Luggy's team was getting on, and to cheer Argyle to the championship.

"We were so taken aback with the response from your fans. As well as a good professional performance from the team, coupled with one of the goals of the season from Marino Keith (better than Zidane's, as my dad said the other night!), it was just such a good day out. We just got the impression that the Argyle fans really know their football, and hold the utmost respect and gratitude for the job that you have done.

"We really did come up the road with smiles on our faces – we'd been entertained by a good footballing side, treated with such high esteem by a top bunch of fans, and seen a United legend once more in the flesh.

In fact, I was so chuffed with what I saw, that I took the road back down to Darlington on the Monday night – this time on my own as my dad had left to go on holiday.

"I managed to make it into the ground with a couple of minutes gone and immediately received applause for wearing my United top. When I took up my position on the terrace, it turned out to be next to one of the blokes I had met on the Saturday I really enjoyed the chat once again, and it was capped by a thoroughly entertaining performance from your lads.

"I ended up swapping tops with Andy Budge (your commercial manager). However, I managed to get it back by the end of the match, as I needed it for the Dundee derby! He was probably thinking that I wouldn't send it to him, but I have enclosed it along with this letter, so no doubt he'll be asking for your autograph on it!

"Basically, I'm just writing to pass on my congratulations to you for doing a top job with Plymouth, and to thank you for a couple of cracking days out that I won't forget in a hurry. As well as a being well-organised, disciplined team, Plymouth play attractive football, with a good front line (any chance of flogging a couple of them to Tannadice?). I can see why you wanted Jason Bent at Tannadice, and big Coughlan looks a quality centre-half. I gather that you have brought in most of the side yourself – well done to you!

"Looking at the potential that exists at Home Park, with the attendances you've been getting, coupled with promotion and genuinely good players, I have high

hopes that you'll do well next season and beyond. I've taken in a lot of English football over the years, and the Plymouth side I have watched this season will be able to handle themselves with the step up to the Second Division.

"On many of the trips down south, I have come back with a fondness for one club or other, either by the way that the team has played, or by the conduct of their fans. I'm happy to say that, in Plymouth's instance, it was a case of both. Congratulations on bringing so much happiness to so many people – and that includes Arabs up here as well! (It was good to see a number of recently-swapped Argyle tops at Dens).

"It only leaves me to say a big 'congratulations' once again – and on your news of being awarded manager of the year. I'm so proud that one of United's favourite sons is having such a big impact with a great club. We'll manage down again next season, whether that to be Blackpool, Tranmere, Stockport or the like. I'll start the chant of "Paul Sturrock's Tangerine Army!"

"Well done again, Luggy.

Ewen Forsyth